TEACHER MANUAL

ESSENTIAL ELEMENTS for Strings

COMPREHENSIVE STRING METHOD

MICHAEL ALLEN • ROBERT GILLESPIE • PAMELA TELLEJOHN HAYES

ARRANGEMENTS BY JOHN HIGGINS

ESSENTIAL ELEMENTS INCLUDES:

Comprehensive Pedagogy
- Address the *process* of teaching and learning.

Melodic Approach
- Early pizzicato tunes develop ear and hand.

Integrated Curriculum
- Theory, history, and multiculturalism in the examples.

Innovative Rhythm System
- Graphics, subdivision, and easy-to-learn sequence.

Easy Note Reading
- Easy notes thoroughly reinforced with note names.

Broad Musical Spectrum
- Classics to contemporary-designed to motivate.

Online Supplemental Material
- Instructional Videos
- Correlated, Popular Bonus Songs
- PDFs of worksheets, duets and trios.

AVAILABLE PUBLICATIONS

Violin
Viola
Cello
Double Bass
Piano Accompaniment
EE String Orchestra Series

To create an account, visit:
www.essentialelementsinteractive.com

Student Activation Code
EEST-3432-8968-7814

ISBN 979-835012073-8

TABLE OF CONTENTS

The *Essential Elements for Strings* Teacher Manual Book 1 is designed to serve as a resource for all your string teaching needs. It contains teaching tips for every page of *Essential Elements for Strings* Book 1. It also includes sample letters for communicating with parents, sample test forms for evaluating students' playing skills, guidelines for instrument care, sizing students for instruments, a keyboard chart, and words to the some of the familiar melodies throughout the book. National standards for teaching strings as well as a resource list of additional materials to help you in your teaching are provided.

SEQUENCE OF

Teacher Page	34	35–36	37–38	39–41	42–45	46–51	52–56	56–59	60–63	64–68	69–74	75–78
Student Page	**1**	**2**	**3**	**4**	**5**	**6**	**7**	**8**	**9**	**10**	**11**	**12**
Bowings							Bow Builder One: Shaping the Right Hand, Pencil Hold	Bow Builder Two: Pencil Hold Exercises Bow Builder Three: Bowing Motions				Bow Builder Four: Shaping the Hand on the Bow
Rhythms				♩ 𝄽								
Theory											Scale	
History	Instrument Histories							Folk Songs				
Terms			*pizz.*	Beat, Music Staff, Bar Line, Measure, Notes, Rest	Clef, Time Signature, Double Bar, Repeat Sign, Counting	Sharp, Keeping Fingers Down Bracket (Bass)			Keeping Fingers Down Bracket (Violin, Viola, Cello)			
Listening Skills						G, F♯, E				D, C♯, B		
Familiar Melodies				At Pierrot's Door				Morning Dance, Rolling Along	Good King Wenceslas, Lightly Row			
Special Features	Welcome to String Playing	Instrument Care, Instrument Parts, Bow Parts, Accessories	Instrument Position, Pizzicato		Counting Introduced	Shaping Left Hand Introduced			New Bass Note: A on G String, Left Hand Rote Exercises		Pizzicato D Major Scale, Bass Shifting	
Quiz Assessments					*pizz.* D/A Strings, Counting, ♩ 𝄽 Steady Beat		*pizz.* D String (G String Bass), Counting, Steady Beat, Square 1st Finger, Time Signature, Clef, Double Bar		*pizz.* D String (G String Bass), Counting, Steady Beat, Square 1st Finger, Keeping Fingers Down, Violin/Viola Shoulder Position	A String Notes	Left Hand Shape, Bass Shifting, *pizz.* D Major Scale	Essential Creativity, Drawing Notes on the Staff
Note Sequence												
Violin												
Viola												
Cello												
Bass												
Correlating St. Orch. Arr. Levels												

ESSENTIAL ELEMENTS

Teacher Page	79-82	83-87	88-92	93-97	98-102	103-106	107-112	113-115	116-119	120-124	125-129	130-133
Student Page	**13**	**14**	**15**	**16**	**17**	**18**	**19**	**20**	**21**	**22**	**23**	**24**
Bowings	Bow Builder Five: Bowing with Rosin Raps			Bow Builder Six: Let's Bow!	String Levels Bow Builder Seven: Bowing Notes of the D Major Scale	Bowing Fingered Notes						
Rhythms												
Theory		Writing D Major Scale Notes	D Major Key Signature						Time Signature: $\frac{2}{4}$ 1st and 2nd Endings	Repeat Signs		Round, Chord, Harmony
History	Israeli Folk Song		Mozart								Beethoven	
Terms	Down Bow, Up Bow			*arco*	Bow Lift			Tempo Markings: Allegro Moderato Andante				Measure Number
Listening Skills				Bowing Open D, A Strings								
Familiar Melodies	Dreidel	Jingle Bells, Old MacDonald Had A Farm	Twinkle, Twinkle, Little Star					Hot Cross Buns, Au Clair De La Lune		At Pierrot's Door, Grandparent's Day, Michael Row The Boat Ashore	Ode To Joy	Frère Jacques, Boil 'Em Cabbage Down
Special Features			Essential Creativity: Composing			Steps For Practicing Music that is Bowed	Special Exercises (Violin, Viola, Cello), Bass C♯ on A String		Conducting Pattern 	4th Finger Pizzicato (Violin, Viola)	Bowing 4th Finger (Violin, Viola)	Performance Spotlight
EE Quiz Assessments					Parallel Bowing, Smooth and Even Tone, Arm Level Changes at String Crossings		Bowing D/A Notes, Bow Markings, Parallel Bowing, String Levels, Half and Whole Steps		Bow Markings, Parallel Bowing, String Levels, Half and Whole Steps, 1st and 2nd Endings		4th Finger (Violin, Viola)	
Note Sequence												
Violin												
Viola												
Cello												
Bass											 4 1 III III	
Correlating St. Orch. Arr. Levels									▲ Explorer Level			

SEQUENCE OF

Teacher Page	133–137	138–142	143–149	150–154	155–161	162–166	167–172	173–177	178–182	183–189	190–194	195–200
Student Page	**25**	**26**	**27**	**28**	**29**	**30**	**31**	**32**	**33**	**34**	**35**	**36**
Bowings		Bowing G String (Violin, Viola, Cello), Bowing E, A Strings (Bass)		Changing Bow Speeds	Slur 2 Notes		Slur 3 Notes					
Rhythms												
Theory		G Major	Common Time $\mathbf{C}$	(dotted half note)	Tie, Slur	Upbeat, D.C. al Fine		♮ Half Step, Whole Step	Chromatics	C Major Key Signature	Theme and Variations	
History	Offenbach Operetta					Latin American Music	Far Eastern Music			Nationalistic Music	16th Century, Thomas Tallis	
Terms		Ledger Lines (Violin)								Duet		
Listening Skills		G, A, B, C						F♮	C♮			C String Notes (Viola, Cello)
Familiar Melodies	Lightly Row, Can-Can		Baa Baa Black Sheep, This Old Man	French Folk Song, Sailor's Song		Banana Boat Song, Firoliralera	Jingli Nona		Bluebird's Song	A-Tisket, A-Tasket, Russian Folk Tune	Bingo, Skip To My Lou, Happy Birthday	
Special Features	Performance Spotlight		Writing G Major Notes, 4th Finger D on G String (Violin, Viola), Conducting 4-Beat Pattern	Time Signature: $\frac{3}{4}$ Conducting 3-Beat Pattern, New Position II $1/2$ (Bass)		Orchestra Arrangement	EE Skill Builders: G Major	New Finger Pattern: Low 2nd Finger on D String (Violin, Viola)	New Finger Pattern: Low 2nd Finger on A String (Violin, Viola)	Duet, New Position II (Bass)	Low and High Second Finger Patterns (Violin, Viola), Essential Creativity: Creating Rhythms, Round	Special Exercises and Orchestra Team Work, C Major Scale
Quiz Assessments			G String Notes (Violin, Viola, Cello), 4th Finger on G String (Violin, Viola), Counting (eighth note), (half note) in $\frac{4}{4}$ Time	$\frac{3}{4}$ Time, Counting (dotted half note), Changing Bow Speeds						F-natural C-natural (Violin, Viola), 4th Finger, Tempo Marking: Andante		
Note Sequence												
Violin												
Viola												
Cello												
Bass												
Correlating St. Orch. Arr. Levels									▲ Performer Level			

ESSENTIAL ELEMENTS

Teacher Page Student Page	201-205 **37**	206-212 **38**	213-217 **39**	218-222 **40**	223-228 **41**	229-233 **42**	234-237 **43**	238-243 **44**	244-249 **45**	250-253 **46**	254-257 **47**	258 **48**
Bowings	Changing Bow Speed					Forte Bowing, Piano Bowing						
Rhythms												
Theory	Arpeggio										Improvisation	
History							African Music	Gioachino Rossini				
Terms				Staccato	Hooked Bowing	Dynamics			Solo			
Listening Skills		D, E, F♮, F♯, G, A	Bowing E String (Violin)									
Familiar Melodies	Long, Long Ago, Monday's Melody		Shepherd's Hey, Big Rock Candy Mountain, Academic Festival Overture Theme	Arkansas Traveler	Pop Goes The Weasel	Surprise Symphony Theme	Cripple Creek	William Tell Overture	Simple Gifts			
Special Features		Upper Octave G Major Scale (Violin)		Staccato, EE Skill Builders: G Major	Hooked Bowing, EE Skill Builders: C Major	Dynamics: *f*, *p* EE Skill Builders: Scales and Arpeggios	Performance Spotlight, Orchestra Arrangement	Performance Spotlight, Orchestra Arrangement	Performance Spotlight, Orchestra Arrangement	Performance Spotlight, Solo with Piano Accompaniment Violin: Bach Minuet No. 1 Viola: Bach Minuet in C Cello: Bach Minuet No. 2 Bass: Bach March in D	Improvising Rhythms and Melodies, Fingering Chart	EE Reference Index
Quiz Assessments			E String Notes, Up-Beat									
Note Sequence												
Violin												
Viola		4										
Cello												
Bass												

Correlating St. Orch. Arr. Levels | ▲ **Artist Level** (at 42)

USING ESSENTIAL ELEMENTS FOR STRINGS

Essential Elements for Strings is a comprehensive method for string musicians, and can be used with heterogeneous and like-instrument classes or individuals. It is designed with fail-safe options for teachers to customize the learning program to meet their changing needs.

The Teacher Manual includes all the music and text from the student books, plus time-saving **EE Teaching Tips** throughout the score. As in the student books, the introduction of a new concept is always highlighted by a **color** box.

STARTING SYSTEM

INSTRUMENT POSITION

- Guitar Position
- Shoulder Position

SHAPING THE LEFT HAND

- Higher numbered fingers first to help shape the hand
- Pizzicato reinforced first so that bowing skills may be developed separately for mastery before combining with left hand skills
- *Work-outs* – rote activities for developing left hand skills

LISTENING SKILLS

- Included for each new pitch to develop intonation skills.

BOW BUILDERS

- Seven carefully sequenced activities for developing string students' beginning bowing skills.

RHYTHM RAPS

After establishing the quarter note pulse, all new rhythms are presented in the innovative **Rhythm Rap** format. Each Rhythm Rap may be clapped, tapped, counted aloud or silently, shadow bowed (bowed in the air), or bowed on an open string. After each Rhythm Rap, the identical rhythms are played on simple pitches in the next exercise.

PLAY-ALONG TRACKS

Play-along tracks are available for all exercises in the book. From the very beginning, students can model tone production and technique by listening to a professional orchestra.

For classroom use, the Teacher Manual includes access to online resources which include play-along tracks of each exercise, with a small string ensemble demonstrating the melody part.

There is a one measure count-off before each track. These tracks are performed on real instruments that support phrasing and dynamics, teaching musicality from the start. They explore a rich variety of musical styles and cultures, including classical, rock, jazz, country, and world music.

Tracks are also available online at **www.myeelibrary.com**.

PERFORMANCE SPOTLIGHTS

Carefully selected music that reviews skills and technique, and may be used for concert performance.

EE SKILL BUILDERS

Technical exercises to reinforce important playing skills.

MUSIC THEORY, HISTORY, AND CROSS-CURRICULAR ACTIVITIES

All the necessary materials are woven into the learning program—right in the student books. With teaching time in short supply, it would normally be impractical to take class time to relate music to history, world cultures or to other subjects in the curriculum. But *Essential Elements for Strings* correlates these activities with the concepts and music throughout the program. These Theory and History features are highlighted by color boxes and appear throughout the book.

As a result, teachers can efficiently meet and exceed the **National Standards for Arts Education**, while still having the time to focus on music performance skills.

CREATIVITY

Essential Creativity exercises appear throughout the book. These are preliminary activities designed to stimulate imaginations, and to foster a creative attitude toward music. Strategies for completing each Essential Creativity exercise are included in the student book. Additional suggestions are included in the Teacher Manual.

ASSESSMENT

ESSENTIAL ELEMENTS QUIZZES

Playing quizzes appear throughout the student books. Objectives highlight the exact elements being reviewed and tested. Review exercises in the Teacher Manual suggest specific examples for students requiring additional practice. Be certain students meet your performance expectations on each quiz.

A Star Achiever chart is provided in the Teacher Manual. It lists all the Essential Elements Quizzes and Essential Creativity exercises. This chart should be reproduced and distributed to each student.

EE CHECKS

EE Checks appear throughout *Essential Elements for Strings*. They are special reminders for students to evaluate the playing skills that have just been introduced.

ADDITIONAL RESOURCES AVAILABLE

PIANO ACCOMPANIMENT BOOK

Piano accompaniments for each exercise are provided in a separate book, but are also printed in the Teacher Manual. They may be used for teaching or performance and offer a variety of styles, from classical to contemporary popular music. You may want to alter these piano accompaniments to meet your specific needs.

CORRELATED MATERIALS

The Essential Elements for Strings Series includes original and popular music, arranged for beginning strings. Each publication is correlated to one of five specific "levels" within Books 1 and 2 (see the Sequence Of Essential Elements chart in the Teacher Manual for details). Contact your music dealer or the publisher for information on the latest releases in this series.

ESSENTIAL ELEMENTS FOR STRINGS BEGINNING SKILLS TEACHING SEQUENCE

Beginning string students need to learn many different skills when first learning to play their string instruments: Left Hand (posture, instrument position, left hand shape, and finger dexterity), and Right Hand (bow hand shape and detache bowing). Each of these skills needs to be introduced separately, and then developed simultaneously. *Essential Elements for Strings* is designed so that students can learn each of these skills sequentially and independently, leading to mastery. For ease of reference, the following diagram outlines the introduction and integration of each of these skills.

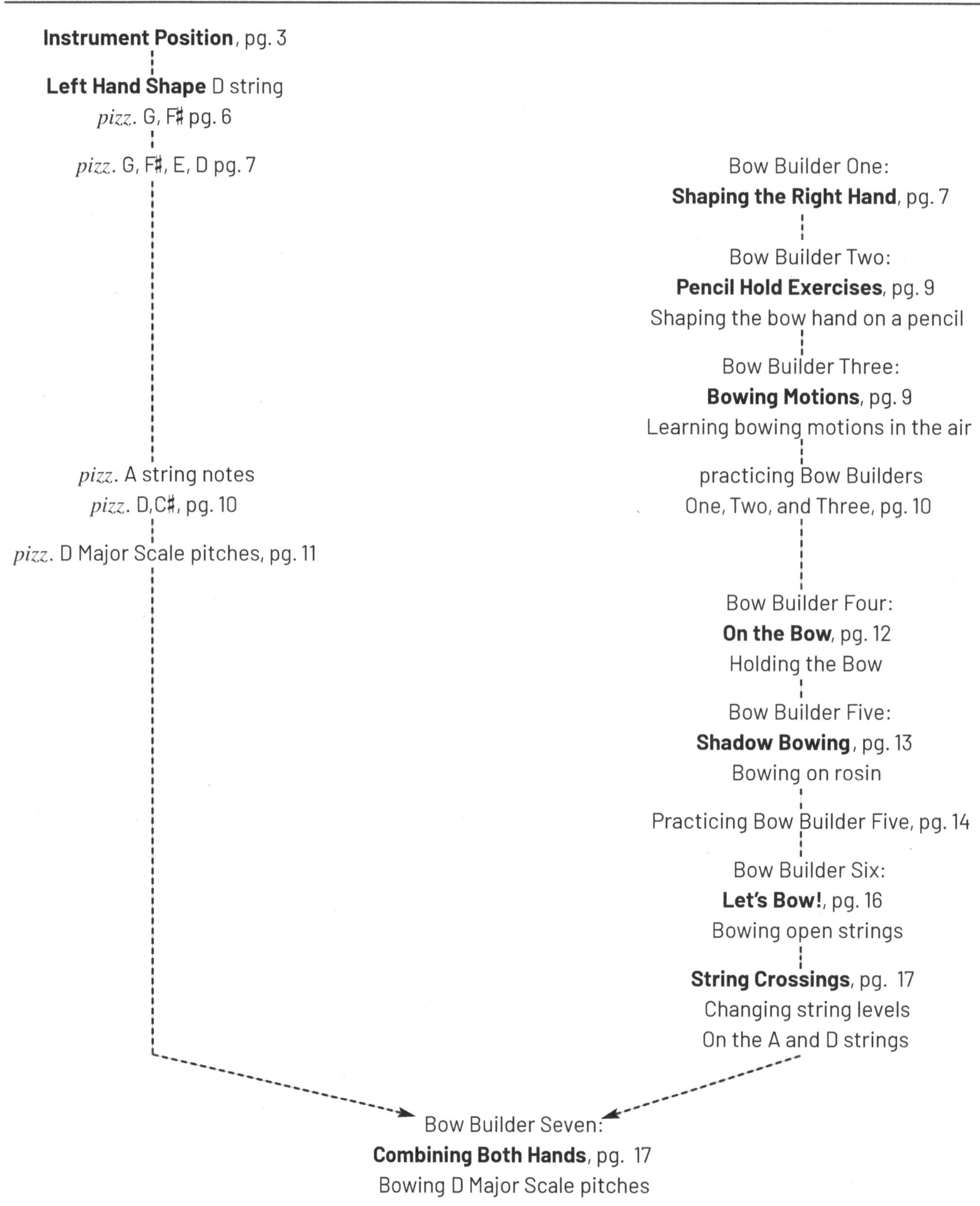

PARENT COMMUNICATION & STUDENT EVALUATION

Teacher

Communication with parents is an essential element for a successful orchestra program. The following letters and "Message For Parents" provide valuable information for orchestra parents. Feel free to adapt or make photocopies of these materials for your use. The letters include the following topics:

- Recruiting students
- "Message To Parents" explaining benefits of string study
- Guidelines for obtaining an instrument
- After the first week of study
- After 3-4 weeks of study
- Midyear practice encouragement
- When a student is discouraged or considering dropping out
- Instrument maintenance needed
- When student forgets instrument for class
- Concert Etiquette
- When students are signing up for next year's classes

The evaluation forms and reports include the following:

- Progress Report
- Position Evaluation
- Orchestra Progress Report
- Orchestra Class Interim Report
- Performance Evaluation (2)
- Practice Record

DATELINE: Distribute to all students when recruiting

Dear Parents:

(Name of school or school district) is pleased to be able to offer beginning strings instruction to students in the (grade level) grade this year. Orchestra classes will meet during the school day and will be free of charge. Instruction will be offered on violin, viola, cello, and bass. In order for your child to participate in these classes, it will be necessary for you to furnish an instrument. Local music stores offer very reasonable rental or lease plans for these instruments. Please do not obtain an instrument until your child has received a written notice of the exact instrument needed.

String instrument instruction will continue to be available to your child through the 12th grade. Learning to play an instrument and belonging to the school orchestra opens up a whole new world of friendship and fun. Your child will be able to take advantage of music performances with orchestras at the (middle school or junior high) and high school levels. The opportunities for playing a string instrument after high school are abundant, with many universities offering scholarships for orchestra participation. Orchestra provides a great foundation for your child in all aspects of life. In addition to music, students learn self-discipline, group cooperation, problem-solving, goal-setting, self-expression, memory skills, concentration, poise, enhanced physcal coordination, high self-esteem, and the importance of teamwork—skills in great demand in almost every aspect of life. Like all the arts, music has a profound effect on the academic success of students as well.

If you wish to enroll your child, please complete and return the application form to the orchestra teacher at the school. If additional information is desired, please feel free to contact me at (phone number and/or e-mail address).

Cordially,

Orchestra Teacher

(Please detach and return)

ORCHESTRA APPLICATION FORM

Name ______________________________

Address ______________________________

Phone ______________ Email ______________

Homeroom __________ Teacher ______________

Parent's Signature ______________________________

DATELINE: Distribute your version of this "Message To Parents" at your first orchestra parents meeting

MESSAGE TO PARENTS

A Parent's Guide To Enhancing Your Child's Musical Experiences

CONGRATULATIONS

Your decision to provide your child with a quality musical instrument is an investment in your child's future. In making it possible for your child to play a musical instrument, you are providing the opportunity for self-expression, creativity, and achievement.

Numerous studies indicate that parental attitude, support and involvement are important factors in a child's ability to successfully learn to play and enjoy music.

These guidelines are designed to assist you in giving your child the best support possible for his or her musical endeavors. Like any skill, interest counts far more than talent. With strong support from you, playing music will become a natural part of your child's life.

BENEFITS

For Your Child

Music participation enhances:

- Problem-solving
- Teamwork
- Goal-setting
- Self-expression
- Physical coordination
- Memory skills
- Self-confidence and esteem
- Concentration
- Poise
- and much, much more!

For Your Family

A child's music study also offers opportunities for shared family experiences, including:

- Musical event attendance
- Family music-making
- Performing for, and with, family and friends
- Learning about the lives of composers and the cultural heritage of many civilizations
- A sense of accomplishment and pride for the entire family

HOW YOU FIT IN

Always keep in mind that your support is an essential element in your child's success with music study.

Schedule Practice Times

Music achievement requires effort over a period of time. The time in orchestra rehearsal is limited. New concepts learned at school need daily personal practice time by your child at home in order for these new skills to be developed. You can help your child by:

- Providing a quiet place in which to practice
- Remaining nearby during practice times as often as possible
- Scheduling a consistent daily time for practice
- Praising your child's efforts and achievements

WHAT TO DO

To give your child the best possible support, you should:

- Remind your child to bring instrument and music to orchestra class
- Encourage your child to play for family and friends
- Offer compliments and encouragement regularly
- Expose your child to a wide variety of music, including concerts and recitals
- Encourage your child to talk with you about classes
- Make sure your child's instrument is always maintained well
- Listen to your child practice, and acknowledge improvement
- Help your child build a personal music library
- Encourage your child to make a commitment to his or her music studies
- Get to know your child's teacher

WHAT TO AVOID

- Using practice as a punishment
- Insisting your child play for others when he/she doesn't want to
- Ridiculing or making fun of mistakes of less-than-perfect playing
- Apologizing to others for your child's weak performance

TO MAINTAIN YOUR CHILD'S INTEREST

- Talk with your child if his or her interest begins to decline
- Discuss with the orchestra teacher ways to maintain your child's enthusiasm for playing
- Increase your enthusiasm and involvement in your child's playing

CREDITS

This message has been adapted from publications by the following organizations in the interest of making music study and participation an enjoyable and richly rewarding experience for children and their families. Hal Leonard Corporation appreciates the cooperation of these organizations for graciously allowing us to reprint this important message.

AMERICAN MUSIC CONFERENCE
303 East Wacker Drive, Suite 1214
Chicago, IL 60601
(312) 856-8820

NATIONAL ASSOCIATION FOR MUSIC EDUCATION
585 Grove Street, Suite 145 #711
Herndon, VA 20170
www.nafme.org

MUSIC TEACHERS NATIONAL ASSOCIATION
617 Vine St., Suite 1432
Cincinnati, OH 45202-2434
(513) 421-1420

NATIONAL ASSOCIATION OF MUSIC MERCHANTS
5140 Avenida Encinas
Carlsbad, CA 92008-4391
(619) 438-8001

DATELINE: Distribute to students once they have been measured for an instrument

PLEASE TAKE THIS FORM WITH YOU TO THE MUSIC STORE

______________________________ is officially enrolled in the (name of school) 'Orchestra Program. An instrument may be obtained from any of our local music stores who have agreed to stock the proper sizes and specifications for our school. These stores have reasonable lease, rental, and/or trial-purchase plans available. You may do business with any store you prefer. They are listed in alphabetical order.

(List names of music stores with addresses, phone numbers, and contact persons)

If you are considering purchasing an instrument from another source, we suggest you call on us to assist you in evaluating it, as one of the principle causes of pupil failure is an inferior instrument. You should obtain the following for your child:

1. Instrument ____________________ Size __________
2. *Essential Elements for Strings*, Book I (be sure the book has the same name as the instrument)
3. A folding metal music stand
4. A shoulder pad for violins and viola
5. A rock stop for cellos and basses (sometimes this is included with the instrument)
6. Stool for basses; if needed
7. A pencil - BRING TO EVERY CLASS!
8. A soft cloth to keep the instrument clean
9. Rosin

Students enrolling in orchestra must understand that they are making a commitment to daily practice at home. Good practice habits and a positive attitude have a great effect on the success your child will achieve through this class.

Parents are urged to consult the teacher any time a question or problem arises. The earlier a positive working relationship is reached between child, parent and teacher, the greater your child's success will be.

SIncerely,

Orchestra Teacher

DATELINE: Send first week of the program

Dear Parents:

Congratulations on enrolling your child in the orchestra! Orchestra is one of the most rewarding and exciting educational opportunities offered by our schools. Your investment will pay tremendous dividends in your child's life for many years to come.

Music provides students with a wealth of benefits. In addition to obtaining the musical skills needed to become a performer, a child learns skills that can be used in every facet of life. Team work, dedication, self-discipline and responsibility prepare a child for a successful future in any profession he/she may choose. A variety of research shows that music students are among the academically strongest in their schools and score higher on the SAT than other students. Most colleges and universities now look for more than good grades on a child's transcript. They want well-rounded students that have been able to accomplish more than textbook knowledge.

You do not have to know anything about music to assist your child in this new endeavor. Arrange a time and place where practice can be done without interruptions. This practice should become a part of each child's daily routine. He/she should never merely put in the required time, but should practice with the goal of always improving. Music should be placed at eye level. Please do not allow your child to put the music on a table, bed, etc. This encourages poor playing posture. Remember, practice doesn't necessarily make perfect, but PERFECT practice does!

Again, I congratulate you on enrolling your child in the orchestra. As the year progresses, I hope you will feel free to contact me whenever necessary.

Sincerely,

Orchestra Teacher

DATELINE: Send 3-4 weeks into the program

Dear Parents:

It is a pleasure to have your child in the (name of school or school district) Orchestra Program. This school district offers string instruction from the (grade level of beginners) through the 12th grade. The program is a continuous one, and I hope to see every student performing in the high school orchestra some day. Your interest and support is a lifetime investment for your child.

All beginning classes are now underway, and I'm sure your child has already performed for you. Proper care of the instrument is encouraged. Students have been shown how to handle the instrument so as not to harm it. I suggest that no one else handle the instrument unless they have your permission and your child's instructions.

During the first several weeks of class the primary emphasis has been on developing good playing position as well as correct posture. Failure to master these concepts can hamper a student's ability and progress for years to come. Thus, these first few weeks are the most critical. This cannot be overemphasized! Practice is needed to develop the coordination and strength necessary to play a stringed instrument. A practice "marathon" cannot accomplish the same results as consistent daily practice. Your encouragement is a very important ingredient for your child's success right now.

Report cards will be sent home every (number) weeks so that you may follow your child's progress. Please encourage (student's name) to demonstrate for you and other supportive family members what he/she has learned and be generous in your praise and encouragement. Help (student's name) to remember his/her instrument and materials for class. A child takes pride not only in learning to play, but in learning to play well.

As questions or problems arise, please feel free to contact me. I hope that your child's experience with the orchestra is a successful one.

Sincerely,

Orchestra Teacher

DATELINE: Send as needed

Dear Parents:

Now that our school year is (nearly halfway completed), I would like to touch base with you regarding your child's participation in the orchestra. We've had a very good year so far, and the orchestra shows a lot of promise. I am very proud of all of the students and the progress they have made.

Keep in mind that the beginning of the year had the excitement of a new instrument and a new activity. Then came the excitement of being able to perform that first tune, followed by the thrill of a public performance complete with lots of applause and proud parents. Now that all of that is gone, we have settled back into the routine of learning to develop new technical skills. Don't be surprised if your child experiences some decrease in interest during this time. It is completely normal. However, with your continued support and encouragement, we can overcome any decline in enthusiasm and reach for the next performance level.

Your child may need EXTRA encouragement during the next few weeks to continue good practice habits and performance in class. These are the formative years and how (he/she) handles situations now can determine the way (he/she) approaches every aspect of life. Though the requirements for learning an instrument often demand a high level of personal discipline, it is this same discipline which will be applied as a habit to all tasks in life, especially (his/her) academic success right now. A child must learn that long range benefits of a task only come from long range commitment and dedication.

Please contact me at your earliest convenience if you would like to discuss any aspect of your child's performance in orchestra class. I am anxious to do all I can to assist you in the successful development of your child's abilities.

Sincerely,

Orchestra Teacher

DATELINE: When a student is discouraged or considering dropping out

Dear (Name of Parent):

I want to express my concern that (name of child) seems to be experiencing some decline in interest in orchestra class. I want you to know that while this is a very normal occurrence, it is important to address immediately. A child experiences a variety of levels of interest during the first year of study. However, it is not common for (him/her) to consider dropping out of the program completely.

As a parent, I ask you for your extra support and encouragement during this time. Do not make a hasty decision, something which you and your child could regret for years to come. Everyone experiences periods of discouragement during (his/her) music study. We all know that it is easy to start a task, but making it to the finish line takes persistence, especially when the going gets rough. I have met countless adults who say, "I wish I hadn't quit" or "I wish I would have had the opportunity to play when I was in school." Of course, there are times when pushing a child too far can have the opposite effect and make the child resentful of music in the future. Neither one of us wants this to happen. There is a fine line between the two, and it is sometimes difficult to distinguish what is best for each child.

Thus, the purpose of this letter is simply to ask that we work together to make the best possible decision for your child's future. Please contact me at your earliest convenience to discuss the matter. I will support whatever decision you feel is best for your child.

Sincerely,

Orchestra Teacher

DATELINE: Send as needed

To the parents of: ______________________________

Proper instrument maintenance and equipment is essential for each student. An instrument must be in excellent condition or it will hamper a student's progress. The checklist below is for your assistance. When the necessary items have been corrected, please return this sheet to the instructor.

____ Clean body of fingerprints, rosin dust, etc. USE ONLY POLISH MADE ESPECIALLY FOR STRINGED INSTRUMENTS WHICH IS AVAILABLE AT A MUSIC STORE.

____ String(s) need to be replaced.

____ Bridge needs to be replaced. Please be sure the bridge is properly fitted by a repair person. You must take the instrument with you to the music store. Simply buying a bridge will not solve the problem.

____ Soundpost must be set-up and adjusted inside the instrument.

____ A shoulder pad is needed to support the instrument properly. It is suggested that the student take the instrument with him/her and try out several to find the one that is the most effective.

____ A rock stop is needed.

____ The bow needs to be rehaired.

____ Rosin is needed.

____ The fine tuner needs to be repaired or replaced.

____ Repair bass stool as needed.

____ A cloth is needed to keep in the case. (Any soft cloth will work.)

____ Other:

Remember to have your child return this letter to me when the above item(s) have been corrected. If you need further information, please feel free to contact me.

Sincerely,

Orchestra Teacher

Date notified: __________

Date corrected: __________

Parent's Signature______________________________

DATELINE: Send when student forgets instruments for class

Dear Parents:

Your child was without an instrument in orchestra class today. In an effort to assure that he/she does not fall behind in class, I asked your child to make detailed notes of the material covered during class. It is important for your child to practice this material at home today so that his/her grade will not be affected. Please have your child return this paper with your signature tomorrow.

Sincerely,

Orchestra Teacher

Parent's Signature____

CLASS NOTES (use back if needed):

DATELINE: Send before concerts - Concert Etiquette

Dear Parents:

The students have made great progress in learning the fundamentals of playing their string instrument. They are so excited to perform for you and friends! As this may be the first time they have ever performed in a formal concert setting, please help them prepare by reviewing these guidelines together for proper concert etiquette. These also include suggestions for audience behavior expectations to help you.

Date of the concert: (day) ______________________, date ____________.

- Students should arrive early enough before the concert begins for tuning and warm-up. Students should arrive at (concert site) ______________________ by (time) ____________.
- Students should arrive at the concert site in proper concert attire. Clothes should be neat and clean . Boys should wear: ______________________; girls should wear: ______________________.
- Be sure your child brings his/her music, instrument, and bow to the concert. The students will be excited, so it will be easy for them to forget.
- Students should sit quietly on stage during the concert and acknowledge applause of the audience as directed by the teacher. During the concert the students should focus their attention on their director. They should avoid looking at the audience. Students should especially watch the director closely for all starting and stopping cues.
- Remind students that it is inappropriate for them to eat, drink, or chew gum during a concert.
- During the concert students should maintain good posture and a positive stage presence at all times when on stage. They are not only representing themselves, but also the entire orchestra.
- Encourage your child to play with his/her best effort. One purpose of a concert is to show the audience the great progress made. Of course, students should must enjoy making beautiful music!

Thanks so much for letting me teach your child. The children have worked very hard and are eager to perform for you and your family and friends. Maybe your child has already played for you some of the music that will be performed. I look forward to seeing you at the concert!

Sincerely,

Orchestra Teacher

DATELINE: Send when student are signing up for next year's classes

Dear Parents:

I know you share my pride in your child's progress in orchestra this year. The personal discipline and commitment have paid off many times over. We've had a GREAT year!

It is now the time of year when students must schedule classes for the coming year. Make certain that orchestra is part of that schedule. If there is ANY indecision or scheduling problems concerning your child's future participation in the orchestra program, please make an appointment with me so we can discuss this matter. Sometimes it may seem that required courses allow no room for electives, but there are many ways to include orchestra in your child's schedule.

I want your child to enjoy continued positive growth during his/her educational career. Group participation enhances self esteem, and there is nothing that brings out a sense of personal contribution quite like being in the orchestra. You have made a great investment in your child's future, and there are many benefits still ahead.

Again, I encourage your communication in this important step. If you have any questions, please feel free to call me at school (#) or e-mail me (e-mail address). I am your partner in seeing that your child has the opportunity to continue his/her important musical development.

Sincerely,

Orchestra Teacher

Dear Parents:

After (number of weeks) in orchestra, we have completed (number) pages in *Essential Elements for Strings* Book 1. We are continuing to have a good year, and I am very proud of our progress. Thank you for all of the support you have offered to this success. What follows is a progress report for your child.

PROGRESS REPORT

Student's Name ______________________________

Letter Grade: ____________

1 = outstanding 2 = above average 3 = average 4 = below average

INSTRUMENT POSITION ____________	1	2	3	4
LEFT HAND POSITION ____________	1	2	3	4
RIGHT HAND POSITION ____________	1	2	3	4
RHYTHM ____________	1	2	3	4
BOWING SKILLS ____________	1	2	3	4
REMEMBERING EQUIPMENT ____________	1	2	3	4

Please check the following:

____ My child always practices without being reminded.

____ My child usually practices without being reminded.

____ My child seldom practices without being reminded.

____ My child practices only when reminded.

____ My child seldom practices at all.

Parent's Signature ______________________________

Please have your child return this letter to me when the above report has been completed and signed by you. I would like to remind you about our upcoming concert on (date/time/location). You and your entire family are invited to hear our performance. Thank you again for your support!

SIncerely,

Orchestra Teacher

POSTION EVALUATION

Name ____

SKILL ♪	CHECK LIST ♪
+ Indicates skill is demonstrated	- Indicates skill needs to be improved

Instrument Hold/Posture
_____ Sitting/standing properly
_____ Instrument at corect angle
_____ Instrument properly supported

Bow hand
_____ Thumb placement
_____ Thumb bent
_____ All fingers placed correctly
_____ Fingers over frog
_____ Pinky curved

Left Hand Position
_____ Fingers properly curved
_____ Thumb placement
_____ No squeezing the neck
_____ Arm/elbow at correct angle
_____ Wrist properly aligned

Comments:

Parent's Signature ____

ORCHESTRA PROGRESS REPORT

First Grading Period

Student's Name ______________________________

Letter Grade: ____________

1 = outstanding 2 = above average 3 = average 4 = below average

INSTRUMENT POSITION ____________	1	2	3	4
LEFT HAND POSITION ____________	1	2	3	4
RIGHT HAND POSITION ____________	1	2	3	4
RHYTHM ____________	1	2	3	4
BOWING SKILLS ____________	1	2	3	4
REMEMBERING EQUIPMENT ____________	1	2	3	4

COMMENTS:

Parent's Signature ______________________________

ORCHESTRA CLASS INTERIM REPORT

First Grading Period

Name ____

1 = outstanding 2 = above average 3 = average 4 = below average 5 = failing

CLASS PERFORMANCE						COMMENTS
1. Proper care of instrument/music	1	2	3	4	5	
2. Remembering equipment	1	2	3	4	5	
3. Correct posture	1	2	3	4	5	
4. Mastery of daily assignments	1	2	3	4	5	
5. Attitude and effort in class	1	2	3	4	5	
LEFT HAND-FINGER DEVELOPMENT						
1. Position	1	2	3	4	5	
2. Intonation	1	2	3	4	5	
BOWING DEVELOPMENT						
1. Right hand position	1	2	3	4	5	
2. Flexibility	1	2	3	4	5	
RHYTHM						
1. Counts or taps toe during class	1	2	3	4	5	
2. Correct rhythms	1	2	3	4	5	
3. Steady beat	1	2	3	4	5	

GRADE ________ **PARENT'S SIGNATURE** ______________________________

PERFORMANCE EVALUATION

Name ______________________________

SKILLS	POINTS POSSIBLE	SCORE
Instrument Position	20	________
Bow Hand Position	20	________
Left Hand Position	20	________
Bowing Skills	20	________
Intonation	20	________

TOTAL: ________

GRADE: ________

COMMENTS:

PERFORMANCE EVALUATION

Name ____________________

SKILLS	POINTS POSSIBLE	SCORE
Instrument Position	30	______
Bow Hand Position	15	______
Bowing Skills	15	______
Left Hand Position	30	______
Correct Notes	5	______
Rhythm	5	______

TOTAL: ______

GRADE: ______

COMMENTS:

PRACTICE RECORD

Name: ____________________________

DUE:

Week: ____________________________

Assignment: ____________________________

Friday	Saturday	Sunday	Monday	Tuesday	Wednesday	Thursday

(number of minutes each day)

TOTAL for the week: ____________ GRADE EARNED ____________

Parent's Signature ____________________________

You can mark your progress through the book on this page.
Fill in the stars as instructed by your orchestra teacher.

1. Page 3, Holding Your Instrument
2. Page 5, EE Quiz, No. 9
3. Page 7, EE Quiz, No. 16
4. Page 9, EE Quiz, No. 22
5. Page 11, EE Quiz, No. 32
6. Page 12, Essential Creativity, No. 35
7. Page 13, Shadow Bowing
8. Page 15, Essential Creativity, No. 46
9. Page 17, EE Quiz, No. 53
10. Page 19, EE Quiz, No. 64
11. Page 21, EE Quiz, No. 76
12. Page 23, EE Quiz, No. 86
13. Pages 24–25, Performance Spotlight
14. Page 27, EE Quiz, No. 102
15. Page 28, EE Quiz, No. 107
16. Page 31, No. 125
17. Page 33, No. 134
18. Page 34, EE Quiz, No. 139
19. Page 35, Essential Creativity, No. 143
20. Page 39, EE Quiz, No. 166
21. Pages 43–46, Performance Spotlight

MUSIC — AN ESSENTIAL ELEMENT OF LIFE

Teacher Discuss with students the key elements in the first paragraph on student book page one. Congratulate students on their decision to play a string instrument. Stress that much of their success as a new musician will depend on the degree and quality of their practice. Point out the life-long learning and playing experiences possible with string instruments. Briefly discuss your musical experiences with string instruments, both as an avocation and career.

A brief instrument history also appears on student book page one. Consider showing students photos of early string instruments. Students like to hear stories about some of the most famous instrument makers such as Guaneri, Amati, and Stradivarius. Also showing photos and playing recordings of famous string instrument performers helps develop students' interests in playing string instruments. Talk about the history of your string instrument and bow.

HISTORY OF THE INSTRUMENTS

VIOLIN

The string family includes the violin, viola, violoncello, and the double bass. The violin dates back to the 16th century. The early ancestors of the violin were the Arabian rebab and rebec, popular during the 14th-16th centuries. During the 1500s, there were two types of viols: the viola da gamba, played on the knee, and the viola da braccia, played on the shoulder.

Gasparo da Salo, an Italian instrument maker, developed the present day violin during the 16th century. Da Salo and Nicolo Amati are credited with establishing the design of today's violin, which has survived with only a few minor changes. Antonio Stradivari, and the Guarneri and Guadagnini families were famous instrument makers from the 17th and 18th centuries, and their violins are still in use today.

Nearly every composer has written music for the violin, including Johann Sebastian Bach, Ludwig van Beethoven, and Peter Ilyich Tchaikovsky. Famous violin performers include Midori, Isaac Stern, Stéphane Grappelli, Itzhak Perlman, Jascha Heifetz, Joshua Bell, Mark O'Connor, Hilary Hahn, and Nicola Benedetto.

VIOLA

The string family includes the violin, viola, violoncello, and the double bass. The early ancestors of the string family were the Arabian rebab and rebec, popular during the 14th-16th centuries. The viola is the oldest of the modern string instruments, and the word "viola" was used to describe many different string instruments until the 18th century. Today's violas look like violins, though they are larger and longer.

The sound of the viola includes notes lower than the violin and has a particular mellow quality that is darker and richer. The viola is often referred to as the alto voice of the orchestra. Antonio Stradivari, and the Guarneri and Guadagnini families were famous instrument makers from the 17th and 18th centuries, and their violas are still in use today.

Many important composers have been violists, including Wolfgang Amadeus Mozart and Paul Hindemith. Other composers known for their viola compositions include Hector Berlioz, Ernest Bloch, and Béla Bartók. Famous viola performers include Walter Trampler, Lionel Tertis, Donald McGinnis, William Primrose, Nobuko Imai, and Kim Kashkashian.

CELLO

The string family includes the violin, viola, violoncello, and the double bass. The early ancestors of the violin were the Arabian rebab and rebec, popular during the 14th-16th centuries. During the 1500s, there were two types of viols: the viola da gamba, played on the knee, and the viola da braccia, played on the shoulder.

The sound of the violoncello, called 'cello' for short, is pitched an octave below the viola. The cello has a warm tone and is capable of playing a wide range of dynamics. It is often referred to as the tenor of the orchestra. Antonio Stradivari, and the Guarneri and Guadagnini families were famous instrument makers from the 17th and 18th centuries, and their cellos are still in use today.

Nearly every composer has written music for the cello, including Johann Sebastian Bach, Ludwig van Beethoven, and Peter Ilyich Tchaikovsky. Famous cello performers include Janos Starker, Leonard Rose, Pablo Casals, Yo-Yo Ma, Sheku Kanneh-Mason, Zuill Bailey, Mischa Maisky, Sol Gabetta, and Kermit Moore.

DOUBLE BASS

The string family includes the violin, viola, violoncello, and the double bass. The double bass (also called the 'string bass', or the 'bass' for short) is the most versatile of all the string instruments. At home in the symphony orchestra, jazz combo, concert band, and the dance band, the double bass provides the harmonic foundation in many styles of music.

The double bass sounds much lower than the cello and is tuned differently than the other instruments of the string family. Gasparo da Salo is credited with being the first to make a double bass in its present form. Other famous double bass makers include Carlo Guiseppe Testore, Carlo Bergonzi, and John Frederich Lott.

Nearly every composer has written music for the double bass, including Johann Sebastian Bach, Ludwig van Beethoven, and Peter Ilyich Tchaikovsky. Famous double bass performers include Gary Karr, Francois Rabbath, Ron Carter, Milt Hinton, Ray Brown, Edgar Meyer, Esperanza Spalding, and Hal Robinson.

Teacher Essential Elements Instructional Design

Students need to develop mastery of their instrument position, left hand shape, and fingering skills before combining with bowing skills. This method has been designed to develop students' right and left-hand skills simultaneously, but independently. This sequence of learning promotes mastery, and greatly helps your students learn to properly play their string instrument.

The following instructions appear on page 2 of each student book. Review the principal parts of the instruments, and point out the need to handle string instruments carefully. They are fragile and easily damaged. Have students state the name of each instrument part as they are touching it.

VIOLIN

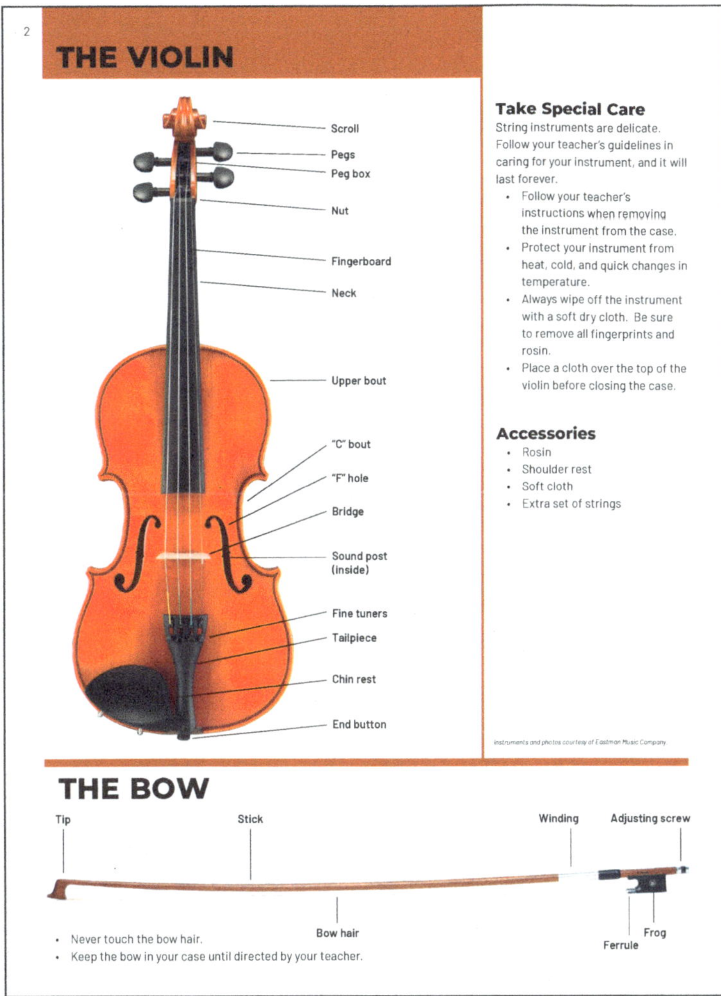

2

THE VIOLIN

Scroll
Pegs
Peg box
Nut
Fingerboard
Neck
Upper bout
"C" bout
"F" hole
Bridge
Sound post (inside)
Fine tuners
Tailpiece
Chin rest
End button

Take Special Care

String instruments are delicate. Follow your teacher's guidelines in caring for your instrument, and it will last forever.

- Follow your teacher's instructions when removing the instrument from the case.
- Protect your instrument from heat, cold, and quick changes in temperature.
- Always wipe off the instrument with a soft dry cloth. Be sure to remove all fingerprints and rosin.
- Place a cloth over the top of the violin before closing the case.

Accessories

- Rosin
- Shoulder rest
- Soft cloth
- Extra set of strings

THE BOW

Tip
Stick
Winding
Adjusting screw
Bow hair
Frog
Ferrule

- Never touch the bow hair.
- Keep the bow in your case until directed by your teacher.

VIOLA

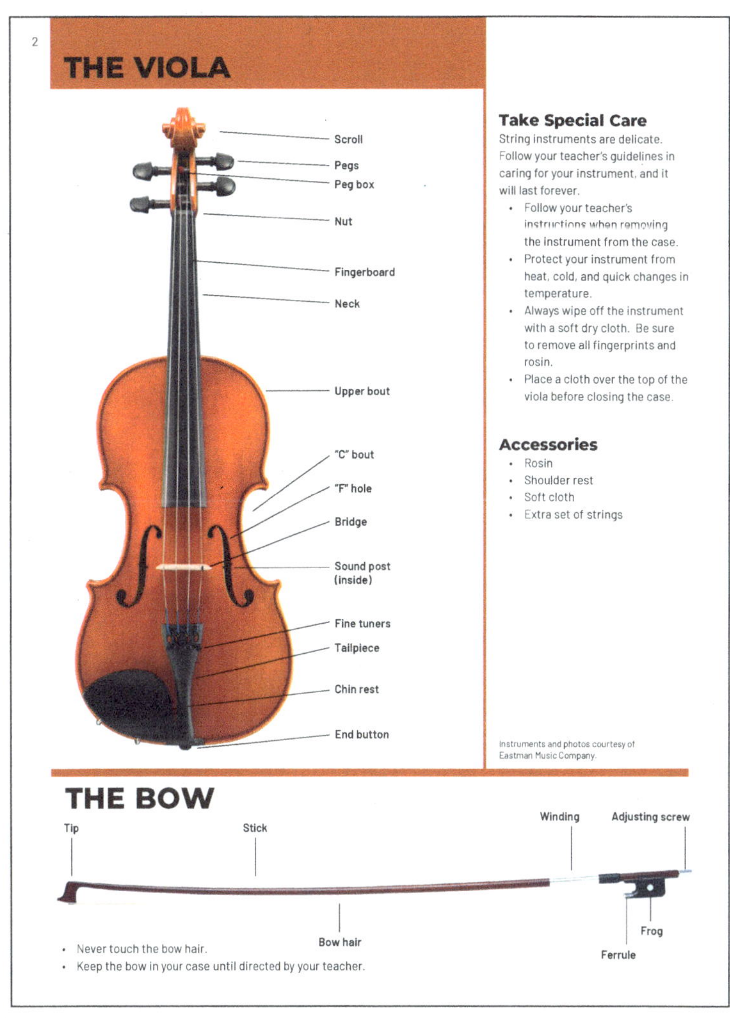

2

THE VIOLA

Scroll
Pegs
Peg box
Nut
Fingerboard
Neck
Upper bout
"C" bout
"F" hole
Bridge
Sound post (inside)
Fine tuners
Tailpiece
Chin rest
End button

Take Special Care

String instruments are delicate. Follow your teacher's guidelines in caring for your instrument, and it will last forever.

- Follow your teacher's instructions when removing the instrument from the case.
- Protect your instrument from heat, cold, and quick changes in temperature.
- Always wipe off the instrument with a soft dry cloth. Be sure to remove all fingerprints and rosin.
- Place a cloth over the top of the viola before closing the case.

Accessories

- Rosin
- Shoulder rest
- Soft cloth
- Extra set of strings

Instruments and photos courtesy of Eastman Music Company.

THE BOW

Tip
Stick
Winding
Adjusting screw
Bow hair
Frog
Ferrule

- Never touch the bow hair.
- Keep the bow in your case until directed by your teacher.

Violin/ Viola Instruct students to leave the bow in their case until they have developed their bow hand shape on a pencil, pen, or straw. Students need to develop mastery of their instrument position, left hand shape, and finger dexterity before combining with bowing skills.

CELLO

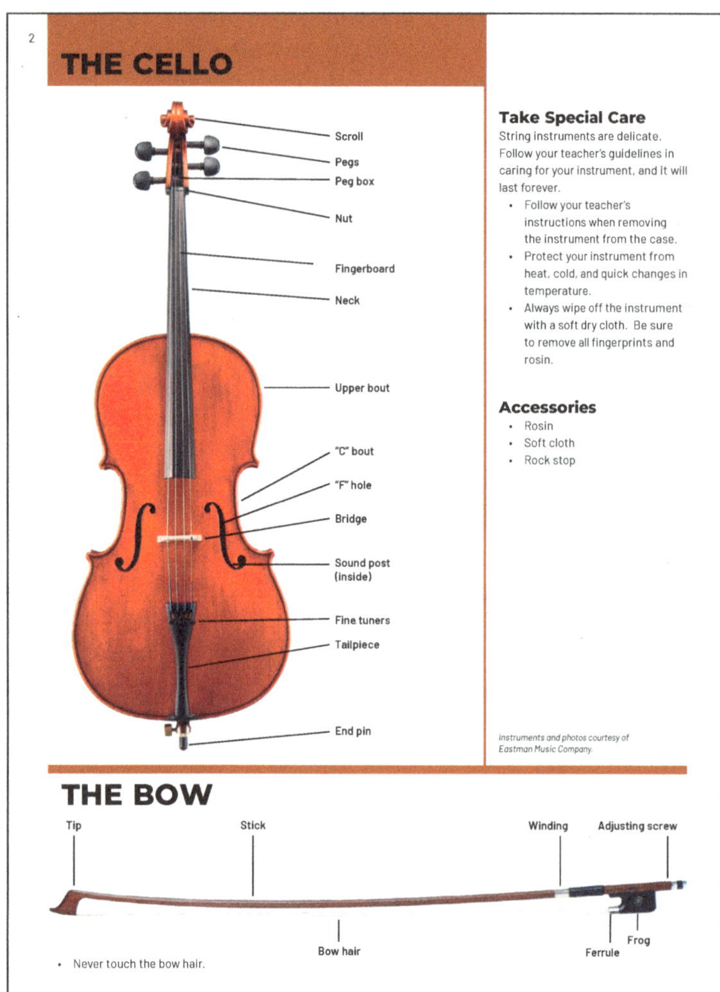

2

THE CELLO

Take Special Care

String instruments are delicate. Follow your teacher's guidelines in caring for your instrument, and it will last forever.

- Follow your teacher's instructions when removing the instrument from the case.
- Protect your instrument from heat, cold, and quick changes in temperature.
- Always wipe off the instrument with a soft dry cloth. Be sure to remove all fingerprints and rosin.

Accessories

- Rosin
- Soft cloth
- Rock stop

Instruments and photos courtesy of Eastman Music Company.

THE BOW

- Never touch the bow hair.

BASS

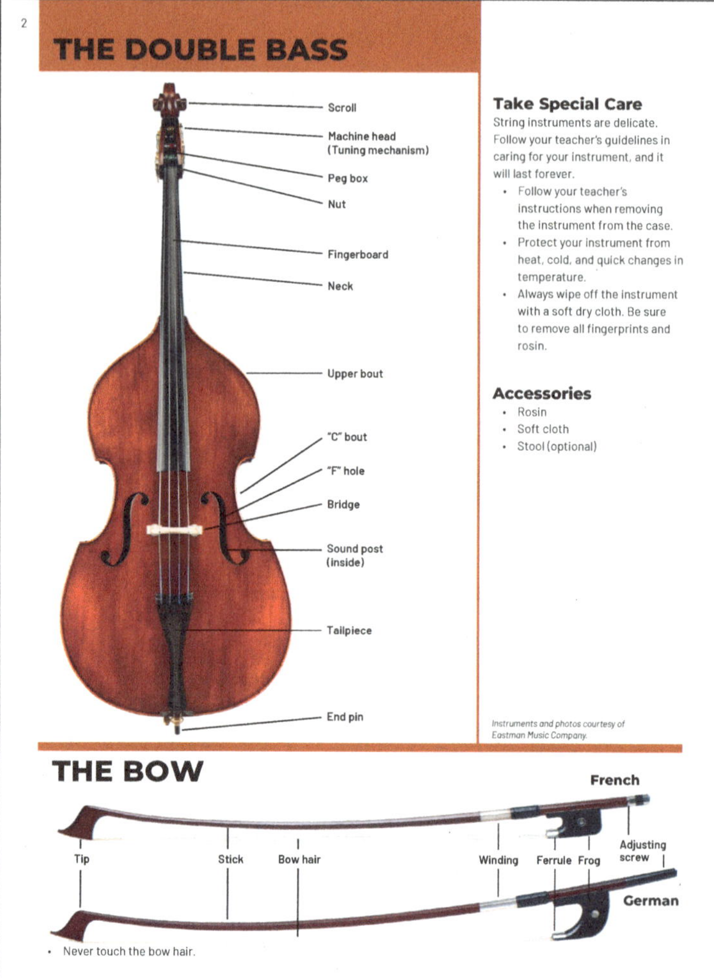

2

THE DOUBLE BASS

Take Special Care

String instruments are delicate. Follow your teacher's guidelines in caring for your instrument, and it will last forever.

- Follow your teacher's instructions when removing the instrument from the case.
- Protect your instrument from heat, cold, and quick changes in temperature.
- Always wipe off the instrument with a soft dry cloth. Be sure to remove all fingerprints and rosin.

Accessories

- Rosin
- Soft cloth
- Stool (optional)

Instruments and photos courtesy of Eastman Music Company.

THE BOW

- Never touch the bow hair.

Cello/ Bass Instruct students to take the bow out of the case before removing the instrument. This will help protect the bow from being damaged. At the end of class, students should loosen the end pin screw, carefully push the end pin in the instrument, put the instrument in the case, and then return the bow to the case.

Teacher Demonstrate and lead each instrument through the four instrument-position steps on student book page 3. Then lead the students as a class through the four steps. Be sure to carefully check each student's instrument position so that an acceptable instrument position may be established right from the start. Practice leading the students through the four steps many times so that correct instrument position habits may be secured.

Have students compare their posture and instrument position to the photos on student book page 3. Students may also assist the teacher by comparing their classmates' posture and instrument to the photos. Actively employing students in the teaching process helps them be aware of their own playing skills.

VIOLIN

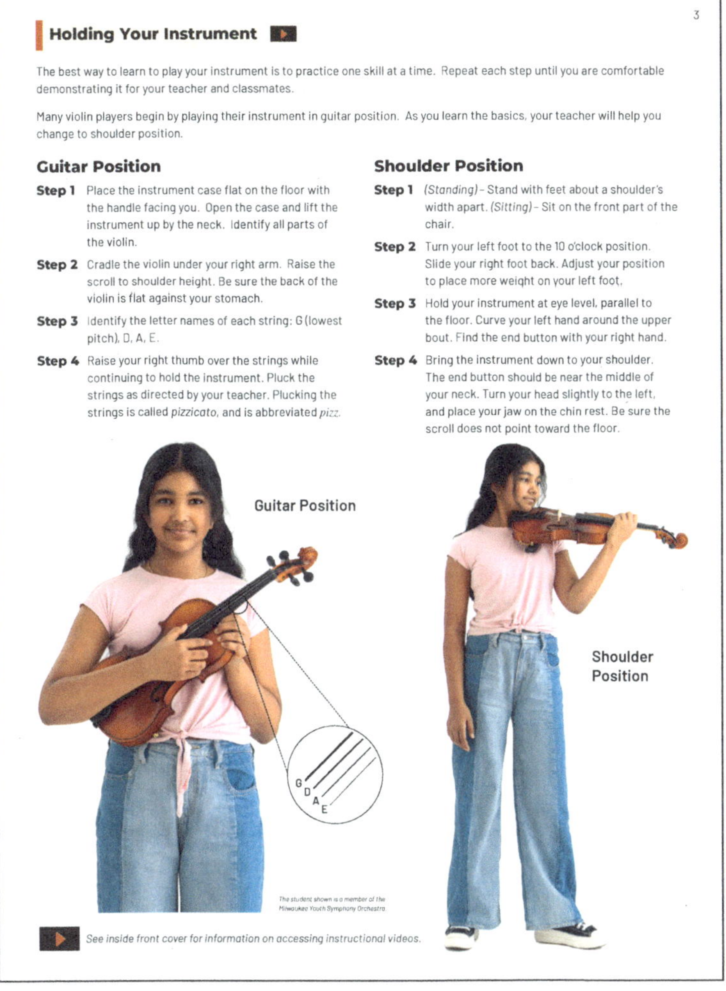

3

Holding Your Instrument

The best way to learn to play your instrument is to practice one skill at a time. Repeat each step until you are comfortable demonstrating it for your teacher and classmates.

Many violin players begin by playing their instrument in guitar position. As you learn the basics, your teacher will help you change to shoulder position.

Guitar Position

Step 1 Place the instrument case flat on the floor with the handle facing you. Open the case and lift the instrument up by the neck. Identify all parts of the violin.

Step 2 Cradle the violin under your right arm. Raise the scroll to shoulder height. Be sure the back of the violin is flat against your stomach.

Step 3 Identify the letter names of each string: G (lowest pitch), D, A, E.

Step 4 Raise your right thumb over the strings while continuing to hold the instrument. Pluck the strings as directed by your teacher. Plucking the strings is called *pizzicato*, and is abbreviated *pizz.*

Shoulder Position

Step 1 *(Standing)* - Stand with feet about a shoulder's width apart. *(Sitting)* - Sit on the front part of the chair.

Step 2 Turn your left foot to the 10 o'clock position. Slide your right foot back. Adjust your position to place more weight on your left foot.

Step 3 Hold your instrument at eye level, parallel to the floor. Curve your left hand around the upper bout. Find the end button with your right hand.

Step 4 Bring the instrument down to your shoulder. The end button should be near the middle of your neck. Turn your head slightly to the left, and place your jaw on the chin rest. Be sure the scroll does not point toward the floor.

See inside front cover for information on accessing instructional videos.

VIOLA

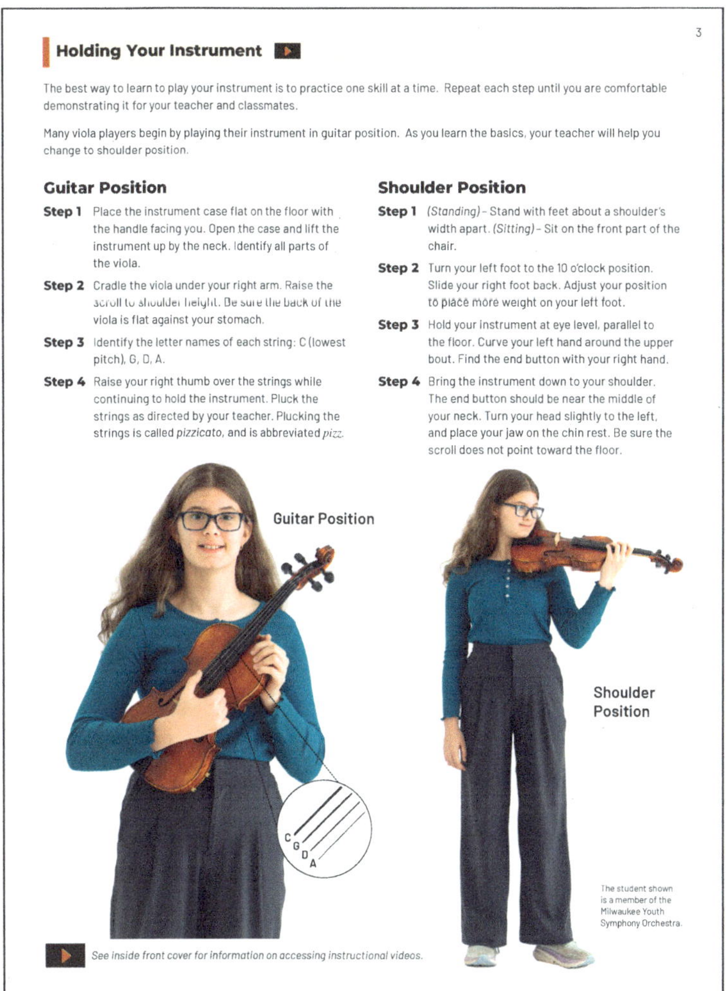

3

Holding Your Instrument

The best way to learn to play your instrument is to practice one skill at a time. Repeat each step until you are comfortable demonstrating it for your teacher and classmates.

Many viola players begin by playing their instrument in guitar position. As you learn the basics, your teacher will help you change to shoulder position.

Guitar Position

Step 1 Place the instrument case flat on the floor with the handle facing you. Open the case and lift the instrument up by the neck. Identify all parts of the viola.

Step 2 Cradle the viola under your right arm. Raise the scroll to shoulder height. Be sure the back of the viola is flat against your stomach.

Step 3 Identify the letter names of each string: C (lowest pitch), G, D, A.

Step 4 Raise your right thumb over the strings while continuing to hold the instrument. Pluck the strings as directed by your teacher. Plucking the strings is called *pizzicato*, and is abbreviated *pizz.*

Shoulder Position

Step 1 *(Standing)* - Stand with feet about a shoulder's width apart. *(Sitting)* - Sit on the front part of the chair.

Step 2 Turn your left foot to the 10 o'clock position. Slide your right foot back. Adjust your position to place more weight on your left foot.

Step 3 Hold your instrument at eye level, parallel to the floor. Curve your left hand around the upper bout. Find the end button with your right hand.

Step 4 Bring the instrument down to your shoulder. The end button should be near the middle of your neck. Turn your head slightly to the left, and place your jaw on the chin rest. Be sure the scroll does not point toward the floor.

See inside front cover for information on accessing instructional videos.

Violin/ Viola Demonstrate your preferred method of holding the instrument. Many teachers instruct their beginning violin and viola students first to play in guitar position. Playing in guitar position requires fewer specific teacher instructions. This helps students easily pizzicato open strings on the first day of class. Guitar position also enables students to more easily develop their left-hand position separately while they are gradually developing shoulder position playing skills.

Playing in shoulder position is a skill that students develop over a period of time. As students' left-hand shapes are developing in guitar position, begin to gradually introduce shoulder position. When ready, have students first learn how to hold the instrument on their shoulder, and then begin to pizzicato. Be sure students have some type of commercial shoulder pad, or material such as foam rubber, to provide adequate instrument support in shoulder position. There should be friction between the material and the student's clothing to help prevent the instrument from slipping. To determine the proper height of the shoulder pad, a student's jawbone should generally be parallel to the floor when the instrument is in shoulder position. Note that the button of the instrument is positioned at or near the center of the player's neck.

CELLO

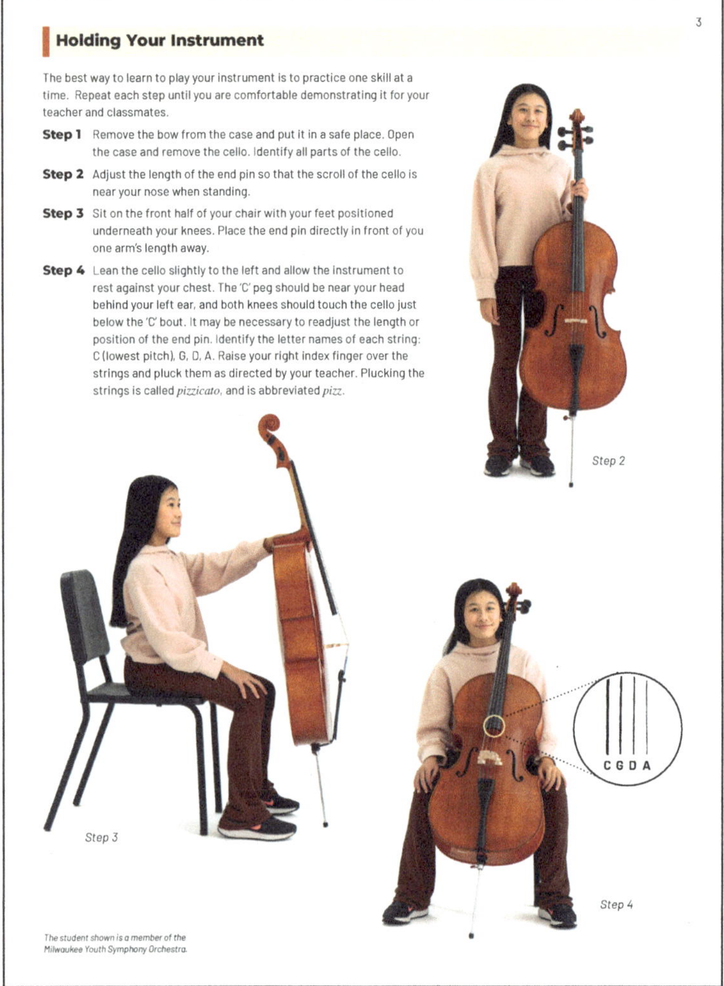

3

Holding Your Instrument

The best way to learn to play your instrument is to practice one skill at a time. Repeat each step until you are comfortable demonstrating it for your teacher and classmates.

Step 1 Remove the bow from the case and put it in a safe place. Open the case and remove the cello. Identify all parts of the cello.

Step 2 Adjust the length of the end pin so that the scroll of the cello is near your nose when standing.

Step 3 Sit on the front half of your chair with your feet positioned underneath your knees. Place the end pin directly in front of you one arm's length away.

Step 4 Lean the cello slightly to the left and allow the instrument to rest against your chest. The 'C' peg should be near your head behind your left ear, and both knees should touch the cello just below the 'C' bout. It may be necessary to readjust the length or position of the end pin. Identify the letter names of each string: C (lowest pitch), G, D, A. Raise your right index finger over the strings and pluck them as directed by your teacher. Plucking the strings is called *pizzicato*, and is abbreviated *pizz*.

The student shown is a member of the Milwaukee Youth Symphony Orchestra.

BASS

3

Holding Your Instrument

The best way to learn to play your instrument is to practice one skill at a time. Repeat each step until you are comfortable demonstrating it for your teacher and classmates.

Holding The Double Bass (sitting)

Step 1 Remove the bow from the case and put it in a safe place. Open the case and remove the bass. Identify all parts of the bass.

Step 2 Adjust the length of the end pin so that the nut of the bass is near the top of your forehead when standing.

Step 3 Sit squarely on the front half of the stool with your right foot on the floor and your left foot on a rung of the stool. Place the end pin in front of your left foot about one arm's length away.

Step 4 Rotate the bass slightly to the right and lean the bass toward your body so that the upper bout rests against the left side of your stomach. Identify the letter names of each string: E (lowest pitch), A, D, G. Raise your right index finger over the strings and pluck them as directed by your teacher. Plucking the strings is called *pizzicato*, and is abbreviated *pizz*.

Holding The Double Bass (standing)

Step 1 Remove the bow from the case and put it in a safe place. Open the case and remove the bass. Identify all parts of the bass.

Step 2 Adjust the length of the end pin so that the nut of the bass is near the top of your forehead when standing.

Step 3 Place the end pin in front of your left foot about one arm's length away. Place your left foot slightly forward.

Step 4 Rotate the bass slightly to the right and lean the bass toward your body so that the upper bout rests against the left side of your stomach. Identify the letter names of each string: E (lowest pitch), A, D, G. Raise your right index finger over the strings and pluck them as directed by your teacher. Plucking the strings is called *pizzicato*, and is abbreviated *pizz*.

The student shown is a member of the Milwaukee Youth Symphony Orchestra.

Bass Students may play the bass standing or sitting. The authors suggest that beginning students play the bass while sitting on a stool. This helps balance the bass, freeing the player's left hand from holding the bass in the beginning stages of playing. Inexpensive thirty-inch stools may be purchased from local hardware stores for students to use. However, be sure that the length of the legs of the stool allows the player's right foot to rest flat on the floor comfortably. This may require either trimming the legs of the stool or purchasing a commercially adjustable stool.

Teacher Elements of reading music are first introduced on student book page 4. Have students say or sing the letter names of the pitches, as well as say "rest" during the quarter rests. Note names appear inside each note on exercises 1–9 to help beginners recognize note names and their location on the staff.

Beat = The *Pulse* of Music The **beat** in music should be very steady, just like your pulse.

Quarter Note ♩ = **1 Beat of Sound** **Notes** tell us how high or low to play, and how long to play.

Quarter Rest 𝄽 = **1 Beat of Silence** **Rests** tell us to count silent beats.

Music Staff The **music staff** has 5 lines and 4 spaces.

Bar Lines **Bar lines** divide the music staff into **measures**.

Measures The **measures** on this page have four beats each.

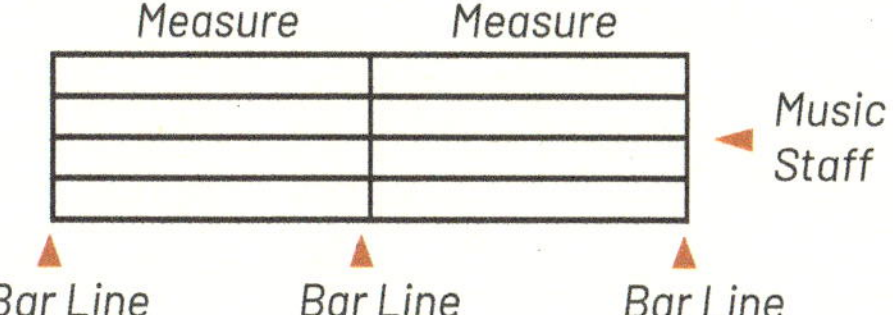

THEORY

Teacher If you are going to use online audio, begin by playing track one: Tuning Track. Compare and tune each of the student's instruments open strings to the audio. To save time, tune only those strings that will be played in class that day. Instruct students to wait quietly while you tune the instruments. As students' playing skills develop, begin teaching them how to tune their own strings using the fine tune tuners or machine-head pegs on their instruments.

Demonstrate to students how to pluck their open strings, either in guitar or shoulder position. For violins and violas it is easier to pluck with the right thumb when holding the instrument in guitar position; in shoulder position it is easiest for students to use their right index finger.

Have students say and spell pizzicato. Point out to students the abbreviation *pizz.* for pizzicato.

Teacher All musical selections in Essential Elements for Strings are accompanied on the online audio. Professional musicians on acoustic instruments perform the recordings. Students may play with the recordings, as they are designed to guide and encourage students' home practice and enliven class rehearsal. Recordings provide a harmonic background for each selection and a performance model for students to emulate. Research strongly suggests that modeling and harmonic accompaniment promotes students' development of intonation.

Play-Along recording accompaniments are recorded at tempos playable by beginning students and include diverse styles of music, including rock, country, and classical. Use of recordings in class frees the string teacher to move throughout the class and assist individual student playing. Please note that the Essential Elements for Strings piano accompaniments are easier to play than those on the recordings, so that you may focus on your students' performance, not your keyboard skills.

1. TUNING TRACK *Wait quietly for your teacher to tune your instrument.*

Teacher Remind violin and viola students to keep their bows in their cases. Request cello and bass students to take the bow out of their case first before removing the instrument. They may place the bow on the floor by their chair or stool, or on their music stand. Students will begin developing bowing skills on student book page 7.

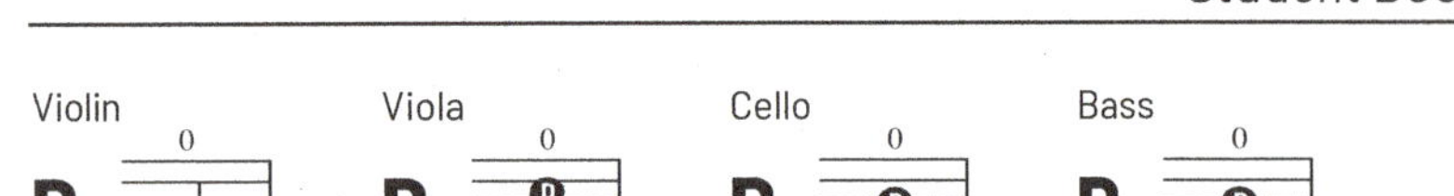

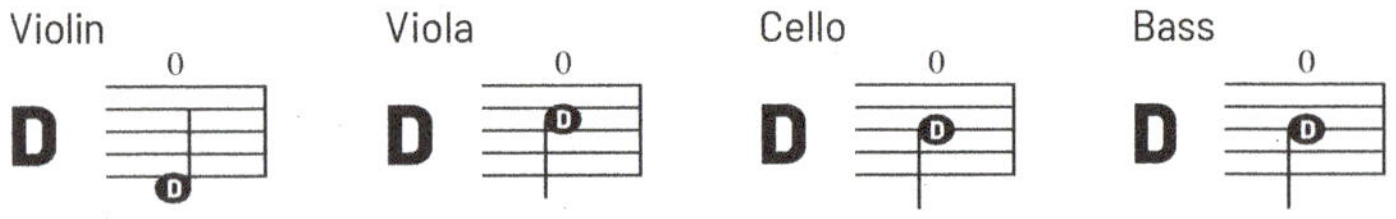

Teacher Instruct students to say and sing the letter names as they are plucking the strings.

2. LET'S PLAY "OPEN D"

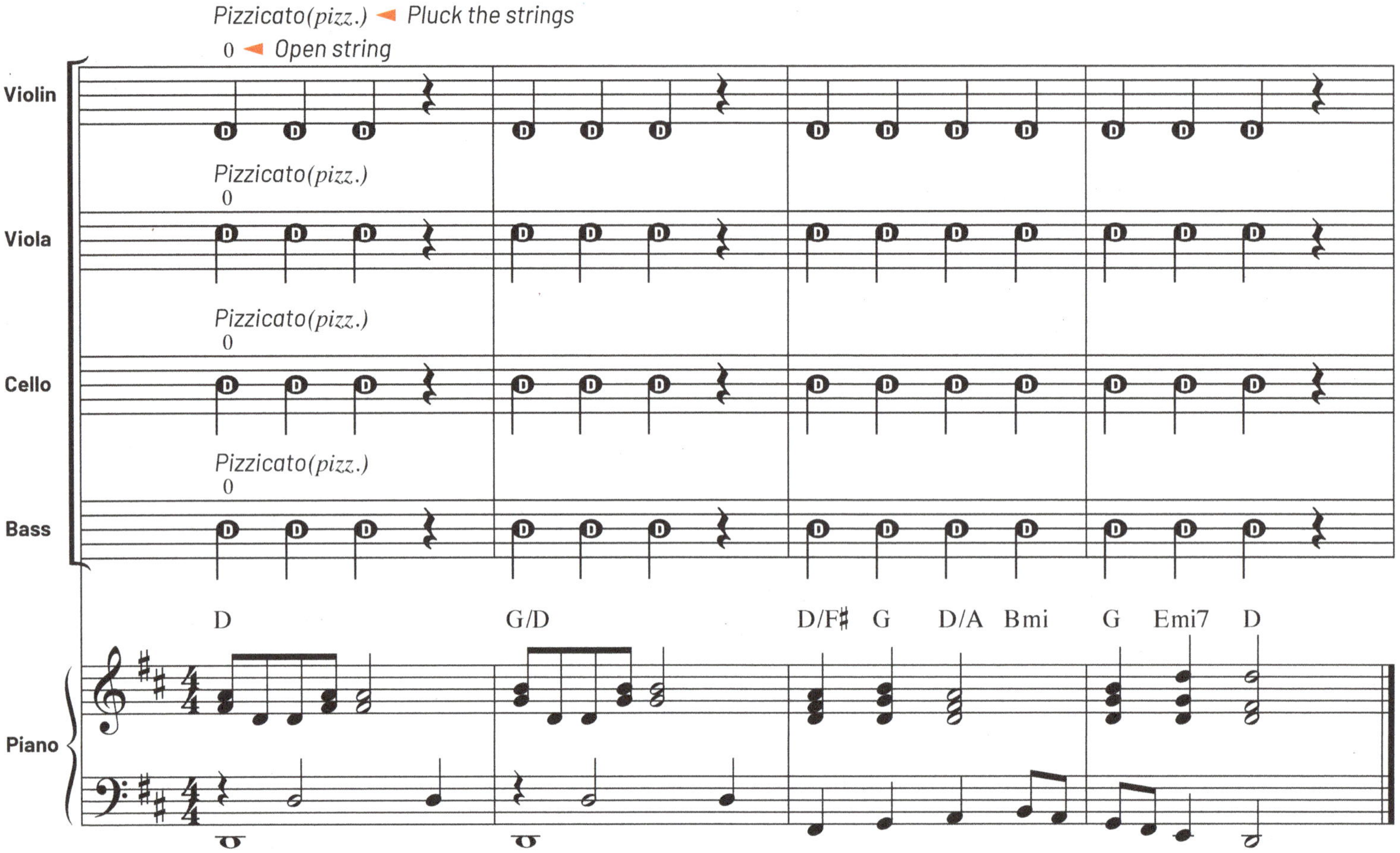

Pizzicato (pizz.) ◄ Pluck the strings

0 ◄ Open string

Violin

Viola *Pizzicato (pizz.)* 0

Cello *Pizzicato (pizz.)* 0

Bass *Pizzicato (pizz.)* 0

Piano: D | G/D | D/F♯ G D/A Bmi | G Emi7 D

Piano accompaniments have been arranged to match the style and harmony of the accompaniments heard on the play-along audio.

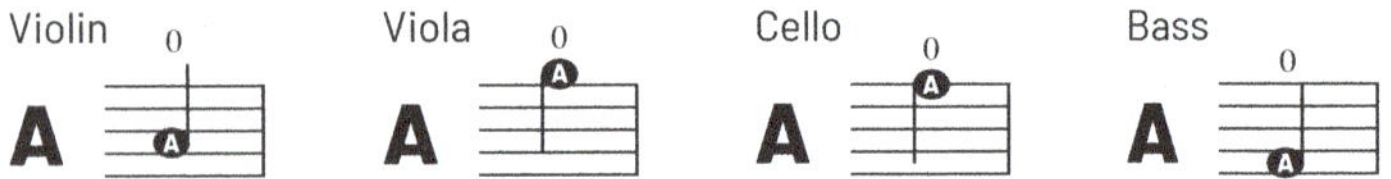

3. LET'S PLAY "OPEN A"

4. TWO'S A TEAM

pizz.

Violin

Viola

Cello

Bass

D G/A D G/A D Gsus2 D

Piano

5. AT PIERROT'S DOOR *The melody is included on the online audio.*

pizz.

Violin

Viola

Cello

Bass

D A/C♯ Bmi7 A G(add9) A G(add9) D

Piano

Teacher Once students can pizzicato the open strings in exercise 5 you may either play the melody on your string instrument while the students are plucking, or play the audio which features the melody on track 5.

Teacher Read the definitions of clef, time signature, and double bar that appear on student book page 5. Point out the note names as they appear in different clefs. Have students point to the time signatures and double bars on the page.

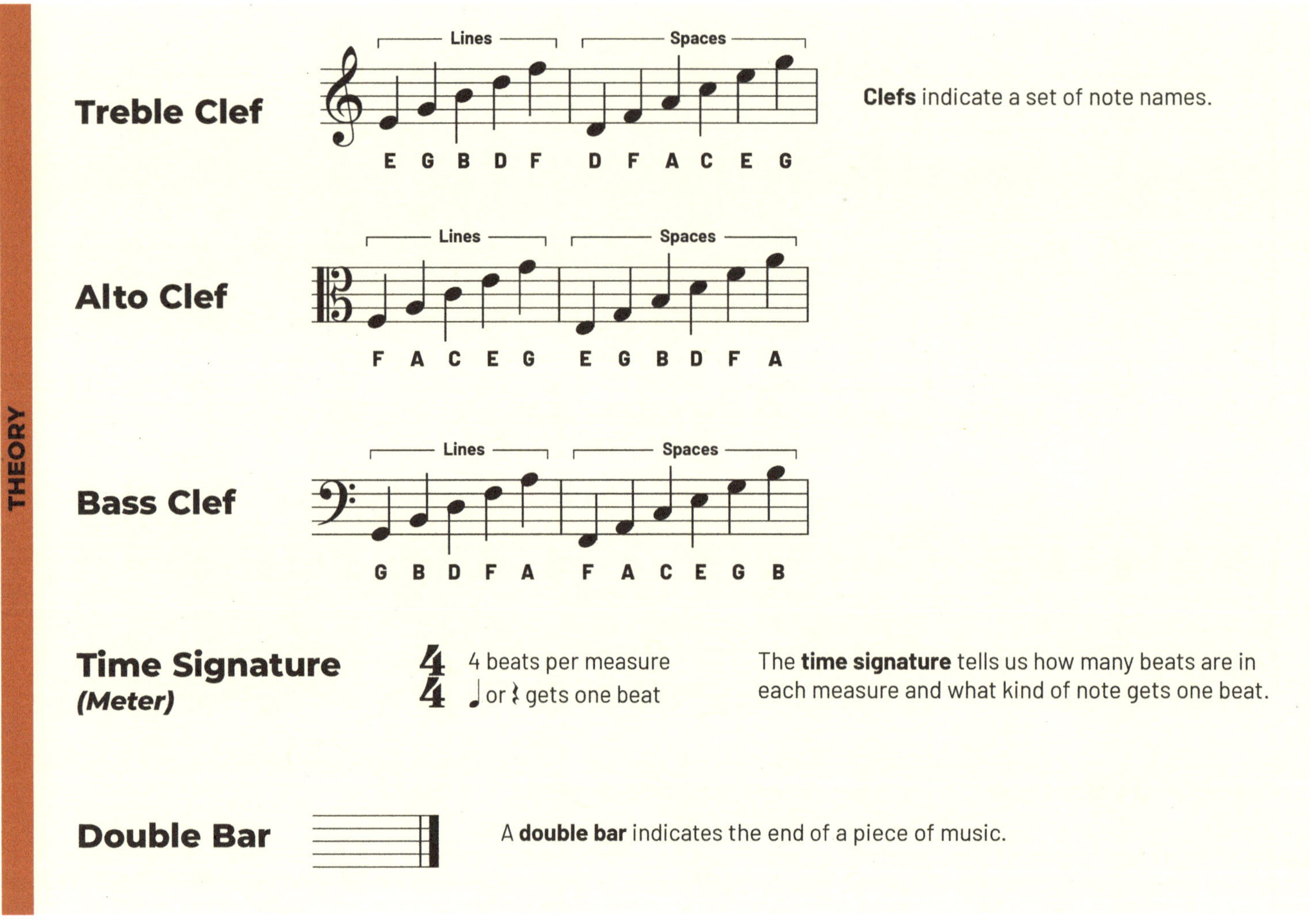

6. JUMPING JACKS *Identify the clef and time signature before playing.*

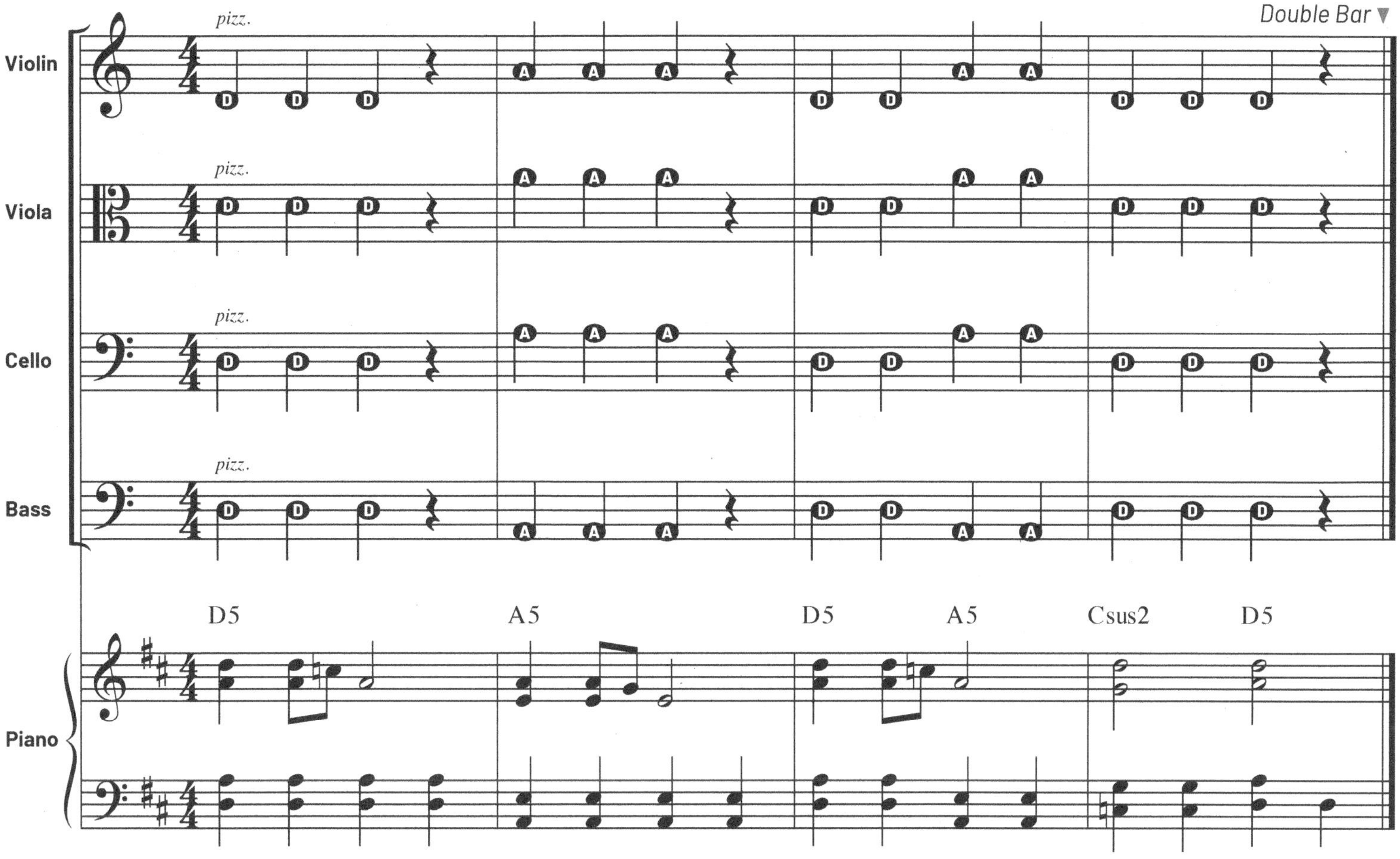

Double Bar ▼

Violin
Viola
Cello
Bass
pizz.

D5 A5 D5 A5 Csus2 D5

Piano

7. MIX 'EM UP

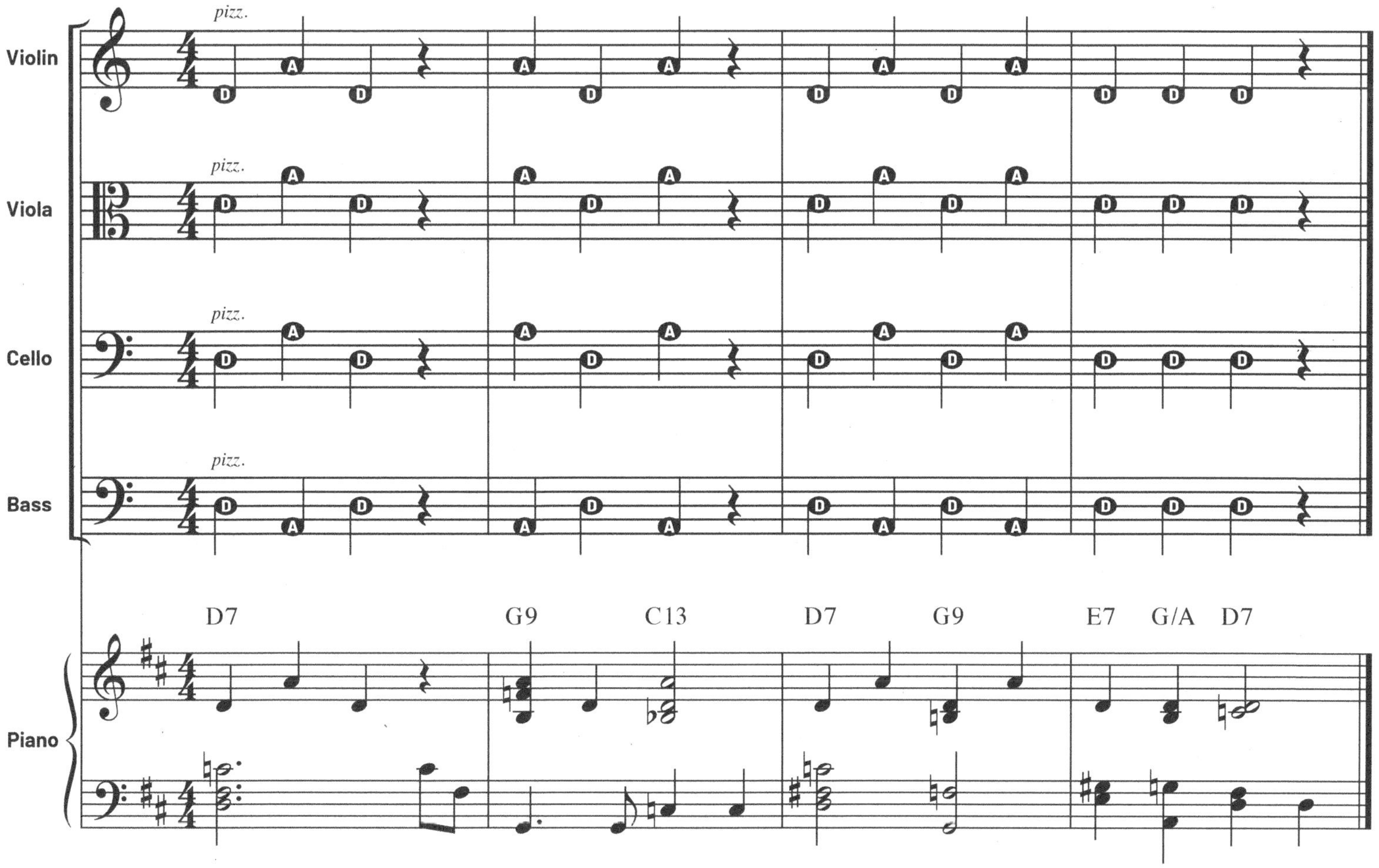

Violin
Viola
Cello
Bass
pizz.

D7 G9 C13 D7 G9 E7 G/A D7

Piano

Teacher Read the definition of repeat sign and note the symbol. Point out the repeat sign in exercise 8.

Demonstrate your preferred method of counting, clapping and tapping. This book uses a traditional counting system and teaches the subdivided beat from the beginning. If you elect to use another counting system, have students write the syllables or system in their books, including subdivided beats.

Counting is shown below the staff in each student book. We strongly encourage you to count, sing, and clap all exercises with your students before playing them. A counting system is not shown below all exercises, so that students will develop rhythmic and counting independence.

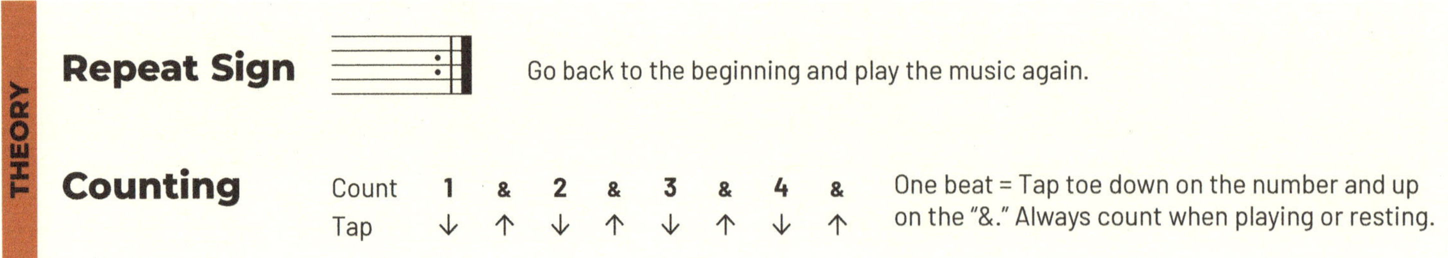

8. COUNT CAREFULLY *Keep a steady beat when playing or resting.*

Student books have repeats, not 1st and 2nd endings (until ex. 76).

1. *Repeat sign* 2.

Violin *pizz.*

Count: 1 & 2 & 3 & 4 & | 1 & 2 & 3 & 4 & | 1 & 2 & 3 & 4 & | 1 & 2 & 3 & 4 & | 1 & 2 & 3 & 4 &

Viola *pizz.*

Cello *pizz.*

Bass *pizz.*

G(add9) D/F♯ G(add9) D/F♯ G(add9) G/A D G(add9) G/A D

Piano

Teacher Performance objectives of each quiz are listed. Objectives highlight the exact elements being reviewed and tested. Review exercises suggest specific examples for students requiring additional practice. Be certain students meet your performance expectations on every quiz.

QUIZ OBJECTIVES

- Pizzicato D and A strings
- Counting quarter notes and rests using subdivided beats
- Steady beat

Review Exercises:

4. *Two's A Team*
6. *Jumping Jacks*
8. *Count Carefully*

Teacher Have students write in the counting for exercise 9. Check to be sure they have written in both the number and subdivided "&" for each pulse.

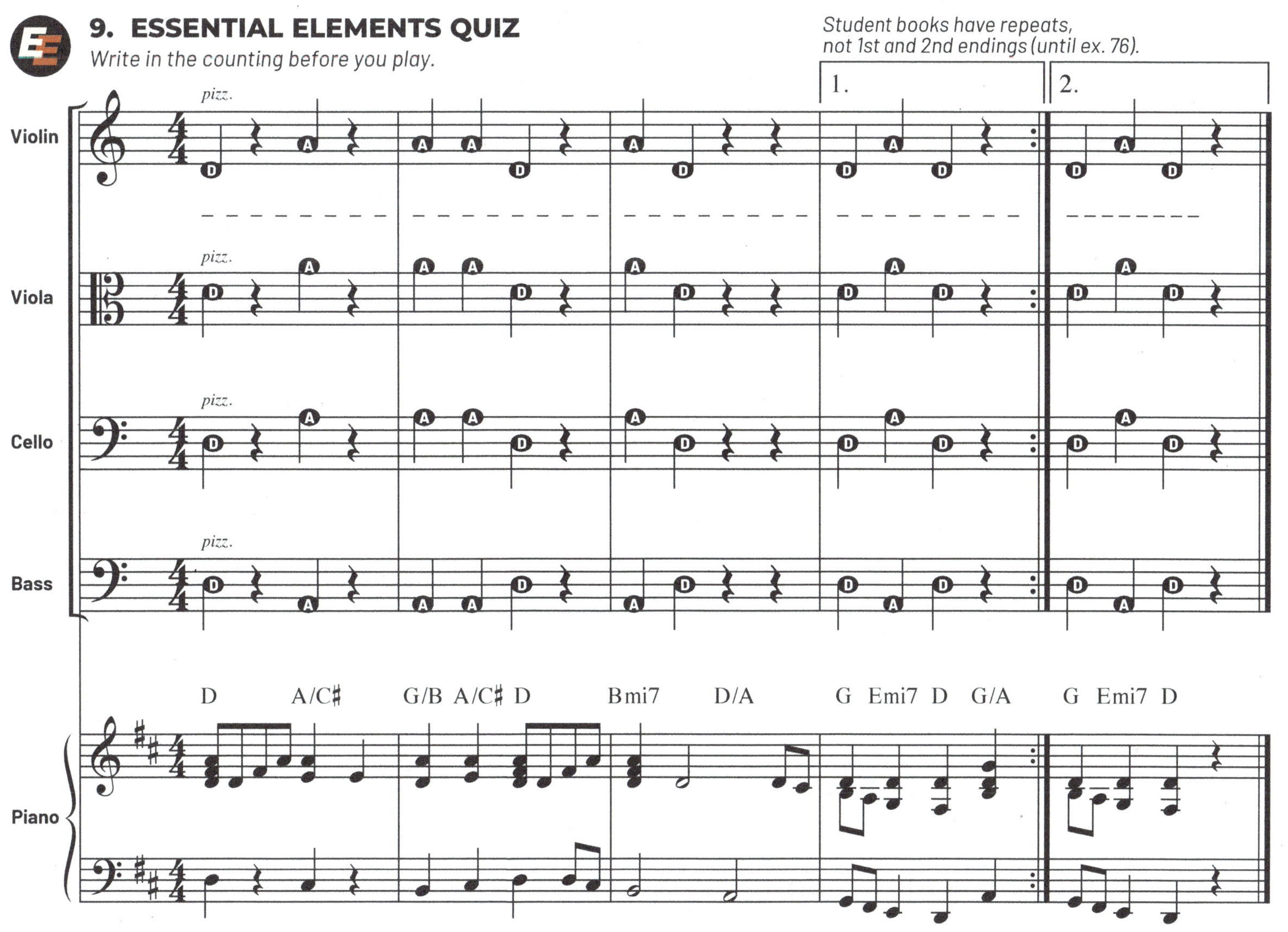

Teacher In string teaching, beginning players first put the sounding finger and all lower numbered fingers on the string together to play a pitch. This is called block fingering. After students' left hand shapes are well established they may begin to use independent fingering, placing only the sounding finger on the string for a pitch.

To help students develop their left-hand shape, the first notes introduced use three fingers for violin/viola and four fingers for cello. Basses should place four fingers on the D string for the pitch F sharp while sounding their open G string when beginning to play. In addition to helping students shape their left hand, playing pitches first that use many fingers is better for students because it is easier to lift off fingers than add them. This approach also helps students establish better intonation.

Have students hold up their left hand and position their fingers as in the drawing on student book page 6. Point out to violin and viola students the second and third fingers touch. Have students say the finger numbers out loud. Notice that the thumb is not a numbered finger in string playing.

Violin/ Viola To help students properly shape their left hand, their index finger should form a square. The square is formed by the fingernail, top of the finger, side of the finger, and the fingerboard. The side of the index finger should touch or be near the side of the fingerboard near the base hand knuckle. This allows the other fingers to be poised over the fingerboard for better playing and intonation, and promotes a straight and relaxed left wrist. Failure to form this square first finger prevents students from properly developing all other left hand skills.

Also notice that the thumb is positioned on the side and is across from the first fingertip. Have students gently tap their thumb on the side of the fingerboard near the first fingertip to find the most natural position of the thumb.

Notice that the player's fingernails are short so that the fingers may be positioned on their tips. Point out to students how the left arm and hand are in a straight line. The wrist should be generally straight, though relaxed.

VIOLIN

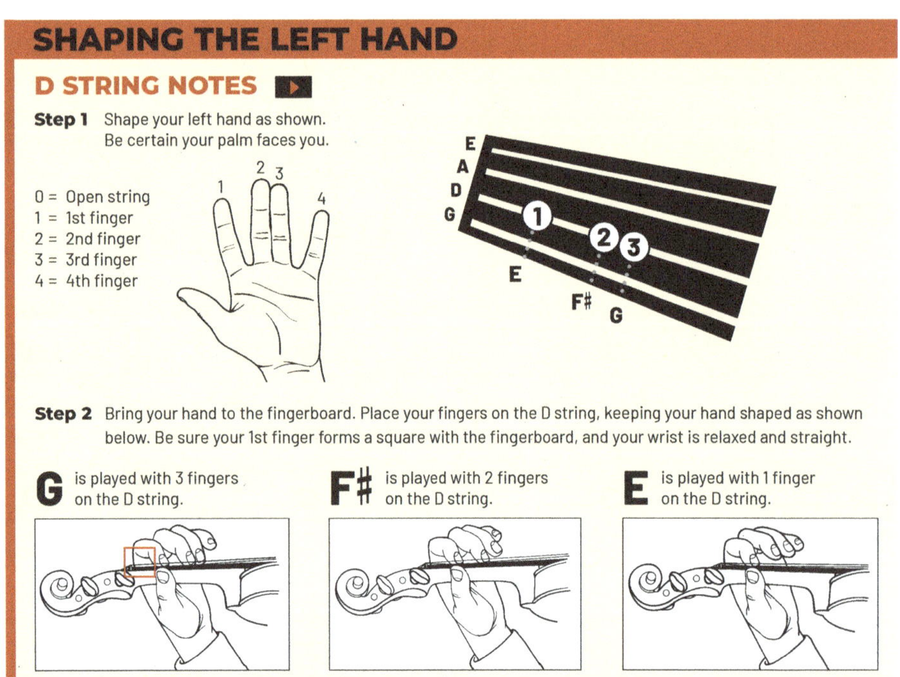

VIOLA

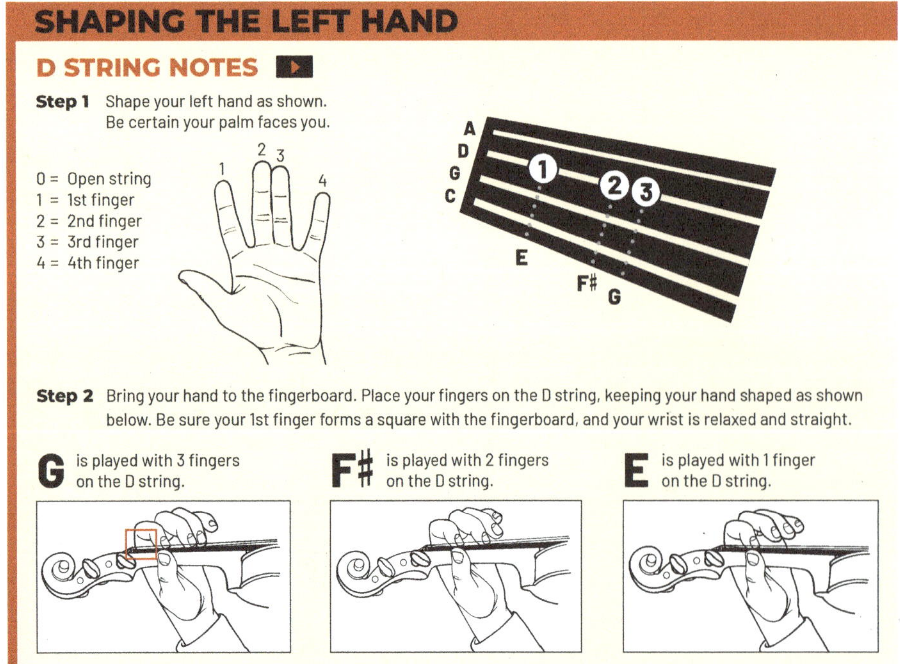

CELLO

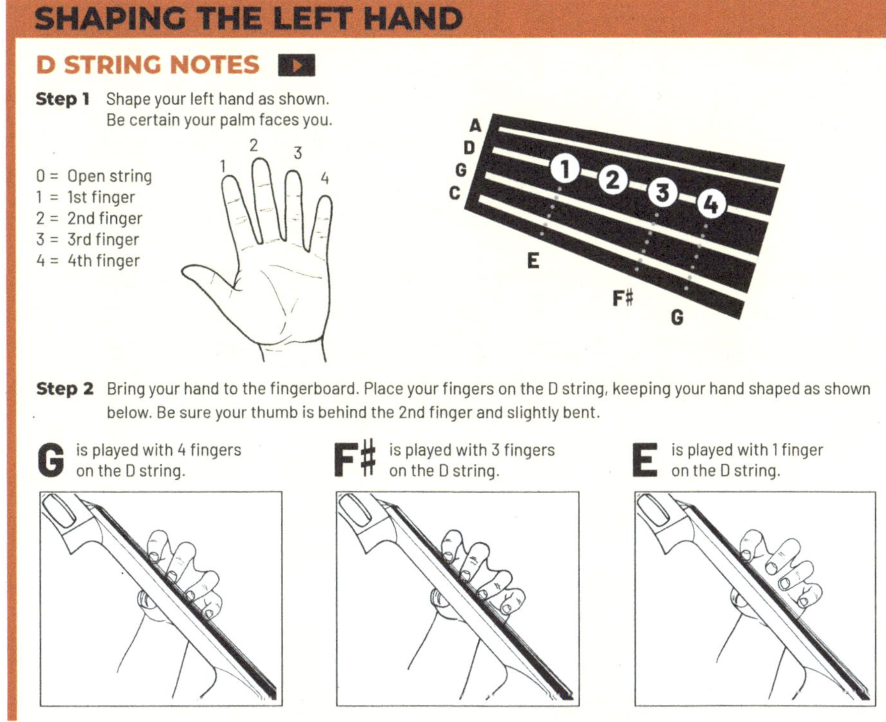

BASS

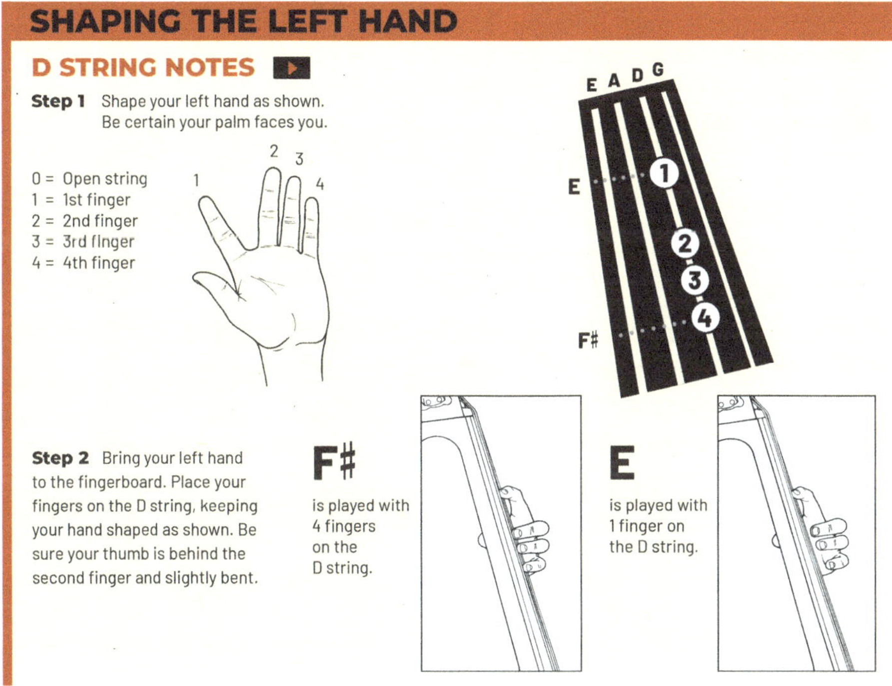

Teacher

Checkpoints Teachers are encouraged to develop checkpoints for quickly evaluating students' playing skills. A list of checkpoints for student skills introduced on student book page 6 would include:

- Body position
- Feet position
- Instrument position
- Fingers curved over strings
- Thumb shape and position
- Violin/Viola: square first finger
- Left wrist straight and relaxed

Listening Skills

Play what your teacher plays. Listen carefully.

Teacher Listening Skills are included every time a new note is introduced. Research suggests that students with well-developed listening skills have better left/right hand coordination, intonation, sound production, and memorization skills.

Teachers are given sample four-beat patterns for students to echo. The echo patterns may be played on any instrument and should be played behind the class so that students cannot see the teacher's fingering. These echo patterns are in treble clef and are only suggestions. Teachers are encouraged to create their own echo patterns. In the beginning, teachers may play echo patterns either pizzicato or with the bow for students to imitate.

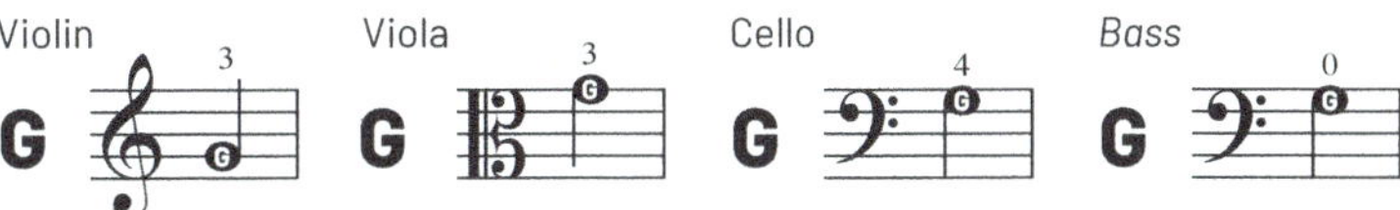

Teacher All finger numbers for pitches appear above the printed notes, and counting symbols below. Each time a new note is introduced, the rhythm in all the exercises immediately following is the same. This allows students to learn one new skill at a time.

Saying letter names out loud, singing letter names, or using solfeggio syllables before and/or during each exercise helps students develop pitch recognition, note reading, and accurate intonation.

As students begin to pizzicato their first left-hand pitches, instruct them to pizzicato quietly, so their left hand will remain relaxed on the fingerboard. Players only need enough weight on the string with their left hand to sound the pitch. No excessive weight or squeezing is needed.

10. LET'S READ "G" *Start memorizing the note names.*

Violin *pizz.* 3

Viola *pizz.* 3

Cello *pizz.* 4

Bass *pizz.* 0

Piano G5 Csus2 G5 Csus2 G5

Teacher In the first part of this method, sharp is being used as an accidental, not as a part of the key signature.

Sharp ♯

A **sharp** sign raises the sound of notes and remains in effect for the entire measure.
Notes without sharps are called **natural** notes.

THEORY

Violin
F♯
2
Viola
F♯
2
Cello
F♯
3
Bass
F♯
4

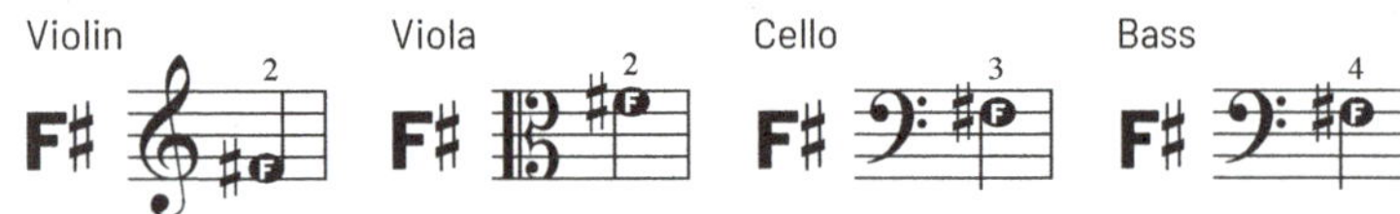

11. LET'S READ "F♯" (F-sharp)

▼ *Play all F♯'s. Sharps apply to the entire measure.*

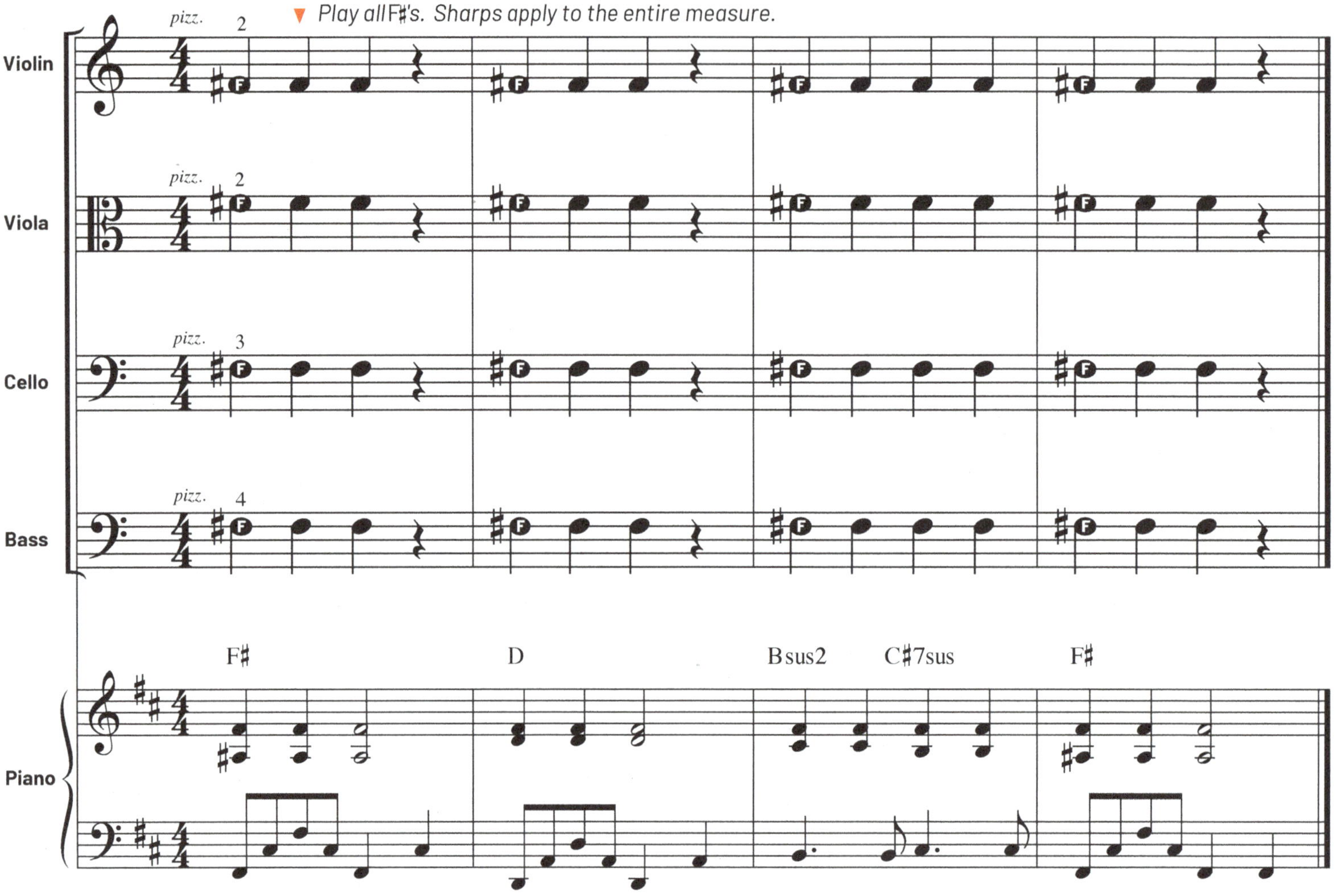
Violin
pizz.
2
Viola
pizz.
2
Cello
pizz.
3
Bass
pizz.
4
Piano
F♯
D
Bsus2
C♯7sus
F♯

Teacher Beginning in exercise 12 the letter name in a repeated note head occurs only in the first pitch. Students should be encouraged to recognize the name of those notes without the alphabet letters as they are note reading and playing.

Encourage students to keep their fingers near the string when lifting off the strings in exercise 12. The fingers that are not on the string should be curved over the strings. The line underneath the staff in the bass part is a bracket indicating that students should keep fingers down while playing additional pitches. This promotes proper left hand shape and intonation. Also, check that violin and viola students are consistently maintaining a square first finger shape as they are playing.

As students are playing the exercises on page 6, encourage them to compare their left hand shape with the drawings.

12. LIFT OFF

Student Is your left hand shaped as shown in the diagrams above?

Teacher The line underneath the staff in exercise 12 in the bass is a bracket indicating that students should keep fingers down while playing additional pitches. This promotes proper left hand shape and intonation. Once students consistently demonstrate an acceptable left-hand shape they may begin to use independent fingering: playing a pitch with only one finger on the string.

Teacher BOW BUILDER ONE appears at the top of student book page 7. The purpose of BOW BUILDERS is to present activities for students to develop their bowing skills independent of their left-hand skills. Students should practice the BOW BUILDER exercises frequently until they are mastered.

The purpose of BOW BUILDER ONE: PENCIL HOLD is to help students develop a well-shaped bow hand position. Shaping the bow hand on a pencil first allows students to focus on the hand shape without having to hold the bow.

Each of the five steps in BOW BUILDER ONE should be practiced daily until the skills are mastered. It is critically important for students to master forming their bow hand shape. The successful combination of bowing with instrument position and left hand skills introduced on student book page 18 depends on how well students master each of the BOW BUILDERS in this book.

VIOLIN

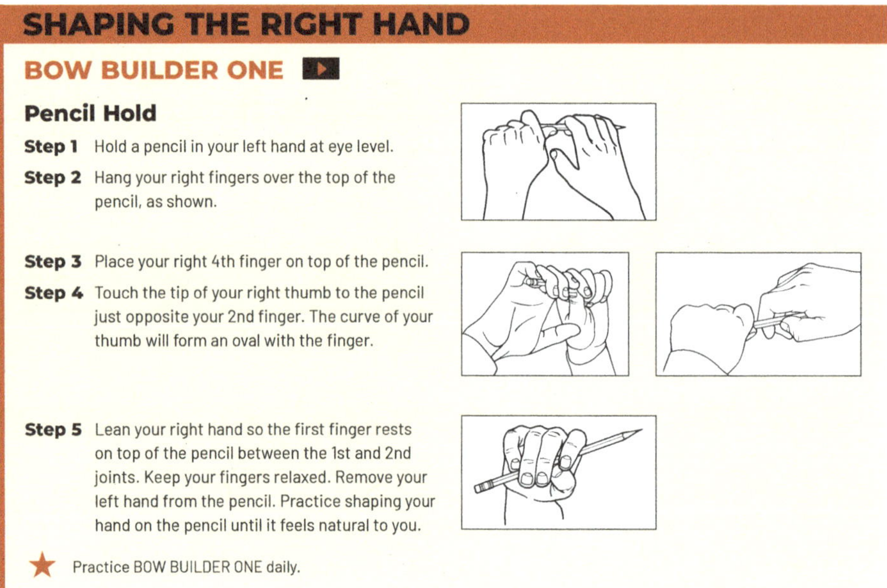

SHAPING THE RIGHT HAND

BOW BUILDER ONE

Pencil Hold

Step 1 Hold a pencil in your left hand at eye level.

Step 2 Hang your right fingers over the top of the pencil, as shown.

Step 3 Place your right 4th finger on top of the pencil.

Step 4 Touch the tip of your right thumb to the pencil just opposite your 2nd finger. The curve of your thumb will form an oval with the finger.

Step 5 Lean your right hand so the first finger rests on top of the pencil between the 1st and 2nd joints. Keep your fingers relaxed. Remove your left hand from the pencil. Practice shaping your hand on the pencil until it feels natural to you.

★ Practice BOW BUILDER ONE daily.

VIOLA

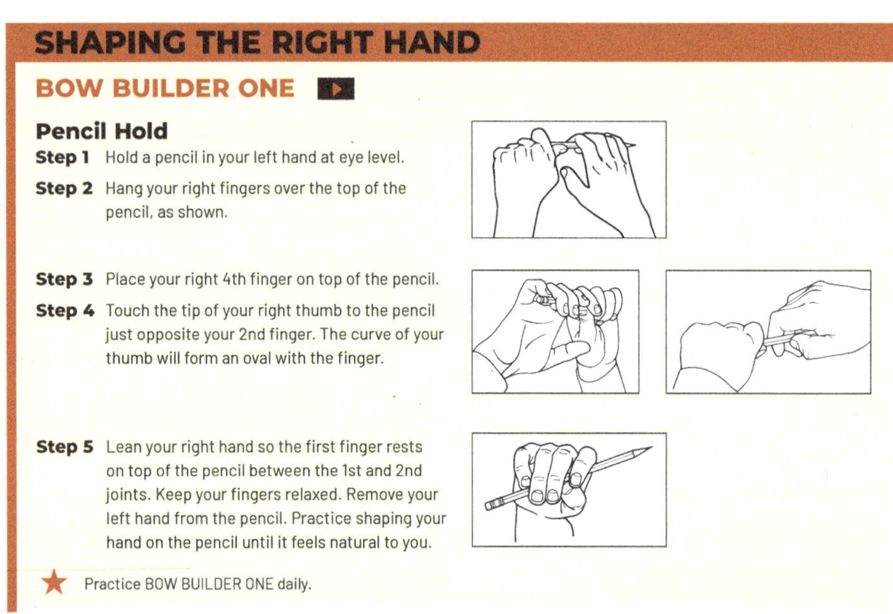

SHAPING THE RIGHT HAND

BOW BUILDER ONE

Pencil Hold

Step 1 Hold a pencil in your left hand at eye level.

Step 2 Hang your right fingers over the top of the pencil, as shown.

Step 3 Place your right 4th finger on top of the pencil.

Step 4 Touch the tip of your right thumb to the pencil just opposite your 2nd finger. The curve of your thumb will form an oval with the finger.

Step 5 Lean your right hand so the first finger rests on top of the pencil between the 1st and 2nd joints. Keep your fingers relaxed. Remove your left hand from the pencil. Practice shaping your hand on the pencil until it feels natural to you.

★ Practice BOW BUILDER ONE daily.

CELLO

SHAPING THE RIGHT HAND

BOW BUILDER ONE

Pencil Hold

Step 1 Hold a pencil in your left hand about waist level.

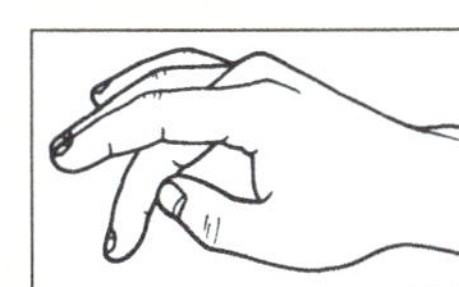

Step 2 Place the tip of your right thumb between the first and second joints of your second finger.

Step 3 Place the pencil between your thumb and second finger, while keeping your thumb gently curved.

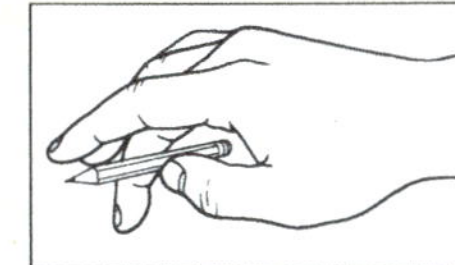

Step 4 The pencil should touch your first three fingers between the first and second joints, and touch the fourth finger at the first joint, as shown.

Step 5 Remove your left hand from the pencil. Keep your fingers relaxed. Practice shaping your hand on the pencil until it feels natural to you.

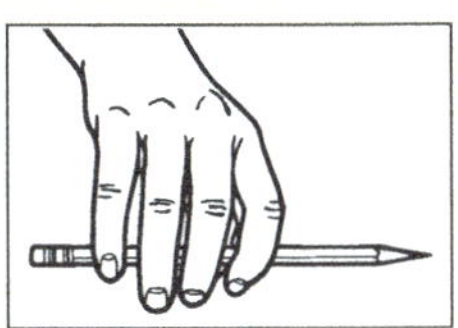

★ Practice BOW BUILDER ONE daily.

BASS

SHAPING THE RIGHT HAND

BOW BUILDER ONE *(French)*

Pencil Hold

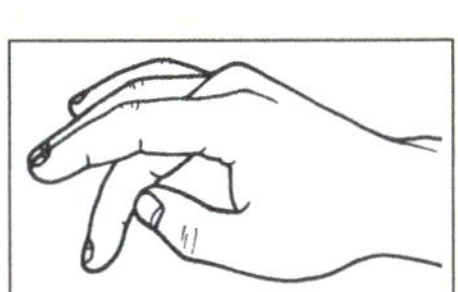

Step 1 Hold a pencil in your left hand about waist level.

Step 2 Place the tip of your right thumb between the first and second joints of your second finger.

Step 3 Place the pencil between your thumb and second finger, while keeping your thumb gently curved.

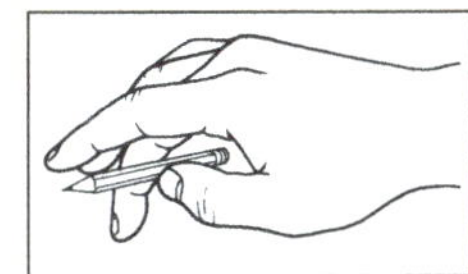

Step 4 The pencil should touch your first three fingers between the first and second joints, and touch the fourth finger at the first joint, as shown.

Step 5 Remove your left hand from the pencil. Keep your fingers relaxed. Practice shaping your hand on the pencil until it feels natural to you.

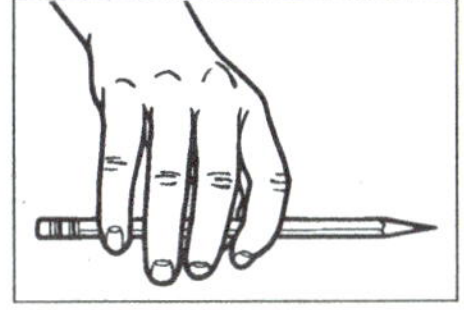

 Practice BOW BUILDER ONE daily.

Violin/ Viola

The following illustrations show acceptable and unacceptable left hand positions. Note the placement of the thumb. Note in acceptable position the thumb is on its side slightly and positioned near the first fingertip. One successful teaching strategy to help students develop an acceptable left hand position is to have them slide their thumb forward as illustrated, promoting a better left hand shape and a straight, but relaxed, wrist position.

Unacceptable

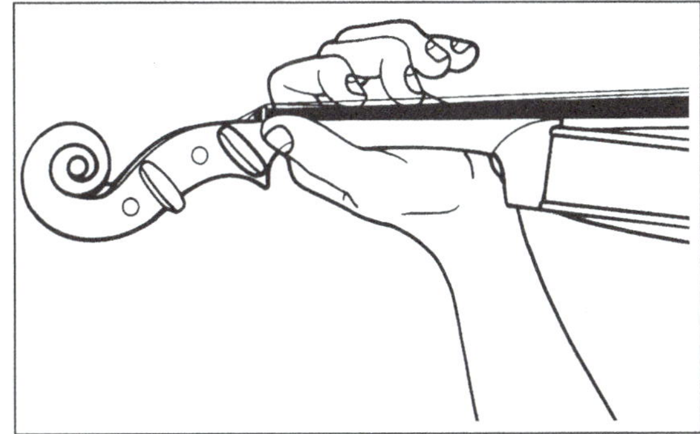

Acceptable

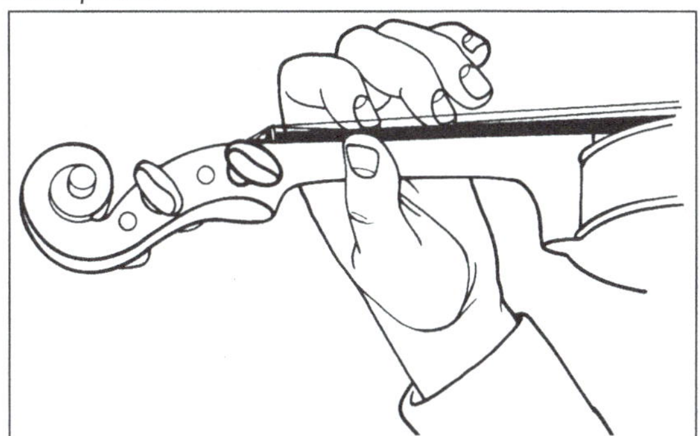

Teacher It is recommended that as students learn to play each new pitch that they also memorize the letter name of each note. Spend time in class reviewing note names as students learn to play new pitches.

Student books have repeats, not 1st and 2nd endings (until ex. 76).

13. ON THE TRAIL *Say or sing the note names before you play.*

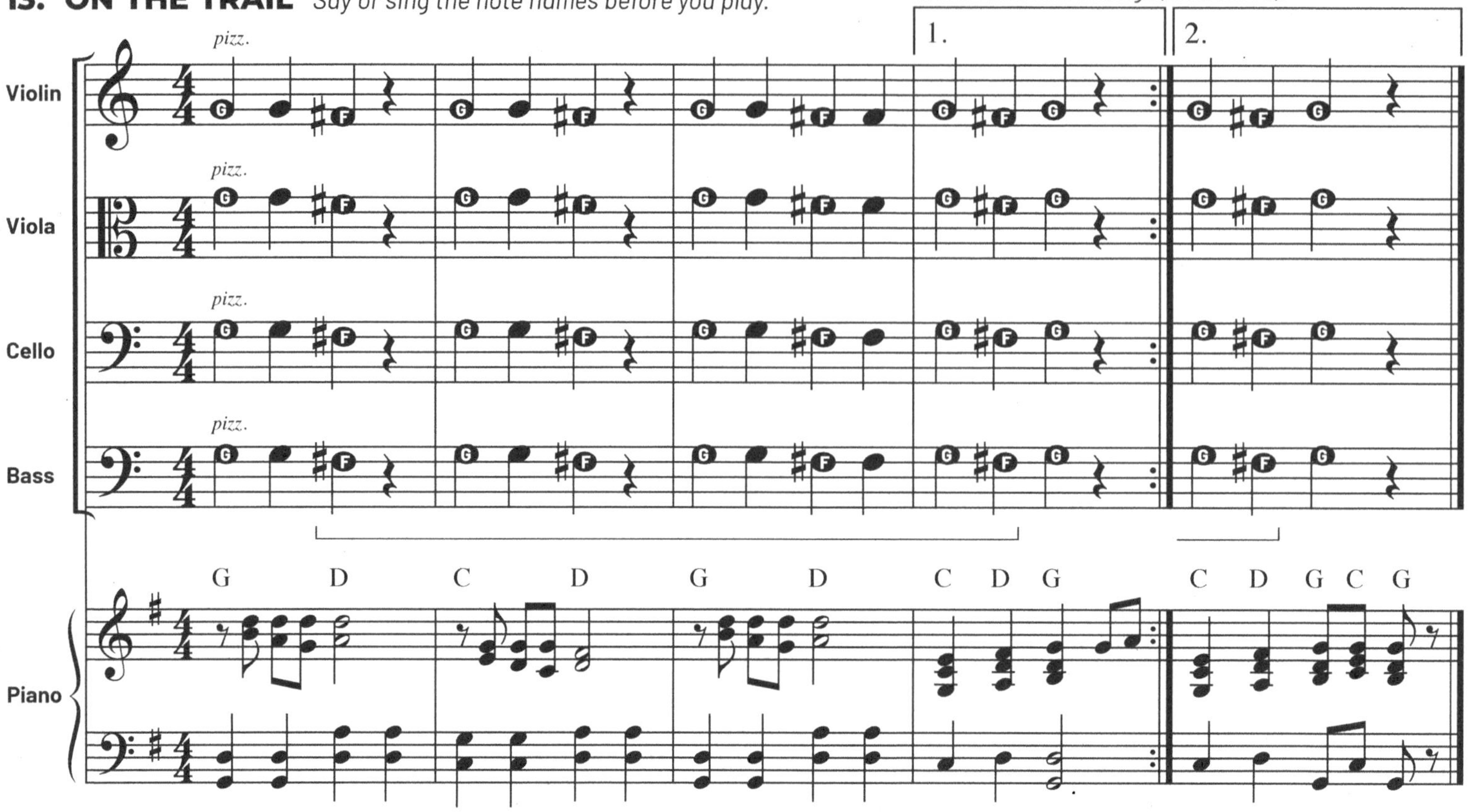
1.
2.
pizz.
Violin
Viola
Cello
Bass
Piano
G D C D G D C D G C D G C G

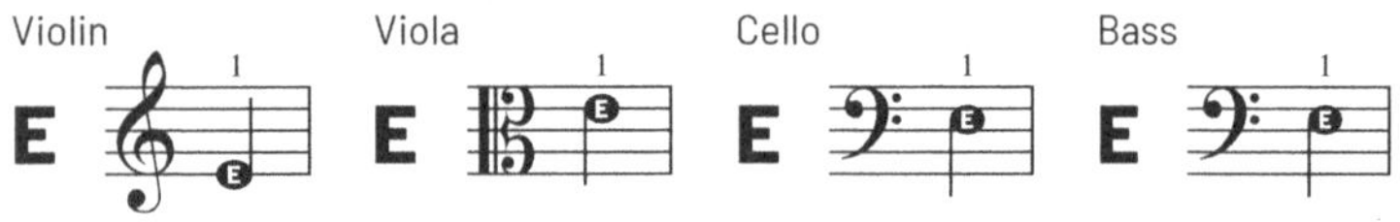
Violin
E
Viola
E
Cello
E
Bass
E
1

Violin/ Viola Remind students to carefully form a square first finger shape as illustrated on page 6. Be sure all other fingers are poised over the string for all instruments.

14. LET'S READ "E"

pizz. 1
Violin
Viola
Cello
Bass
Piano
C
Ami7
Fma7
G6
C

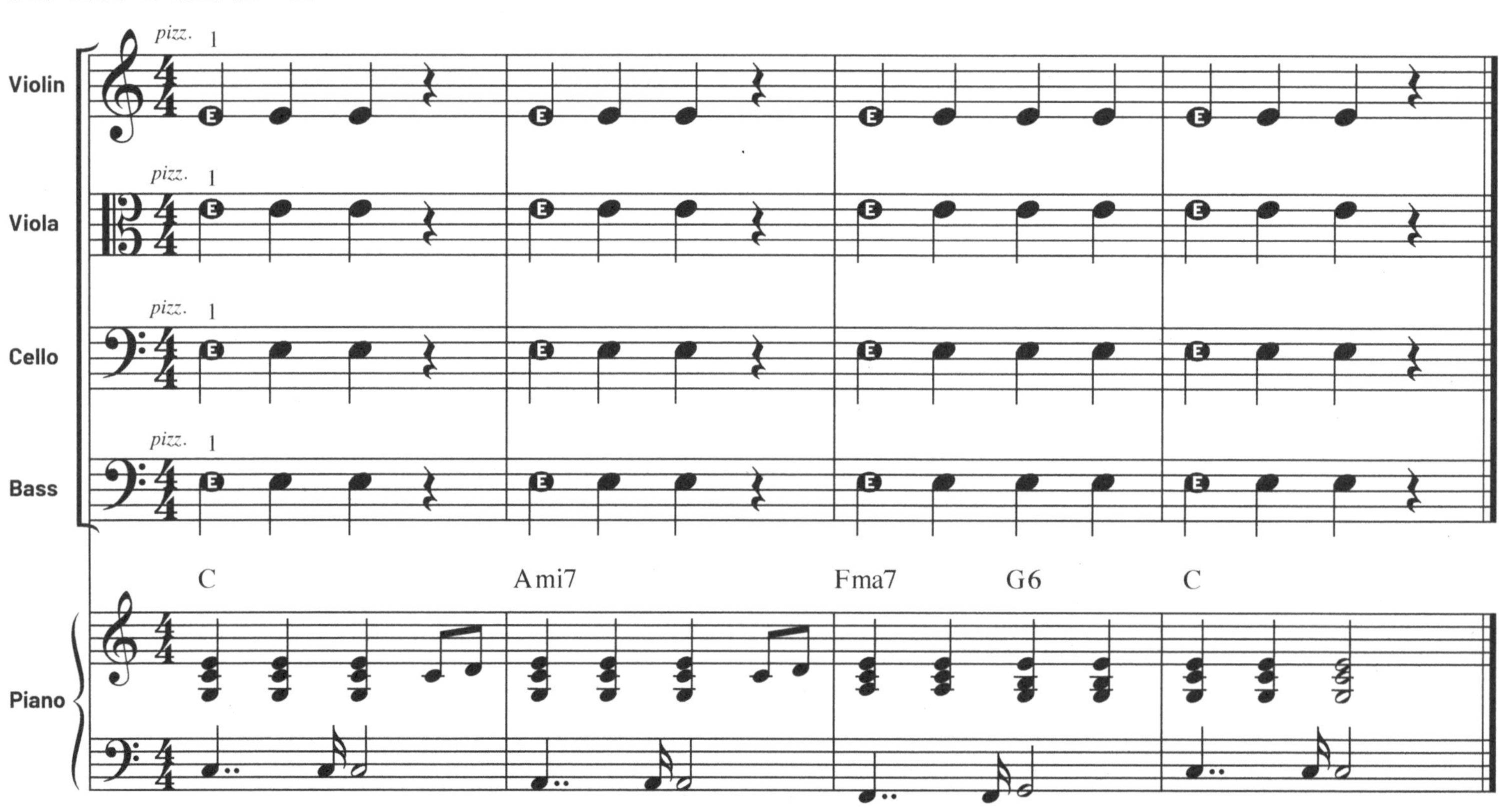

Teacher Be sure students review their counting, including subdivisions, when playing exercise 15.

Student books have repeats, not 1st and 2nd endings (until ex. 76).

15. WALKING SONG

QUIZ OBJECTIVES – ICE DANCING

- Pizzicato notes on D string (pizzicato G string on Bass)
- Counting
- Steady beat
- Square first finger shape (Violin/Viola)
- Recognizing, writing, and reading clef signs, time signatures, and double bar lines

Review Exercises:

13. *On the Trail*
14. *Let's Read "E"*
15. *Walking Song*

- Have students write the clef sign for their instrument
- Have students write $\frac{4}{4}$ time signatures

16. ESSENTIAL ELEMENTS QUIZ

Draw the missing symbols where they belong before you play:

Violin — *pizz.* G G F♯ F♯ | E E D 𝄽 | D D E E | F♯ F♯ G 𝄽

Viola — *pizz.* G G F♯ F♯ | E E D 𝄽 | D D E E | F♯ F♯ G 𝄽

Cello — *pizz.* G G F♯ F♯ | E E D 𝄽 | D D E E | F♯ F♯ G 𝄽

Bass — *pizz.* G G F♯ F♯ | E E D 𝄽 | D D E E | F♯ F♯ G 𝄽

Piano — G D/G | C/G D/G | G/B C | D Gsus G

Teacher BOW BUILDER TWO and BOW BUILDER THREE are introduced at the top of student book page 8. Have students master BOW BUILDER TWO before proceeding to BOW BUILDER THREE. BOW BUILDER TWO: PENCIL HOLD EXERCISES will help students develop curved, relaxed, flexible fingers and thumbs. BOW BUILDER THREE: BOWING MOTIONS will help students develop proper violin/viola bowing motion from the elbow, not the shoulder. *Elbow Energy* develops cello students bowing skills, as does *The Pendulum* for basses.

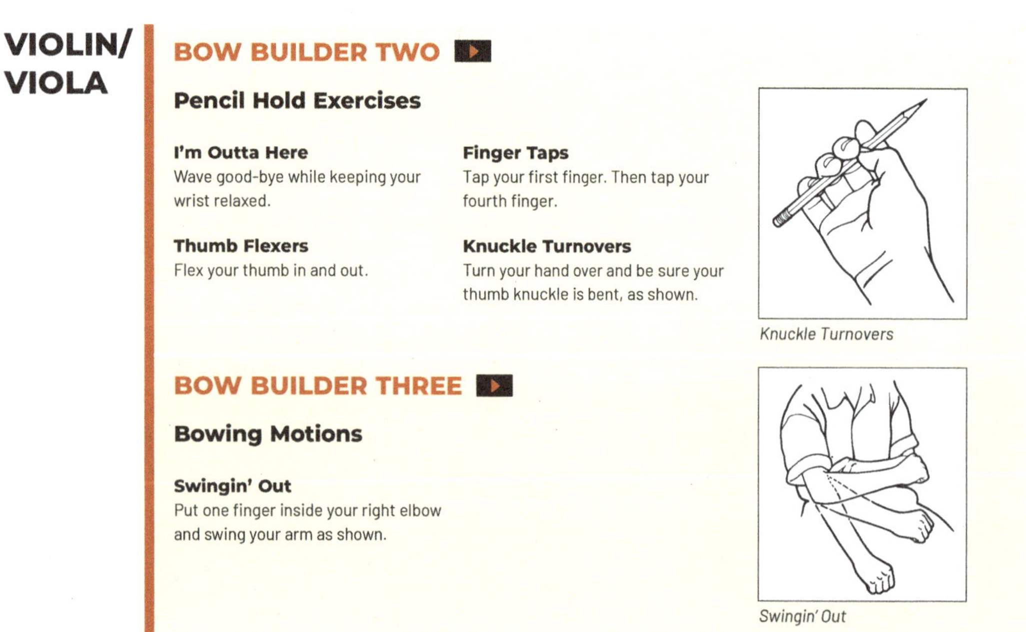

VIOLIN/ VIOLA

BOW BUILDER TWO

Pencil Hold Exercises

I'm Outta Here
Wave good-bye while keeping your wrist relaxed.

Finger Taps
Tap your first finger. Then tap your fourth finger.

Thumb Flexers
Flex your thumb in and out.

Knuckle Turnovers
Turn your hand over and be sure your thumb knuckle is bent, as shown.

Knuckle Turnovers

BOW BUILDER THREE

Bowing Motions

Swingin' Out
Put one finger inside your right elbow and swing your arm as shown.

Swingin' Out

CELLO

BOW BUILDER TWO

Pencil Hold Exercises

I'm Outta Here
Wave good-bye while keeping your wrist relaxed.

Thumb Flexers
Flex your thumb in and out.

Finger Taps
Tap your first finger. Then tap your fourth finger.

Knuckle Turnovers
Turn your hand over and be sure your thumb knuckle is bent, as shown.

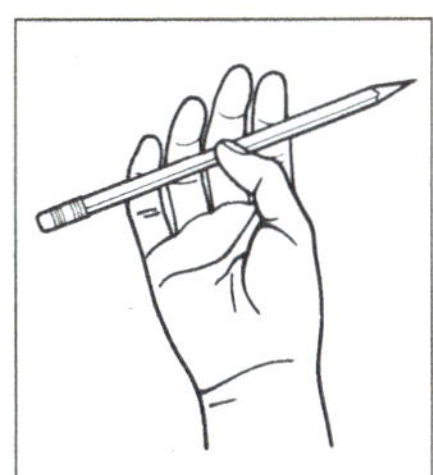
Knuckle Turnovers

BOW BUILDER THREE

Bowing Motions

Elbow Energy
- Swing your right elbow away from your body.
- Open your right forearm, as shown.
- Close your right forearm.
- Swing your elbow back toward your body.

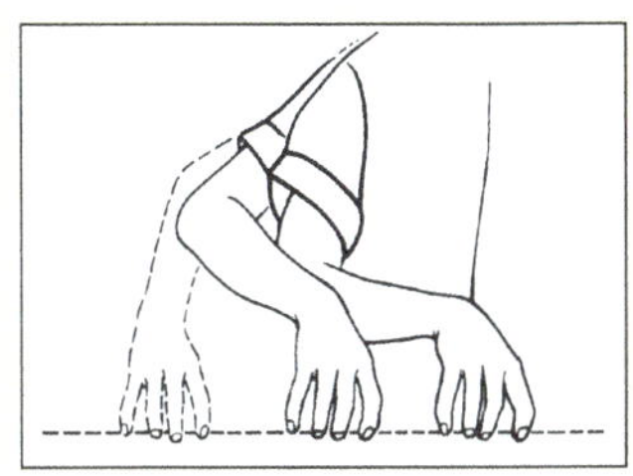
Elbow Energy

BASS

BOW BUILDER TWO

Pencil Hold Exercises *(French Bow Only)*

I'm Outta Here
Wave good-bye while keeping your wrist relaxed.

Thumb Flexers
Flex your thumb in and out.

Finger Taps
Tap your first finger. Then tap your fourth finger.

Knuckle Turnovers
Turn your hand over and be sure your thumb knuckle is bent, as shown.

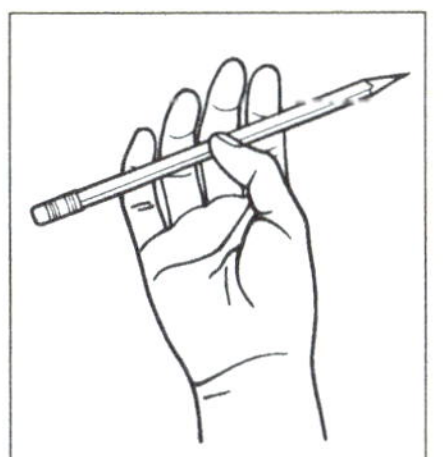
Knuckle Turnovers

BOW BUILDER THREE

Bowing Motions

The Pendulum *(French and German Bow)*
Let your arm hand down to your side. While keeping your elbow straight, swing your arm back and forth like a pendulum.

The Pendulum

17. HOP SCOTCH

HISTORY

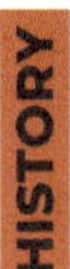

Folk songs have been an important part of cultures for centuries and have been passed on from generation to generation. Folk song melodies help define the sound of a culture or region. This folk song comes from the Slavic region of eastern Europe.

Teacher Familiarize students with different types of folk music by playing recorded examples of Slavic folk music. Discuss examples of American folk music, e.g. *Skip To My Lou, Long Long Ago.*

18. MORNING DANCE

Slavic Folk Song

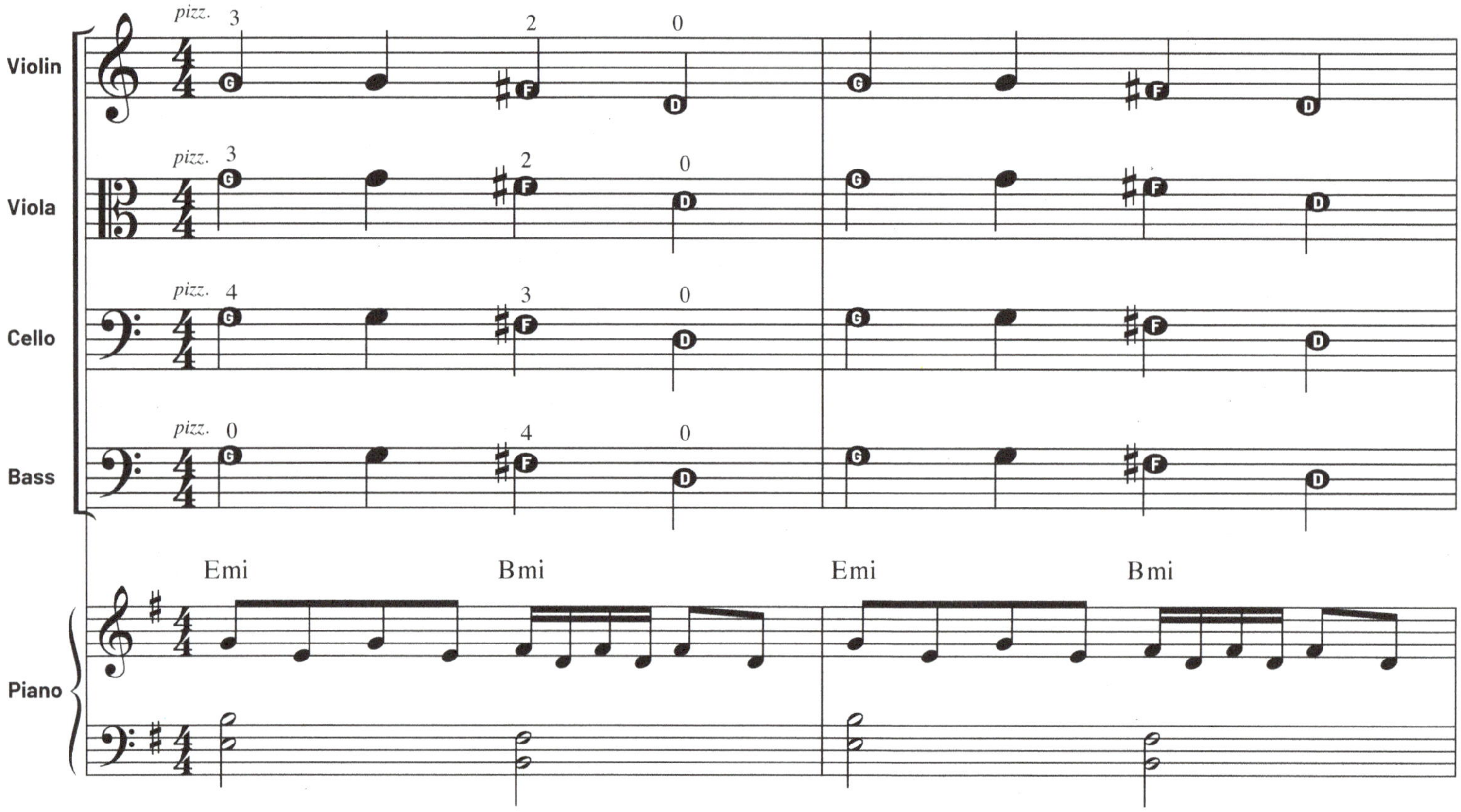
Violin
Viola
Cello
Bass
Piano
pizz.
Emi
Bmi
Emi
Bmi

Student books have repeats, not 1st and 2nd endings (until ex. 76).

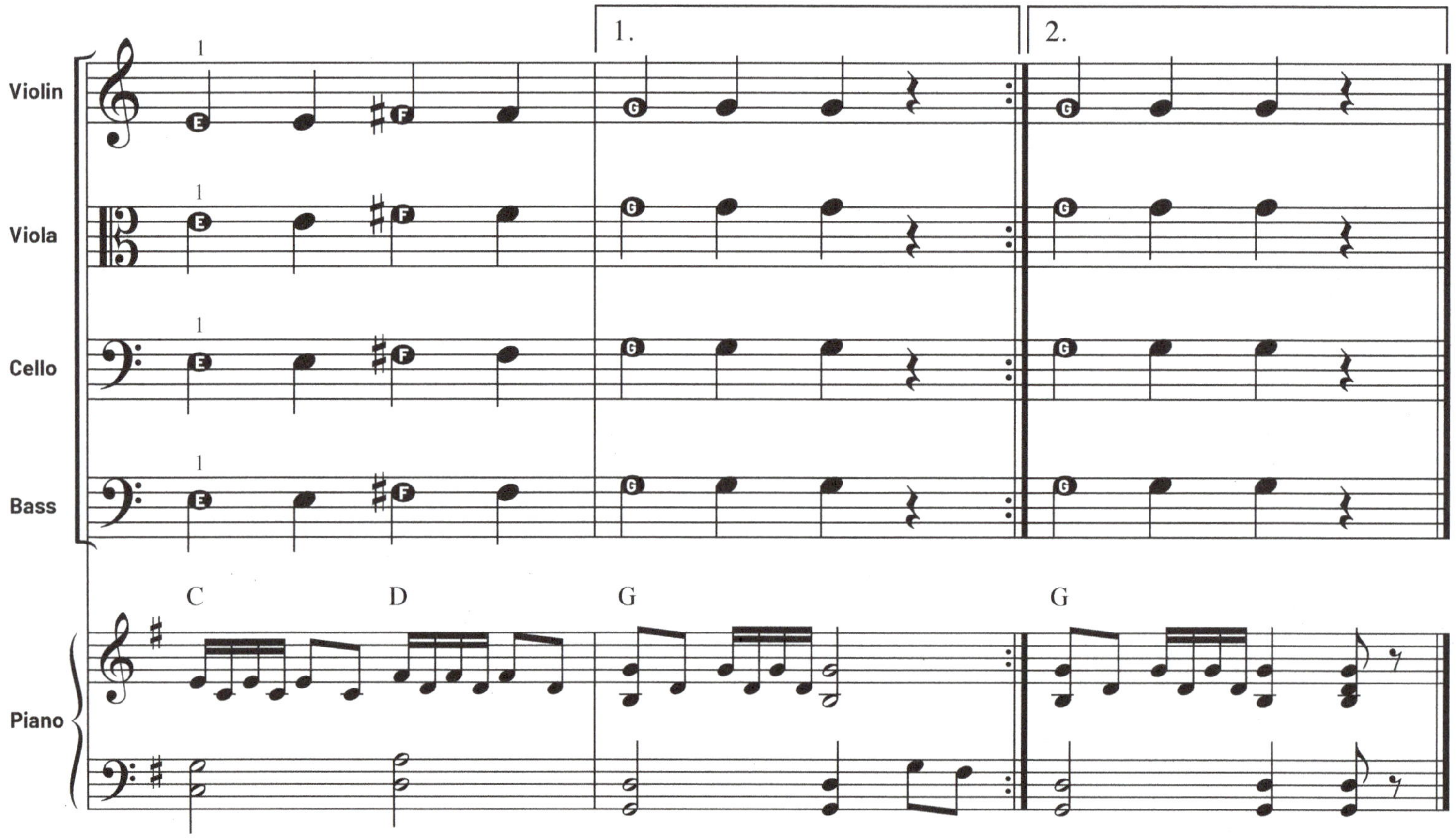
Violin
Viola
Cello
Bass
Piano
1.
2.
C
D
G
G

19. ROLLING ALONG

Violin/ Viola Review holding the violin or viola in shoulder position as shown on page 3. Check to see if the scroll is generally parallel to the floor and positioned over the left foot. Also check the location of the instrument button. It should be either near or touching the middle of the neck, with the side corner of the jaw resting on the chin rest and the head erect.

Violin/ Viola/ Cello The following *Workouts* will help your students develop a relaxed left hand. Violin/Viola students should now be spending more time playing in shoulder position than in guitar position. Left-hand exercises were not included in the student bass book because of the space devoted to the two different bow holds: French and German. However, bass students can do these exercises also, and they are demonstrated on the online video.

Practice each of the *Workout* exercises with students until they have mastered them. The foundation for more advanced left-hand skills is being established by successfully mastering each of the Workouts. Demonstrate each of the Workouts for the students before they practice them.

VIOLIN

WORKOUTS 

Place your instrument in shoulder position as shown on page 3. Then practice the following exercises with your left hand:

Finger Taps
Tap fingertips on any string. Practice in different combinations of fingers.

Pull Aways
Pull your left hand away from the side of the neck, while keeping the thumb and fingers on the instrument.

Strummin' Along
Strum the strings with your 4th finger while swinging your elbow under the violin, as shown.

Strummin' Along

VIOLA

WORKOUTS 

Place your instrument in shoulder position as shown on page 3. Then practice the following exercises with your left hand.

Finger Taps
Tap fingertips on any string. Practice in different combinations of fingers.

Pull Aways
Pull your left hand away from the side of the neck, while keeping the thumb and fingers on the instrument.

Strummin' Along
Strum the strings with your 4th finger while swinging your elbow under the viola, as shown.

Strummin' Along

CELLO

WORKOUTS

Practice the following exercises with your left hand:

Finger Taps 
Tap fingertips on any string. Practice in different combinations of fingers.

Strummin' Along 
Strum the strings with your 4th finger while swinging your elbow, as shown.

Strummin' Along

BASS

NEW NOTE

A

is played with 1 finger on the G string.

E A D G
A
1
2
3
4

Bass

A
1

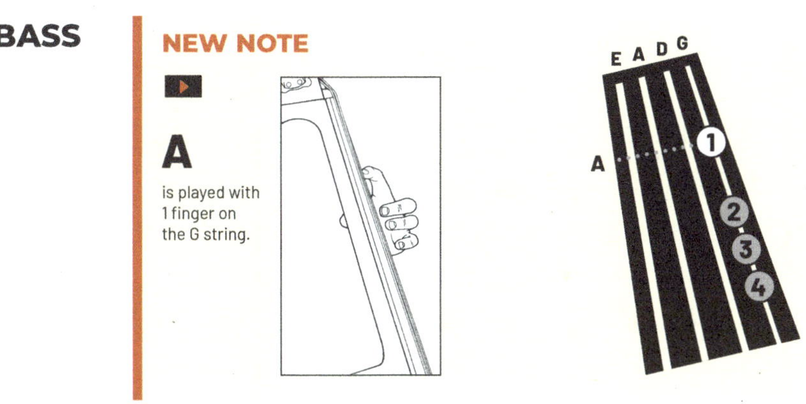

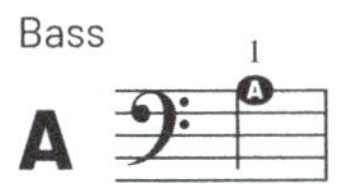

Bass The note A played in first position on the double bass is introduced in exercise 20. There are no new notes introduced in the violin, viola, or cello student books. Those instruments are playing their open A string while the bass is fingering the A on the G string.

In exercise 20, *Good King Wenceslas*, for the first time the violin, viola, and cello students should keep their fingers down on some pitches while playing others. Basses did this first in exercise 12. This helps students develop a well-shaped left-hand position when first learning to play.

The words to *Good King Wenceslas* are provided on page 262. Have students say and sing the words to *Good King Wenceslas* as they are learning to play the melody.

20. GOOD KING WENCESLAS

Welsh Folk Song

Student books have repeats, not 1st and 2nd endings (until ex. 76).

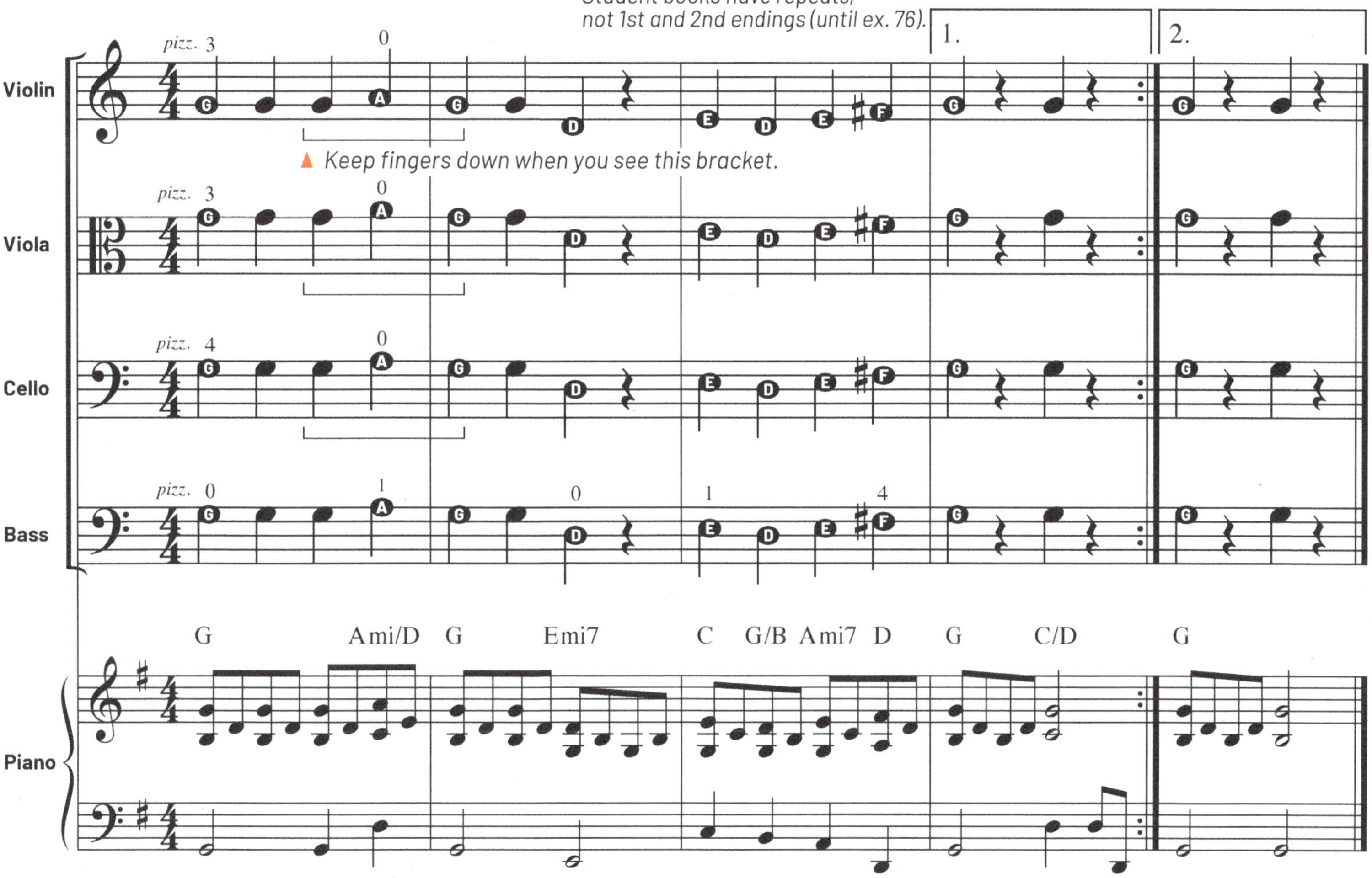

1.
2.
Violin
pizz. 3
0
Keep fingers down when you see this bracket.
Viola
pizz. 3
0
Cello
pizz. 4
0
Bass
pizz. 0
1
0
1
4
G Ami/D G Emi7 C G/B Ami7 D G C/D G
Piano

21. SEMINOLE CHANT

Student books have repeats, not 1st and 2nd endings (until ex. 76).

QUIZ OBJECTIVES – LIGHTLY ROW

- Pizzicato notes on D string (and the G string on Bass)
- Counting
- Steady beat
- Square first finger shape (Violin/Viola)
- Keeping fingers down while playing pitches on another string
- Violin and Viola shoulder position

Review Exercises:

Page 9 *Workouts*
19. *Rolling Along*
20. *Good King Wenceslas*
21. *Seminole Chant*

22. ESSENTIAL ELEMENTS QUIZ – LIGHTLY ROW

Teacher The pitches D, C♯, and B are introduced. D and C♯ notes are in third position on the double bass so that bass students will be able to avoid octave displacements. Research suggests that students have difficulty recognizing and understanding a melodic line that contains octave displacements. Point out to bass students that their finger spacing in third position is the same as in first position, and that the thumb remains behind the second finger.

For developing student listening skills, sample four-beat patterns are provided that incorporate the new pitches introduced on student book page 10. Play the pitch patterns provided, or ones you create, for students to echo so that they may continue to develop their listening skills. Remember the echo patterns may be played on any instrument and should be played behind the class so that students cannot see the teacher's fingering.

Remind students to memorize the names of the new notes they are learning to play.

VIOLIN/ VIOLA

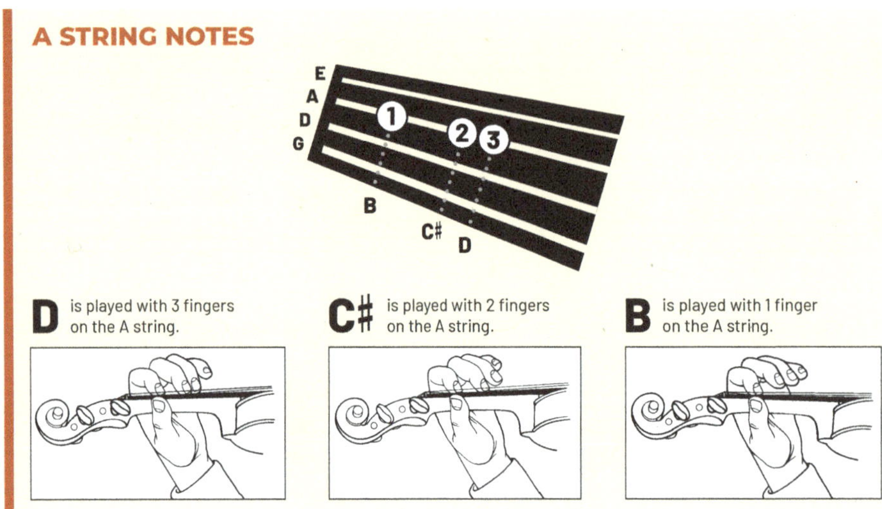

CELLO

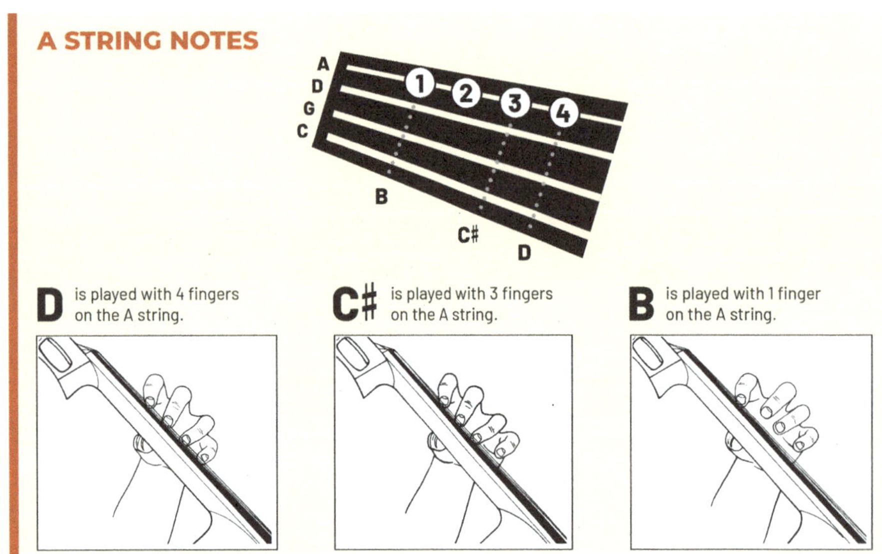

BASS

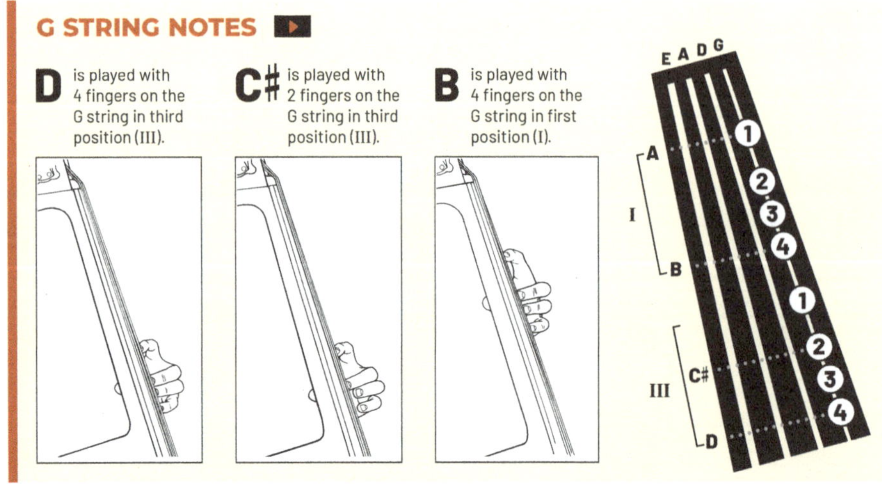

Listening Skills

Play what your teacher plays. Listen carefully.

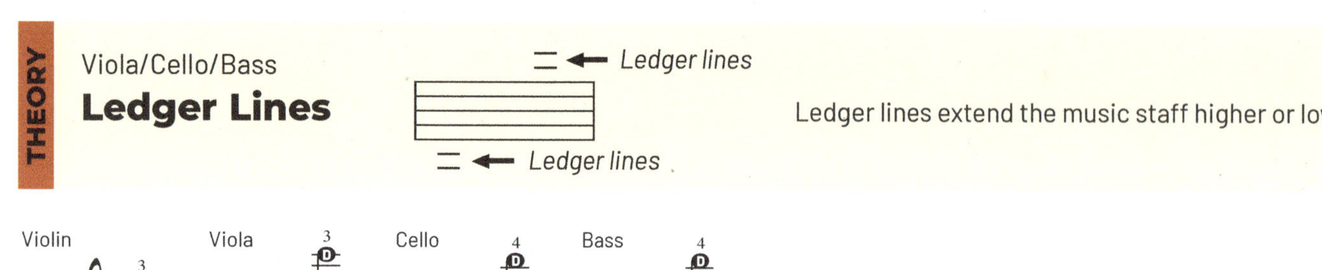

Violin D · Viola D · Cello D · Bass D (III)

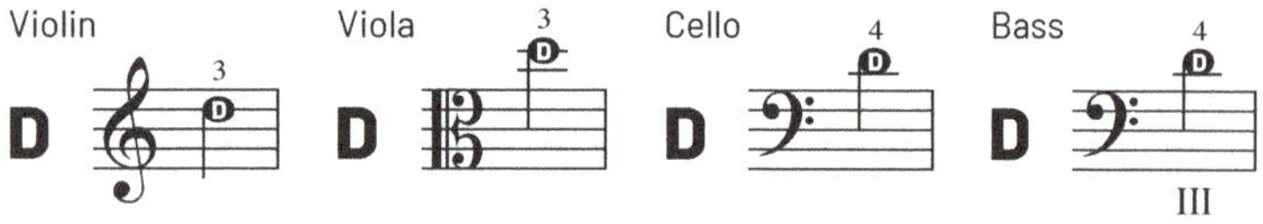

23. LET'S READ "D"

Violin (pizz.) · Viola (pizz.) · Cello (pizz.) · Bass (pizz., III)

Piano: D(add9) · G(add9) · F6 · G(add9) · D(add9)

Violin
C♯
2
Viola
C♯
2
Cello
C♯
3
Bass
C♯
2
III

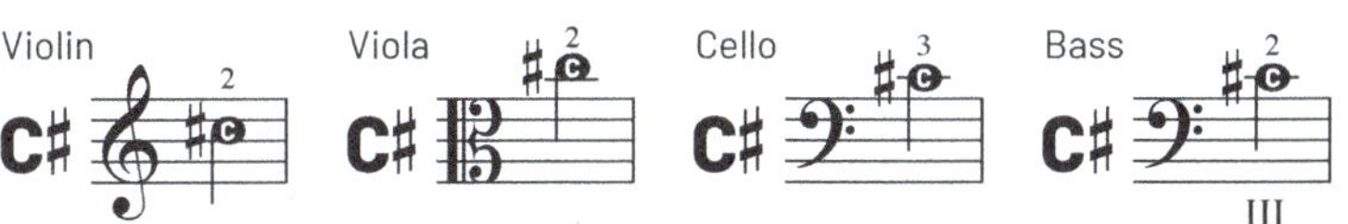

24. LET'S READ "C♯" (C-sharp)

▼ *Play all C♯'s. Sharps apply to the entire measure.*

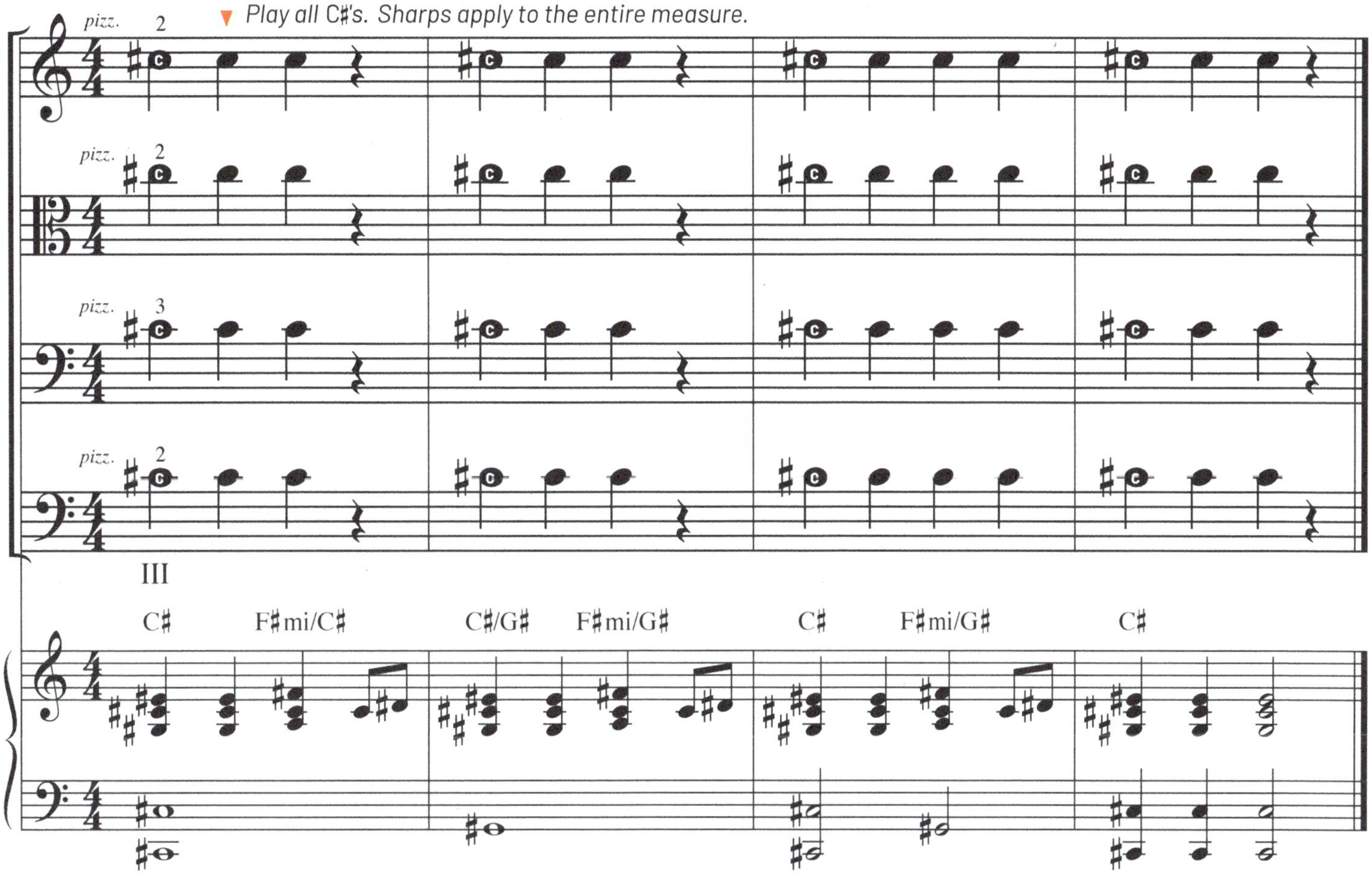

pizz.
Violin
Viola
Cello
Bass
III
C♯
F♯mi/C♯
C♯/G♯
F♯mi/G♯
C♯
F♯mi/G♯
C♯
Piano

25. TAKE OFF

pizz.
Violin
Viola
Cello
Bass
III
Dsus
D
F♯sus
F♯/A♯
G(add9)
G
A
G
A
Dsus
D
Piano

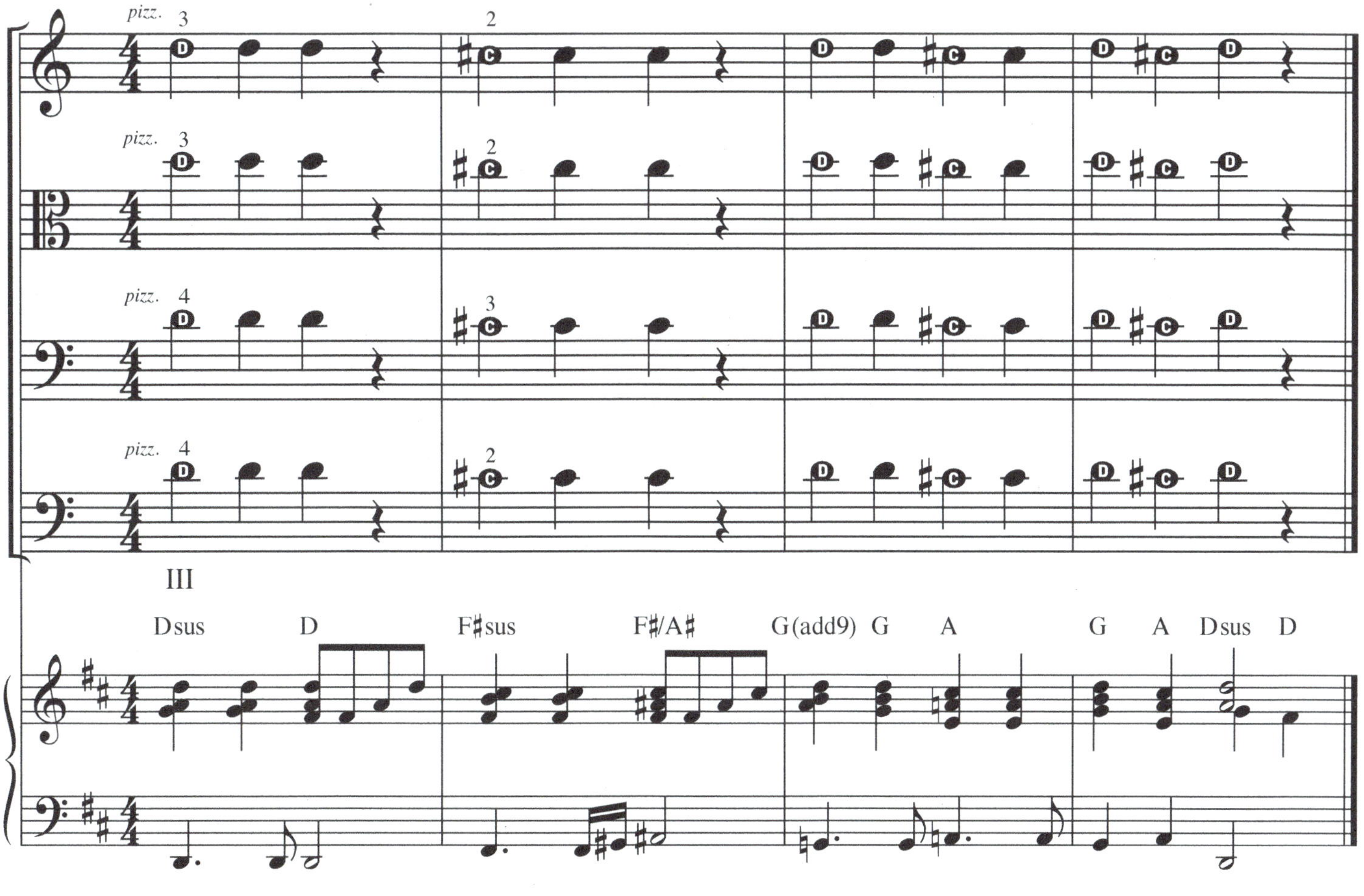

26. CARIBBEAN ISLAND

Student ★ Practice BOW BUILDERS ONE, TWO, and THREE daily.

Teacher Continually review the counting system you have selected with students as they learn to play each exercise. It is recommended that students count aloud each exercise while they are playing. Review BOW BUILDERS ONE, TWO, and THREE daily with students until they are mastered.

Teacher Have students compare their fingered D to the open D string in measures 1, 4 of exercise 27, *Olympic High Jump*. Point out to students that both pitches are D, only an octave apart. Ask students to find another D on their instrument by moving their left hand along the fingerboard, using their ear to guide them.

27. OLYMPIC HIGH JUMP

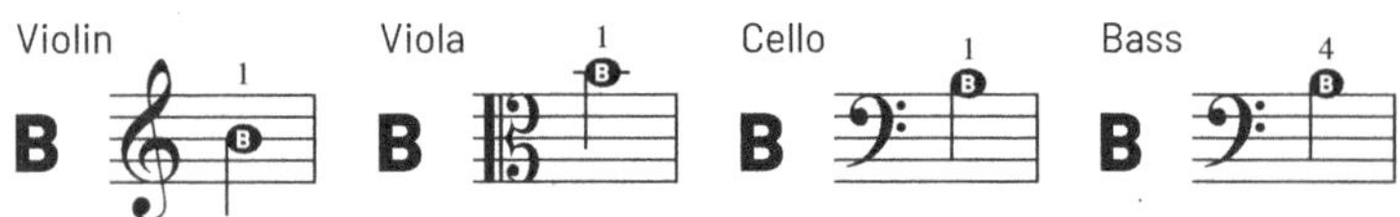

Teacher Students learn a new note, B, in exercise 28. Remind students to memorize the note name as they are learning to play the note.

28. LET'S READ "B"

Violin *pizz.* 1

Viola *pizz.* 1

Cello *pizz.* 1

Bass *pizz.* 4

Piano

B E/B B E/B B B/D♯ E C♯mi7 E/F♯ B

Bass In exercise 29, *Half Way Down*, basses shift for the first time. They shift from third to first position in measure 3 to play B. Instruct basses to release their hand weight on the string before and during the shift and that the thumb and hand move together as a unit. The thumb should remain by the second finger. Students may practice the shifting motion in the air away from the bass to help develop their shifting skill. Bass students should also practice shifting back and forth from C♯ to B and from B to C♯ in preparation for exercise 30, Right Back Up.

Dashes before finger numbers are used to indicate both ascending and descending shifts. Four positions are used in Book I and are indicated in students books by Roman Numerals:

I = First position (first finger plays A on the G string)
II = Second position (first finger plays B♭ on the G string)
III = Third position (first finger plays C on the G string)

Bass
Shifting Sliding your left hand smoothly and lightly to a new location on the fingerboard, indicated by a dash (-).

29. HALF WAY DOWN

Violin

Viola

Cello

Bass

Piano

Bass Basses shift from first to third position.

30. RIGHT BACK UP

Teacher Read the definition of scales. Demonstrate examples of various scales. Point out that scales begin and end on the same note.

A descending scale is introduced first because it helps promote the left-hand shape of the violins, violas, and cellos. Also, it is easier for students to lift off fingers while maintaining an acceptable left-hand shape as they are playing a descending scale.

Reviewing the names of the notes with students is an excellent activity while students are practicing their D major scale on student book page 11.

THEORY

Scale

A **scale** is a sequence of notes in ascending or descending order. Like a musical "ladder," each note is the next consecutive step of the scale. This is your D Scale. The first and last notes are both D.

31. DOWN THE D SCALE *Remember to memorize the note names.*

Violin — *pizz.* 3 D, 2 C, 1 B, 0 A, 3 G, 2 F, 1 E, 0 D

Viola — *pizz.* 3 D, 2 C, 1 B, 0 A, 3 G, 2 F, 1 E, 0 D

Cello — *pizz.* 4 D, 3 C, 1 B, 0 A, 4 G, 3 F, 1 E, 0 D

Bass — *pizz.* 4 D, 2 C, –4 B, 1 A, 0 G, 4 F, 1 E, 0 D

III I

Piano — D, F♯mi, G, F♯mi, G, D/A, Emi/A, D

QUIZ OBJECTIVES

- Left-hand shape
- Bass shifting
- Pizzicato D major scale

Review Exercises:

29. *Half Way Down*
30. *Right Back Up*

32. ESSENTIAL ELEMENTS QUIZ – UP THE D SCALE

Teacher

BOW BUILDER FOUR: ON THE BOW is introduced on the top of student book page 12. The purpose of this BOW BUILDER is to apply the hand shape previously positioned on a pen, pencil, or straw to the bow stick. Notice that the bow hand is positioned at the balance point of the bow for violin and viola. Students are able to hold the bow lightly if the hand is positioned first at the balance point. As students master the bow hand shape at the balance point they may begin to gradually move the hand to the frog.

The skills of holding the bow with an acceptable hand shape takes time for students to master. The authors recommend that students wait until their hand shape is mastered before setting the bow on the string to begin to learning bowing motions. While the bow hand is being mastered students may continue to work on their left hand, counting, listening, and note reading skills.

Violin/ Viola

BOW BUILDER FOUR 

On the Bow (Early Bow Hold)

Step 1 Identify all parts of the bow (see page 2). Hold the bow in your left hand near the tip with the frog pointing to the right.

Step 2 Put your right thumb and 2nd finger on the bow stick near the middle of the bow.

Step 3 Shape your right hand on the bow stick, as shown.

Step 4 Turn your right hand over, and be sure your thumb and fingers are curved.

Step 5 Hold the bow and repeat the exercises on page 8.

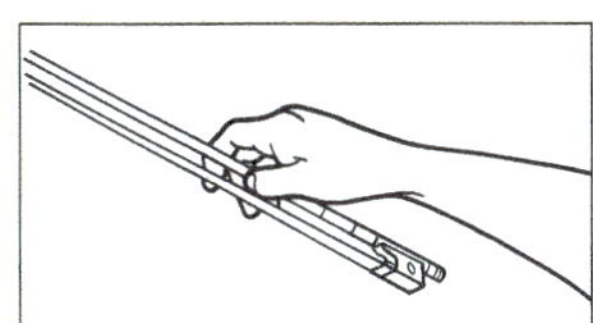

Balancing The Bow

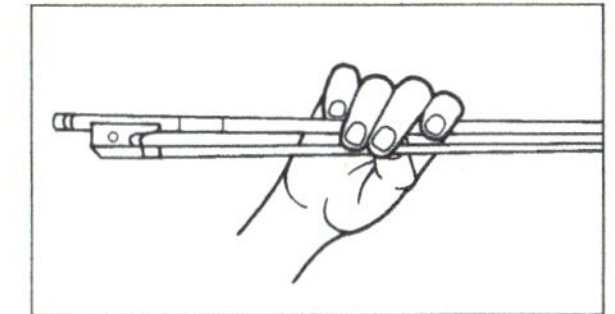

Early Bow Hold

Cello

BOW BUILDER FOUR 

On the Bow

Step 1 Identify all parts of the bow (see page 2). Hold the bow in your left hand near the tip with the frog pointing to the right.

Step 2 Place the bow between your right thumb and second finger. The tip of your thumb will contact the stick next to the frog, and your second finger will extend to the ferrule.

Step 3 Shape the remaining fingers on the bow stick, as shown.

Step 4 Turn your right hand over, and be sure your thumb is curved.

Step 5 Hold the bow and repeat the exercises on page 8.

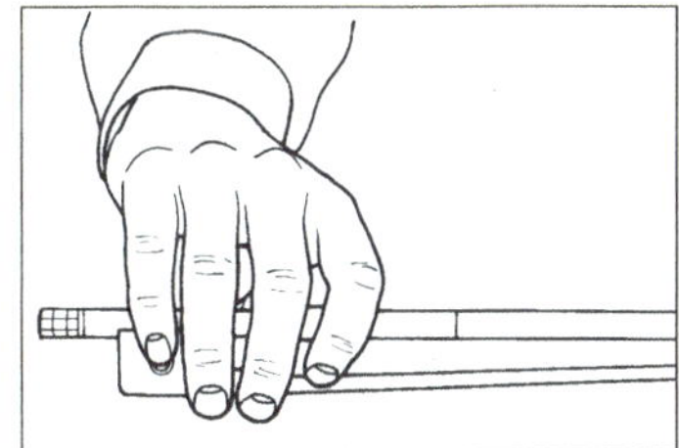

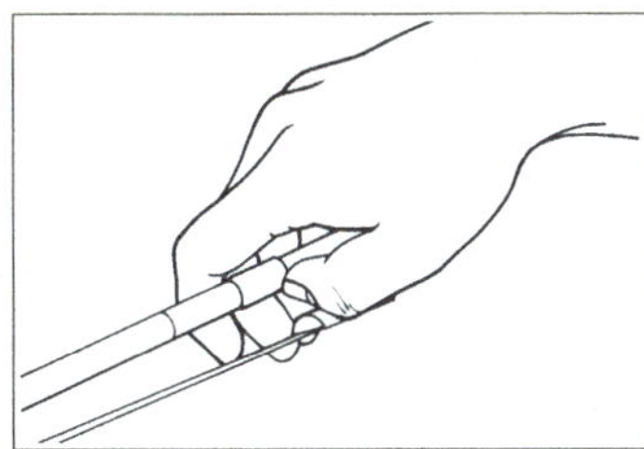

Bass

BOW BUILDER FOUR

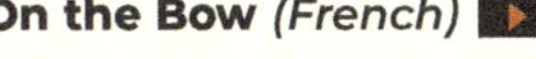

On the Bow *(French)*

Step 1 Identify all parts of the bow (see page 2). Hold the bow in your left hand near the tip with the frog pointing to the right.

Step 2 Place the bow between your right thumb and second finger. The tip of your thumb will contact the stick next to the frog, and your second finger will extend to the ferrule.

Step 3 Shape the remaining fingers on the bow stick as shown.

Step 4 Turn your right hand over, and be sure your thumb is curved.

Step 5 Hold the bow and repeat the exercises on page 8.

On the Bow *(German)*

Step 1 Identify all parts of the bow (see page 2). Hold the bow in your left hand near the tip with the frog pointing to the right.

Step 2 Place the frog in your right hand at the base joints of your fingers.

Step 3 Put your thumb on top of the bow while the tips of the first and second fingers touch the side of the stick and frog.

Step 4 Hook your fourth finger underneath the frog touching the ferrule. Allow the third finger to curve and relax.

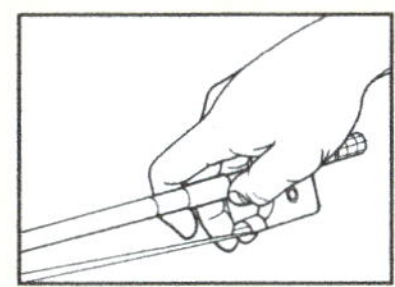

French Bow

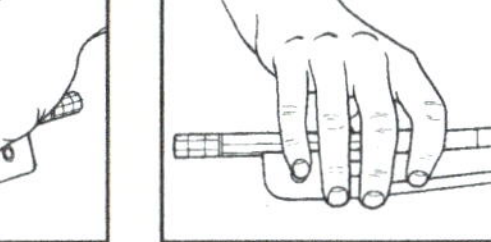

French Bow

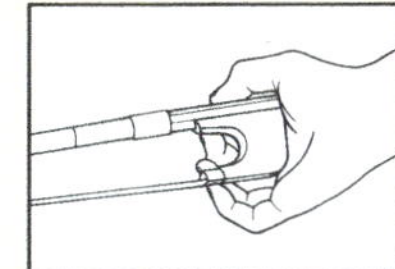

German Bow

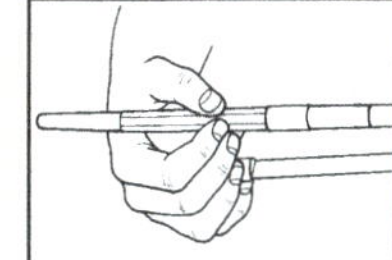

German Bow

Alert Do not place your bow on the instrument until instructed to do so by your teacher.

33. SONG FOR CHRISTINE

Violin *pizz.*

Viola *pizz.*

Cello *pizz.*

Bass *pizz.*

D(add9) A/D G/D D G(add9)/B Dma7/A E/G♯ G/A A

Piano

Violin

Viola

Cello

Bass

Bmi7 D/A Gma7 D(add9)/F♯ Emi7 A7sus G/C D

Piano

34. NATALIE'S ROSE *Remember to count.*

Teacher The goal of exercise 35, *ESSENTIAL CREATIVITY*, is to reinforce students note reading skills in a creative manner. Students are asked to spell words using the pitches they have learned to play. Answers may include egg, bed, dad, fad, dog, cab, etc.

35. ESSENTIAL CREATIVITY *How many words can you create by drawing notes on the staff below?*

Teacher The well-known folk song, *Dreidel*, is presented at the beginning of student book page 13. Familiarize students with other traditional Jewish folk songs by playing recorded examples in class. Discuss the history of Israel and its relationship to the United States.

Please note that *Dreidel* is the last exercise that includes alphabet letters in note heads to aid students in their note reading. Review students' note reading again, so that they will be successful in reading notes from this point on.

HISTORY

Folk songs often tell stories. This **Israeli folk song** describes a game played with a dreidel, a small table-top spinning toy that has been enjoyed by families for centuries. The game is especially popular in December around the time of Hanukkah.

36. DREIDEL

Israeli Folk Song

Violin

Viola

Cello

Bass

(D) Dsus D A7

Piano

Violin

Viola

Cello

Bass

D A7 D

Piano

Teacher The purpose of BOW BUILDER FIVE: SHADOW BOWING is to help students develop beginning bowing skills away from the instrument. This teaching strategy allows students to concentrate on only one skill at a time. The steps to begin teaching shadow bowing are the same for all four instruments.

Point out to students the definition of shadow bowing: bowing without the instrument. In BOW BUILDER FIVE, shadow bowing is done on rosin so that students will learn to pull the bow in a straight line. Shadow bowing may also be done by bowing in the air, through a PVC tube or paper product tube held in the air (cello/bass), or on the shoulder or arm (violin/viola).

First, demonstrate for students how to tighten and loosen the bow hair. Turn the screw of the bow clockwise to tighten, and counter-clockwise to loosen. Instruct students to always loosen the bow hair when they are finished playing.

Next, have students shadow bow on their rosin as illustrated on student book page 13. Basses should wait to use real bass rosin until page 16, or later, so that they can learn how to pull the bow in a straight line on a rectangular cake of rosin as illustrated.

Another way to practice shadow bowing is to bow through a PVC tube or paper product tube. Violin and viola students may hold the tube with their left hand over their left shoulder. They can place their bow inside the tube and bow through it to help learn their bowing motion. Cello and bass students may hold the tube in front of themselves where the bow would be contacting the string while bowing through the tube.

Review the definition and symbols for down and up bow. Demonstrate up and down bow directions for students.

Violin/ Viola

BOW BUILDER FIVE

Shadow Bowing

Shadow Bowing is bowing without the instrument.

Step 1 Tighten the bow hair as instructed by your teacher.

Step 2 Place the rosin in your left hand. Hold the bow at the balance point.

Step 3 Shadow bow by slowly moving the bow back and forth on the rosin. Be sure to move the bow, not the rosin.

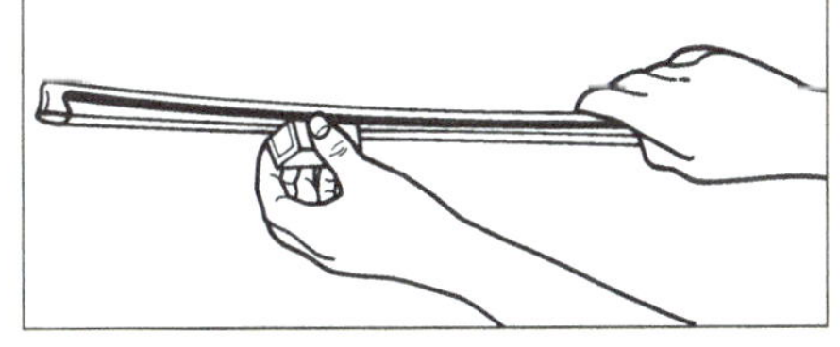

Cello

BOW BUILDER FIVE

Shadow Bowing

Shadow Bowing is bowing without the instrument.

Step 1 Tighten the bow hair as instructed by your teacher.

Step 2 Place the rosin in your left hand. Hold the bow in your right hand.

Step 3 Shadow bow by slowly moving the bow back and forth on the rosin. Be sure to move the bow, not the rosin.

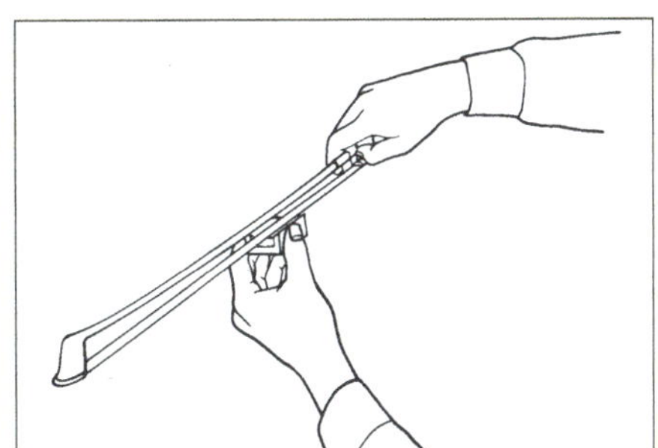

Bass

BOW BUILDER FIVE 

Shadow Bowing

Shadow Bowing is bowing without the instrument.

Step 1 Tighten the bow hair as instructed by your teacher.

Step 2 Place the rosin in your left hand. Hold the bow in your right hand.

Step 3 Shadow bow by slowly moving the bow back and forth on the rosin. Be sure to move the bow, not the rosin.

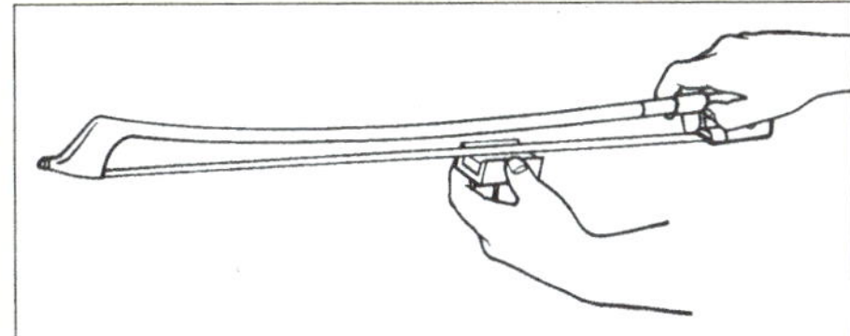

Down Bow  Move the bow away from your body (to the right).

Up Bow V Move the bow toward your body (to the left).

Teacher *Rosin Raps* 37–39 promote development of bowing skills away from the instrument so that students need to learn only one kinesthetic skill at a time. Rosin Raps also help students develop the physical coordination of reading music while bowing at the same time. Bowing on rosin is one way for students to shadow bow.

Have students say or sing "down" and "up" for bow direction and "rest" as indicated in the student book while bowing the following Rosin Raps. Have violin and viola students first bow the Rosin Raps with their bow hand positioned at the balance point. Once students can consistently bow the raps while keeping an acceptable bow-hand shape they may begin to gradually move their bow hand position to the frog.

As students are practicing the Rosin Raps encourage them to frequently compare their bow hand shape to the one in the illustration.

Student ✔ Is your bow hand shaped as shown in the diagram above?

Teacher Have students write the letter names of the notes in the theory exercise that appears at the top of student book page 14.

Review these notes. Write the letter names in the spaces below.

THEORY

Teacher All remaining exercises will use regular music notation. Students should name the notes of the following examples to reinforce note reading skills.

While students are learning to pizzicato and read the note names in exercises 40–42 they should be continuing to practice BOW BUILDER FIVE in preparation for bowing on the string beginning on student book page 16.

40. CAROLINA BREEZE

Violin *pizz.*

Count: 1 & 2 & 3 & 4 & | 1 & 2 & 3 & 4 & | 1 & 2 & 3 & 4 & | 1 & 2 & 3 & 4 & | 1 & 2 & 3 & 4 &

Viola *pizz.*

Cello *pizz.*

Bass *pizz.*

Piano

C9 Bmi7 Ami7 G7 C9 Bmi7 Ami7 D7 G7 Ami7 D7 G7

41. JINGLE BELLS

J. S. Pierpont

Violin
Viola
Cello
Bass
Piano
D(add9) D D(add9) D D(add9) G/A D(add9) D
G(add9) G Dsus D Bmi7 Emi7 A7sus A7 D(add9) D

42. OLD MACDONALD HAD A FARM

American Folk Song

Violin

Viola

Cello

Bass

G C G A7 D7 G D7 G

Piano

Student  Practice BOW BUILDER FIVE daily.

HISTORY

Austrian composer **Wolfgang Amadeus Mozart** (1756-1791) was a child prodigy who first performed in concert at age 6. He lived during the time of the American Revolution (1775-1783). Mozart's music is melodic and imaginative. He wrote hundreds of compositions, including a piano piece based on this familiar song.

Teacher Familiarize students with music of Mozart by playing recorded examples of his works. You may also want to use the movie Amadeus as a resource.

43. A MOZART MELODY

Adapted by W. A. Mozart

Violin
Viola
Cello
Bass
Piano
D/F♯ A7sus/E A/E D Asus A D/F♯ A7sus/E A/E D Asus A
D D/F♯ G/B G D/F♯ D G/B A7/C♯ D D/F♯ Asus/G A7 D

Key Signature D MAJOR

A **key signature** tells us what notes to play with sharps and flats throughout the entire piece. Play all F's as F♯ (F-sharp) and all C's as C♯ (C-sharp) when you see this key signature, which is called "D Major."

Teacher Read the definition and example of key signature as presented on student book page 15. Give students examples of other key signatures and have them practice writing them. Be sure students are counting, including subdivisions, when learning to play each exercise.

44. MATTHEW'S MARCH

Violin *pizz.*

▲ *Play F♯'s and C♯'s when you see this key signature.*

Viola *pizz.*

Cello *pizz.*

Bass *pizz.*

III I III I

D A7 D Bmi F♯ Bmi E7 A7sus A7

Piano

Violin

Viola

Cello

Bass

G A/G G D/F♯ G/B D/A G6 A7 D G/D D

Piano

45. CHRISTOPHER'S TUNE

Violin *pizz.* 0 2 1 3 1 3

Viola *pizz.* 0 2 1 3 1 3

Cello *pizz.* 0 3 1 4 1 4

Bass *pizz.* 0 4 1 0 1

Piano D A7 D

Violin

Viola

Cello

Bass 4 1 0 4 1 4 −2 4 III

Piano D G A7 D

Teacher Have students create and write notes they choose to complete the melody in ESSENTIAL CREATIVITY, exercise 46. This allows students to begin composing their own melodies while reinforcing their note reading and rhythm reading skills. Give them the opportunity to play their completed melodies in class. Consider allowing students to play them on a concert.

46. ESSENTIAL CREATIVITY

Play the notes below. Then compose your own music for the last two measures using the notes you have learned with this rhythm:

Teacher BOW BUILDER SIX: LET'S BOW! is introduced at the top of student book page 16. The purpose of this exercise is to give students the opportunity to begin bowing on the string, using all the skills learned in the previous BOW BUILDERS.

Violin/ Viola

BOW BUILDER SIX

Let's Bow!

Early Bow Hold

Regular Bow Hold

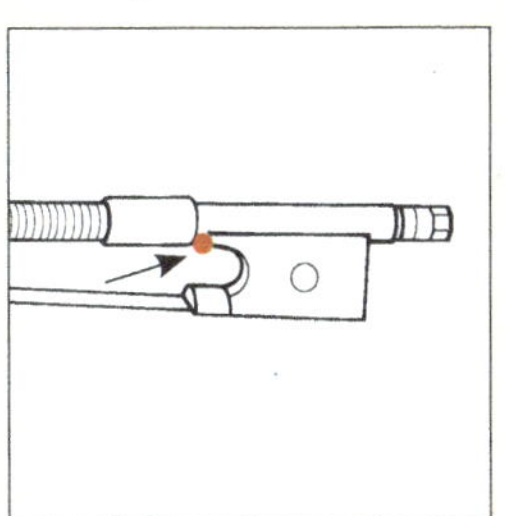

Thumb Placement

Cello

BOW BUILDER SIX

Let's Bow!

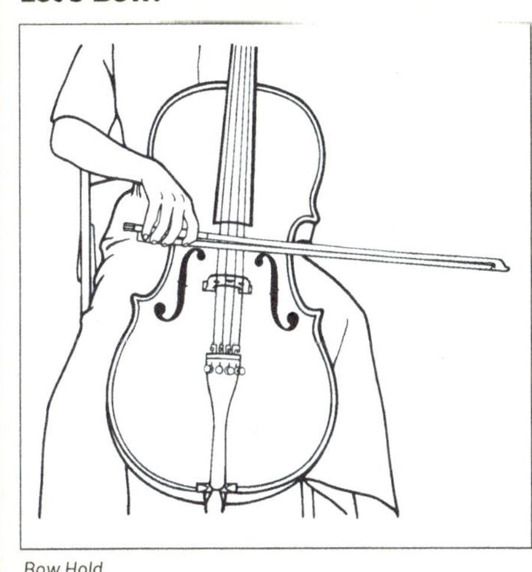

Bow Hold

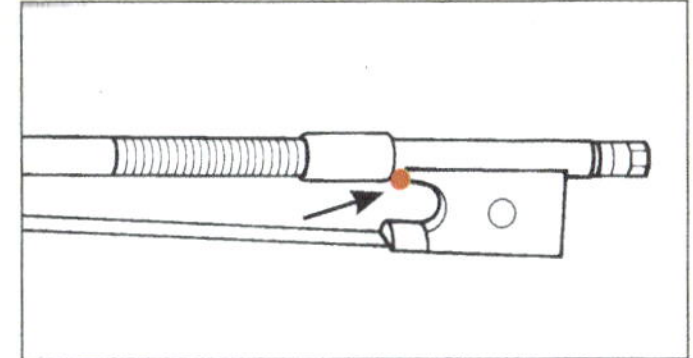

Thumb Placement

Bass

BOW BUILDER SIX

Let's Bow!

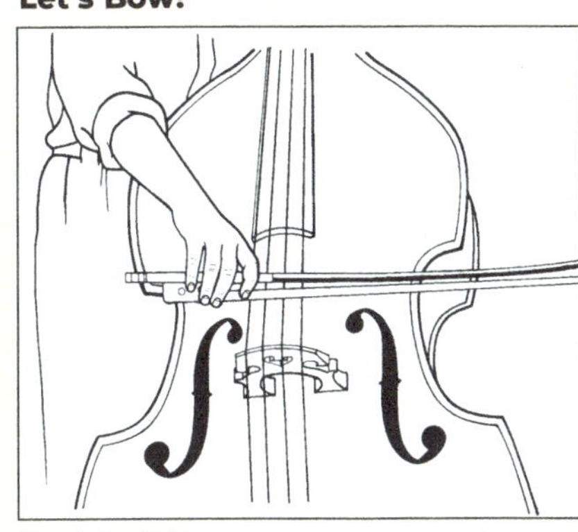

French Bow Hold

German Bow Hold

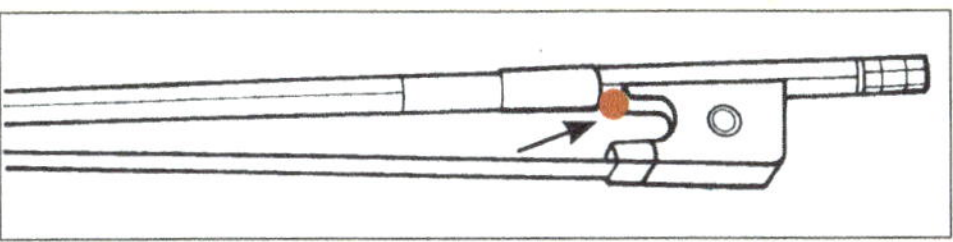

Thumb Placement (French)

Violin/ Viola

Even though students will only be bowing open strings first, be careful that they keep the proper shape and position of their left hand while bowing. Notice in the illustration that the left hand is on the bout where the neck and instrument meet and that all the fingers are curved. This finger position helps reinforce students left hand shape as they get ready to bow fingered notes.

Examine the illustration with a straw in the "F" hole. Notice that the straw is placed in the "F" hole near the low string of the student's instrument. The bow is placed between the bridge and the straw. The straw helps the student bow in a straight line parallel to the bridge. This bow placement will produce the best sound for students.

This illustration is in the Teacher Manual only.

Straw in the "F" hole

This illustration is in the Teacher Manual only.

Bowing through a tube

Teacher

Also notice the illustration with the bow traveling through a tube attached to the string. Bowing through a tube will help all string students learn the proper bowing motion. Either plastic PVC tubes or paper product tubes may be used. Place a rubber band under the strings and then loop the ends around each end of the tube.

Students should begin bowing with short bow strokes: violins and violas in the middle of the bow; cellos and basses in the lower half of the bow. As students' bowing skills develop, they should gradually lengthen their bow strokes.

Violin/Viola
Step 1 Hold the instrument with your left hand on the upper bout as illustrated.

Violin/Viola
Step 2 Hold the bow at the balance point (Early Bow Hold). Your right elbow should be slightly lower than your hand.

Your teacher will suggest when to begin moving your bow hand toward the frog, as shown in the Regular Bow Hold illustration. The tip of your thumb will move to the place on the stick where it touches the frog.

Teacher Model open D's and A's for students to echo. Evaluate the tone of students' echoes. The tone should be smooth, even, and pleasant to hear. Sample open string examples for echo practice with students are provided.

Listening Skills

Play what your teacher plays. Listen carefully.

Teacher As students develop their bowing skills, have them do some of the exercises on student book page 8 to relax their hand during the rests. For exercise 47, check to make sure that students' elbows are at the proper height when their bow is on the D string.

47. BOW ON THE D STRING

Teacher Check to make sure that students' elbows are at the proper height for the A string.

48. BOW ON THE A STRING

Teacher String levels, for string crossing motions, are introduced on student book page 17. Note that the motion to change string levels is the opposite for upper and lower strings, i.e., a player raises the right arm to play lower-pitched strings for violin/viola, but lowers the right arm to play lower-pitched strings on the cello/bass.

Be sure that students raise and lower their arms during the rests for each new string level in the following exercises.

Violin/ Viola

WORKOUTS

String Levels

Your arm moves when bowing on different strings. Memorize these guidelines:

- **Raise** your arm to play **lower**-pitched strings.
- **Lower** your arm to play **higher**-pitched strings.

Raise arm = lower string

Lower arm = higher string

Cello

WORKOUTS

String Levels

Your arm moves when bowing on different strings. Memorize these guidelines:

- Move your arm **forward** and **up** to play **higher**-pitched strings.
- Move your arm **back** and **down** to play **lower**-pitched strings.

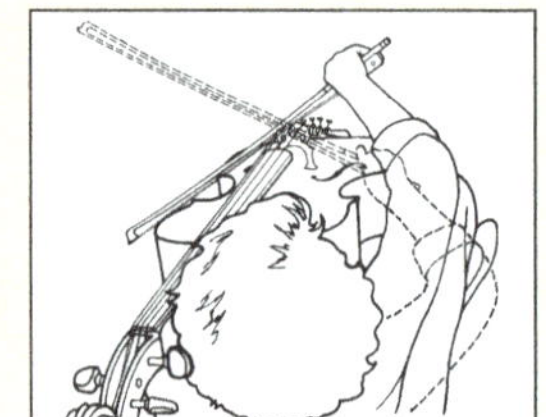

Raise arm = higher string

Lower arm = lower string

Bass

WORKOUTS

String Levels

Your arm moves when bowing on different strings. Memorize these guidelines:

- Move your arm **forward** and **up** to play **higher**-pitched strings.
- Move your arm **back** and **down** to play **lower**-pitched strings.

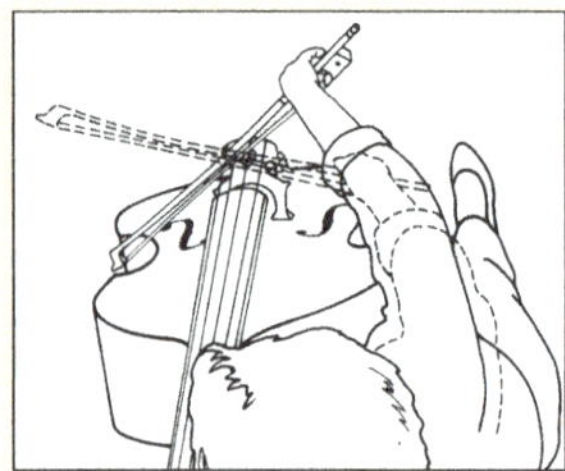

Raise arm = higher string

Lower arm = lower string

49. RAISE AND LOWER

Student books have a repeat sign in measure 4.

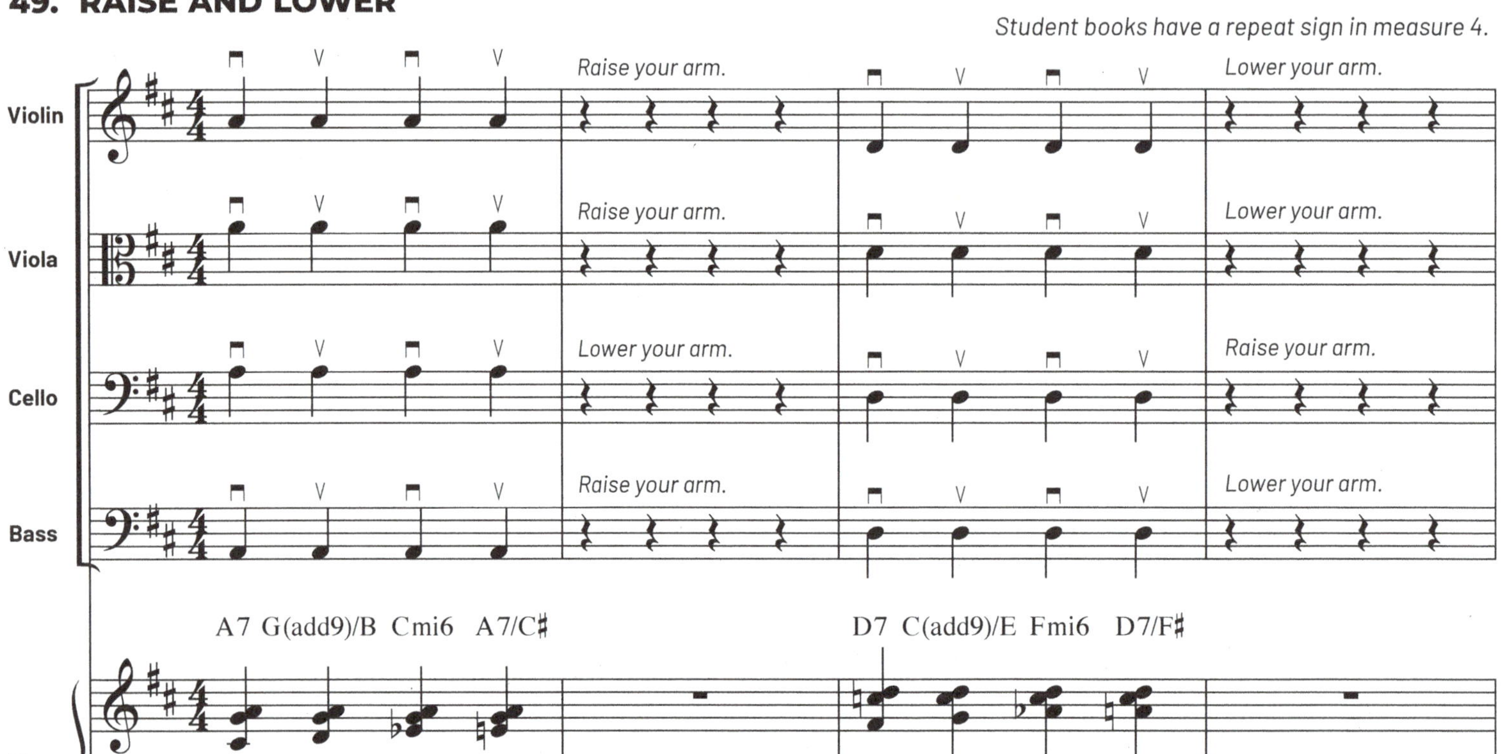

Violin — Raise your arm. — Lower your arm.

Viola — Raise your arm. — Lower your arm.

Cello — Lower your arm. — Raise your arm.

Bass — Raise your arm. — Lower your arm.

Piano — G/A F♯mi/A Emi/A D/A A7 G/A F♯mi/A Emi/A D/A D

50. TEETER TOTTER

Violin

Viola

Cello

Bass

Piano — Asus D5 Asus D5 C5 D5

51. MIRROR IMAGE

Bow Lift

Lift the bow and return to its starting point.

Teacher Read the definition and show students the symbol for bow lift. Practice lifting and setting the bow on the string with students. Be sure that students relax their shoulder, arm, wrist, and bow hand after they set the bow on the string each time before pulling the bow.

Be sure that students raise and lower their arms during the rests for each new string level in the following exercises. Notice that violin/viola and cello/bass levels are reversed.

52. A STRAND OF D 'N' A

QUIZ OBJECTIVES – OLYMPIC CHALLENGE

- Parallel bowing
- Smooth and even tone
- Arm level changes at string crossings

Review Exercises:

49. *Raise and Lower*
50. *Teeter Totter*
52. *A Strand of D'N'A*

53. ESSENTIAL ELEMENTS QUIZ – OLYMPIC CHALLENGE

BOW BUILDER SEVEN

Combining Both Hands

Using notes from the D major scale, echo what your teacher plays.

Teacher BOW BUILDER SEVEN: COMBINING BOTH HANDS involves the teacher playing pitch patterns and the students echoing those patterns. Before students proceed to page 18, be sure that they have mastered proper bow hand shape, beginning open string motions, and changing string level skills in the echo patterns. On page 18 students will begin to bow fingered notes for the first time. This is an important skill and students must first master bowing open string skills before they begin bowing fingered pitches.

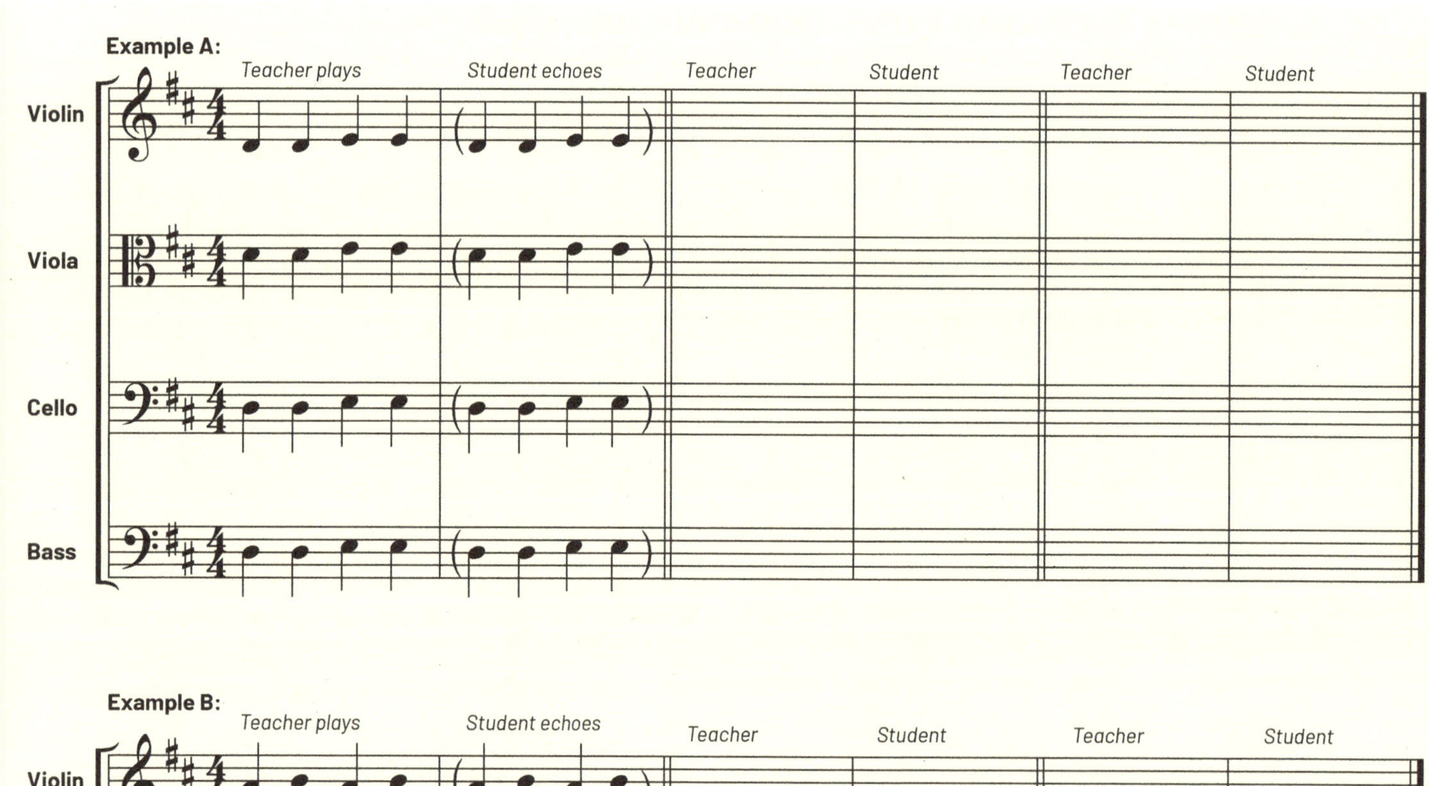

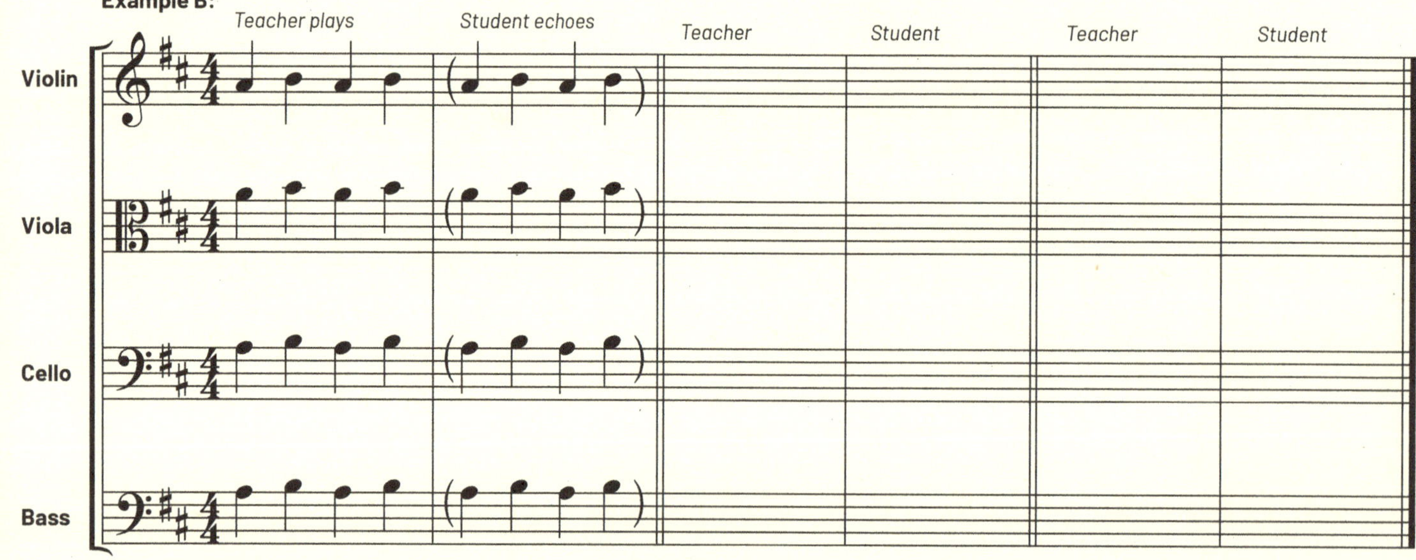

Teacher Students should now be ready to begin learning to bow fingered pitches while reading music. A suggested practice routine is provided for them in the student text. These sequential practice steps are important for students to follow because they will help them develop successful playing skills and home practice skills. Lead students through these steps carefully for each of the remaining playing exercises, and encourage students to use these steps while practicing at home. Create and substitute additional practice steps as needed.

Remember, there are many different ways to shadow bow that can be used in Step 3, e.g. bowing in the air, bowing on rosin, or bowing through tubes attached to the instrument or held over the left shoulder (violin and viola) or in front (cello and bass). One way is to ask students to bow vertically in the air, being careful that the down bow motion is toward the floor and the up bow motion is toward the ceiling. Bowing vertically helps eliminate tension in the right hand, which will occur if the bow is held in the air horizontally while shadow bowing. Of course, you may always have students practice bowing their open strings.

PUTTING IT ALL TOGETHER

Congratulations! You are now ready to practice like an advanced player by combining left and right hand skills while reading music. When learning a new line of music, follow these steps for success:

Step 1 Tap your toe and say or sing the letter names.

Step 2 Play *pizz.* and say or sing the letter names.

Step 3 Shadow bow and say or sing the letter names.

Step 4 Bow and play as written.

54. BOWING "G"

Violin

Viola

Cello

Bass

Piano

G C/G Csus/G C G

55. BACK AND FORTH

56. DOWN AND UP

57. TRIBAL LAMENT

Student books have repeats, not 1st and 2nd endings (until ex. 76).

58. BOWING "D"

59. LITTLE STEPS

Violin

Viola

Cello

Bass

III

D A G A G A D

Piano

60. ELEVATOR DOWN

Violin

1 & 2 & 3 & 4 & 1 & 2 & 3 & 4 & 1 & 2 & 3 & 4 & 1 & 2 & 3 & 4 &

Viola

Cello

Bass

III I

D A D F♯7 G D G D A D

Piano

Teacher Counting and playing eighth notes will be introduced on student book page 20. Counting quarter note subdivisions was first introduced on page 5, with additional examples on successive pages. Give students further preparation for page 20 by counting aloud as a class, including subdivisions, for each of the exercises on page 19. The authors also recommend that students review their toe tapping skills as they play each exercise.

61. ELEVATOR UP

62. DOWN THE D MAJOR SCALE

63. SCALE SIMULATOR *Remember to count.*

QUIZ OBJECTIVES – THE D MAJOR SCALE

- Bowing and fingering D and A string notes
- Playing correct bow markings
- Bowing parallel to the bridge
- String Levels
- Half steps and whole steps

Review Exercises:

60. *Elevator Down*
62. *Down the D Scale*
63. *Scale Simulator*

Teacher As students are practicing for exercise 64. *Essential Elements Quiz – The D Major Scale*, encourage them to constantly evaluate their intonation. The half and whole steps must be in tune. Assisting students as they develop self-assessment skills is critical to developing effective practice skills.

64. ESSENTIAL ELEMENTS QUIZ – THE D MAJOR SCALE

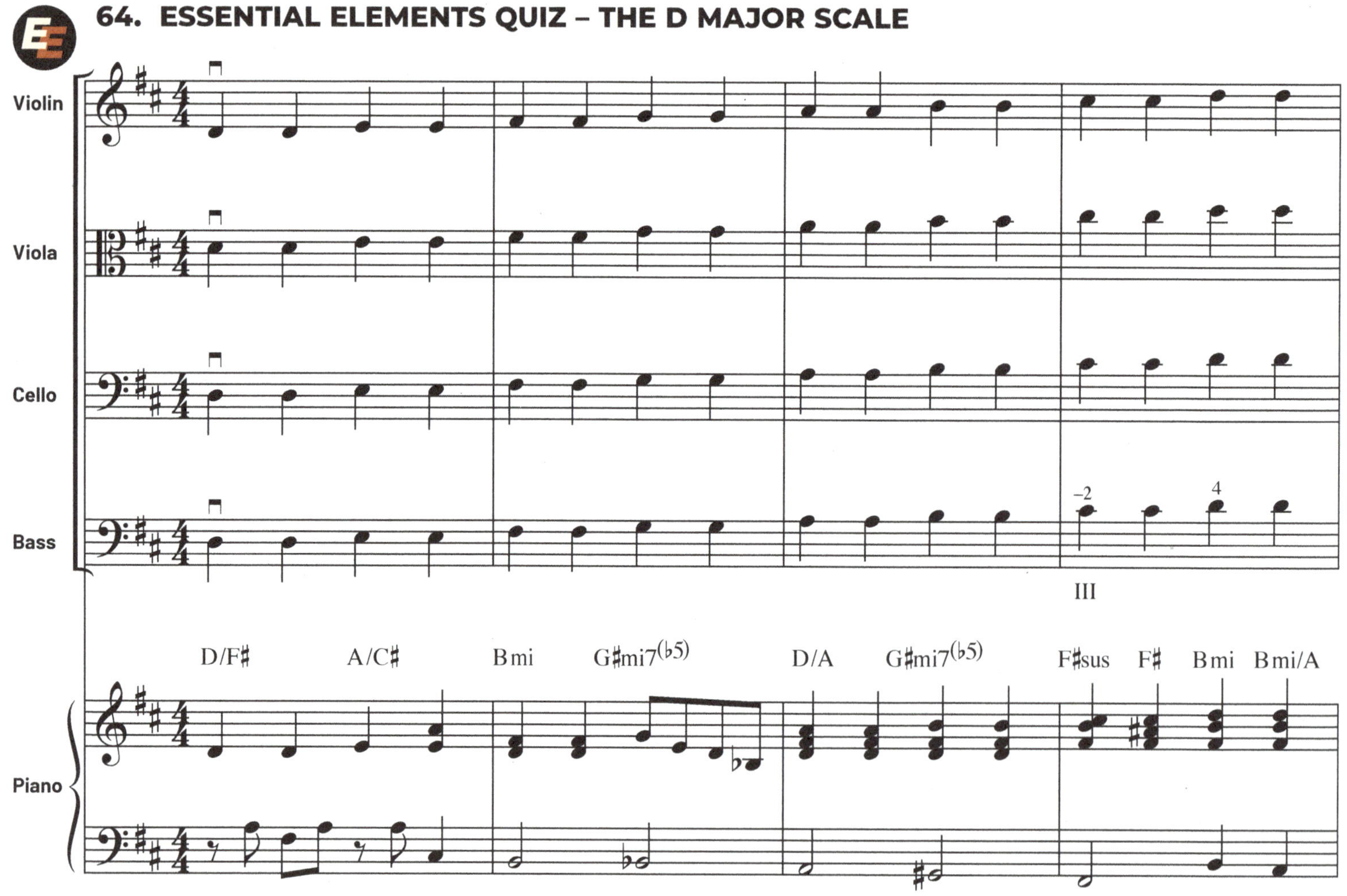

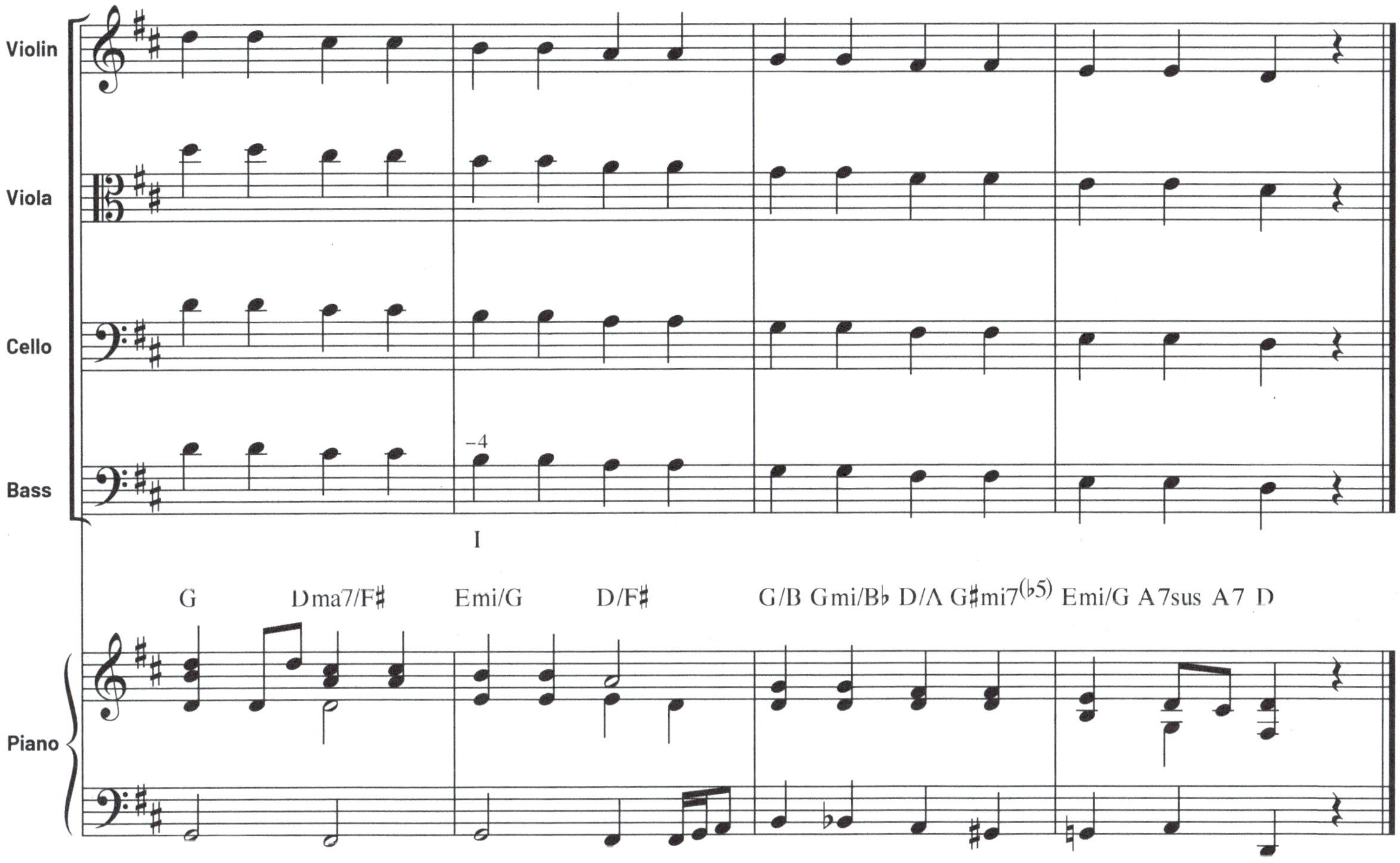
Violin
Viola
Cello
Bass
-4
I
G Dma7/F♯ Emi/G D/F♯ G/B Gmi/B♭ D/A G♯mi7(♭5) Emi/G A7sus A7 D
Piano

Teacher The basses learn the new note C♯ while the other instruments review note reading, bar lines, and counting through a written exercise.

Special Exercise (Violin/Viola/Cello)

While the basses learn a new note, draw the bar lines in the music below. Then write in the counting.

Violin
Viola
Cello

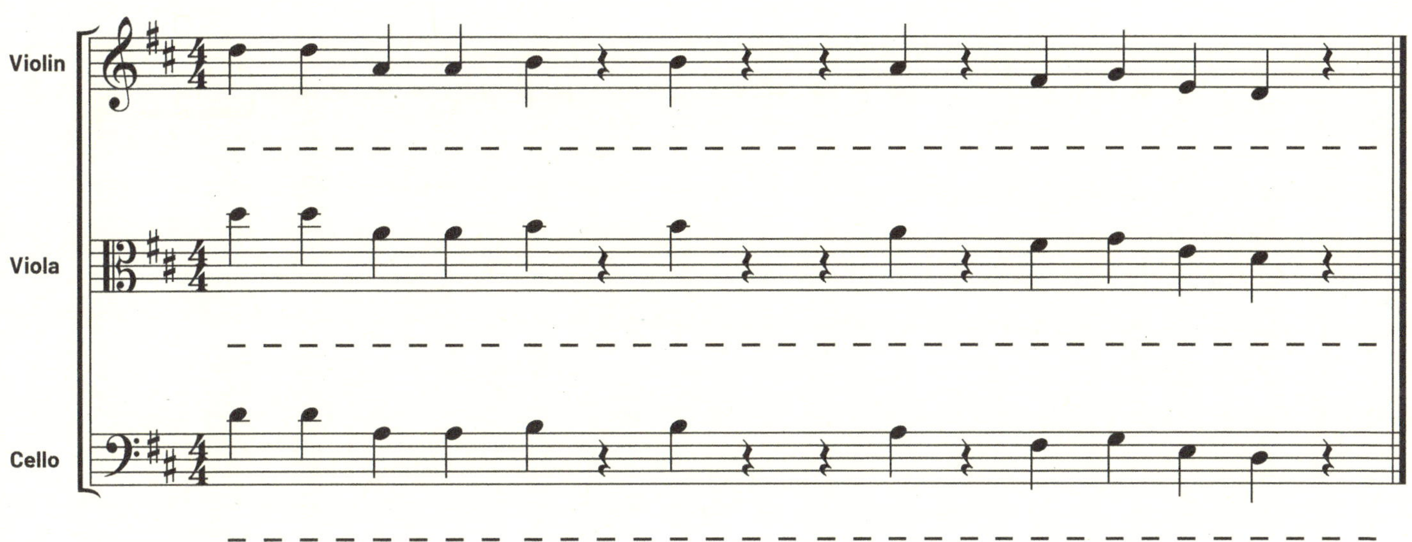

Bass

NEW NOTE

C♯

is played with 4 fingers on the A string.

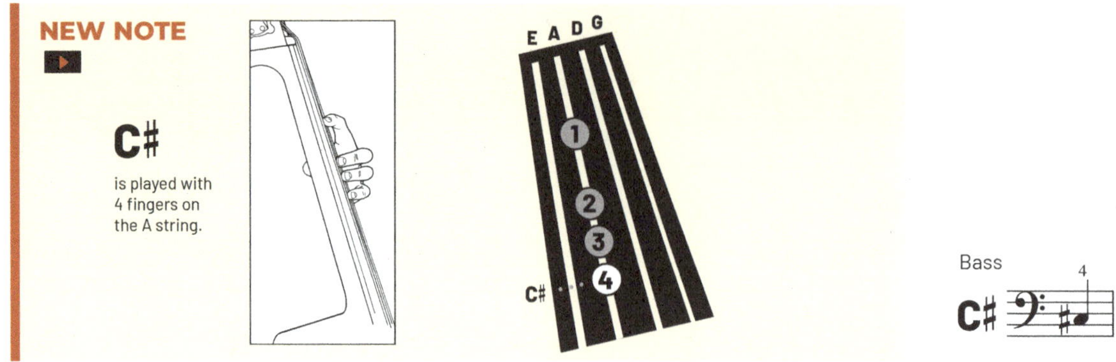

65. LET'S READ "C♯" – Review

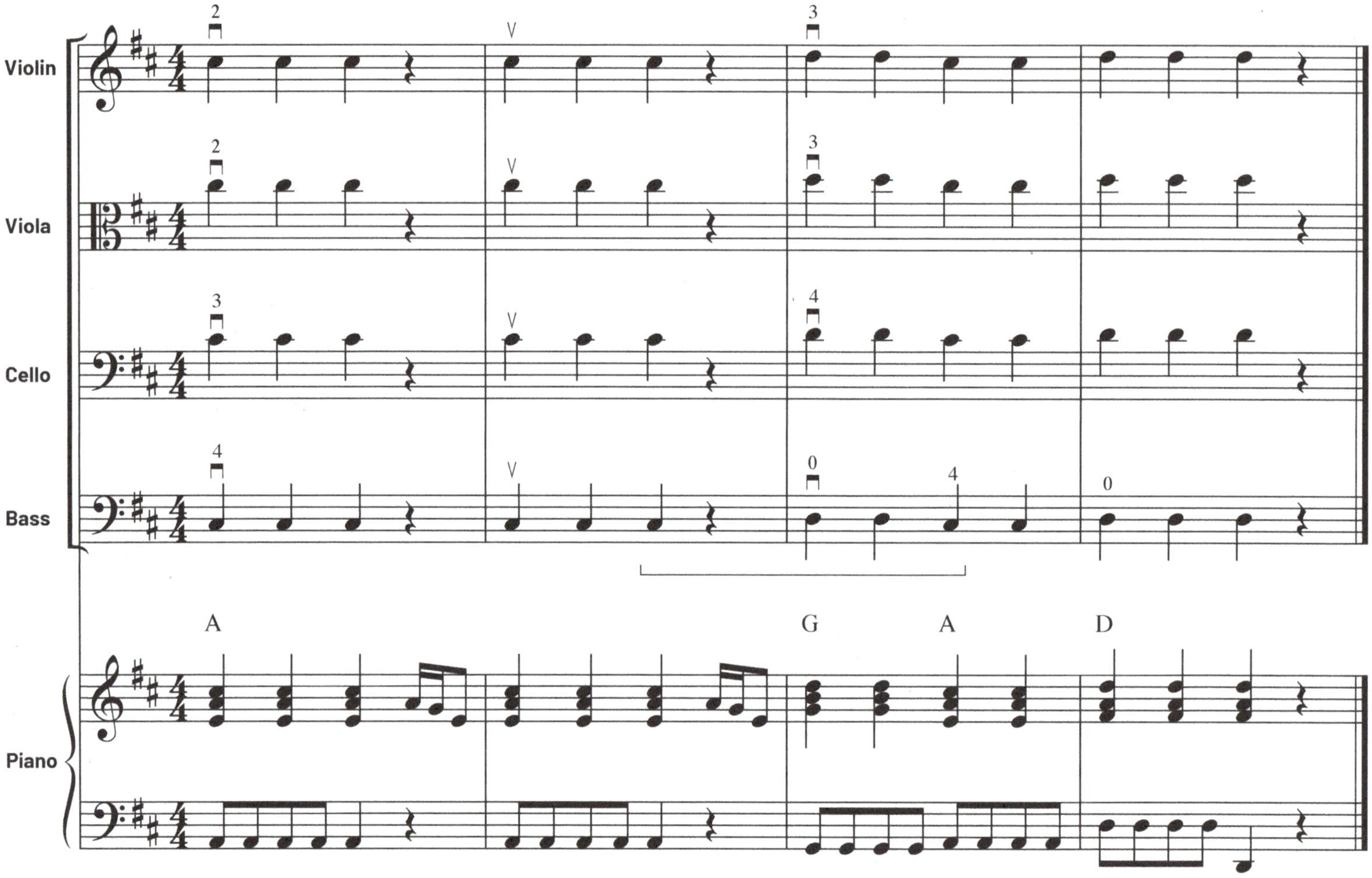

THEORY

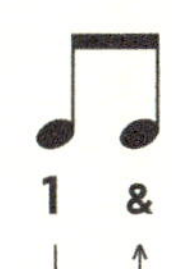

Each Eighth Note = 1/2 Beat
2 Eighth Notes = 1 Beat

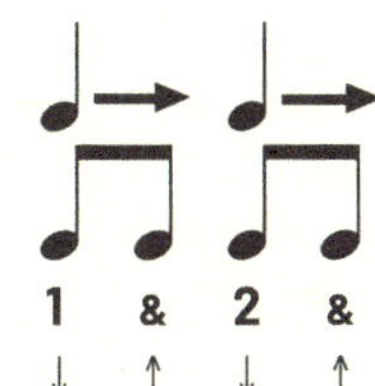

Two or more Eighth Notes have a *beam* across the stems.

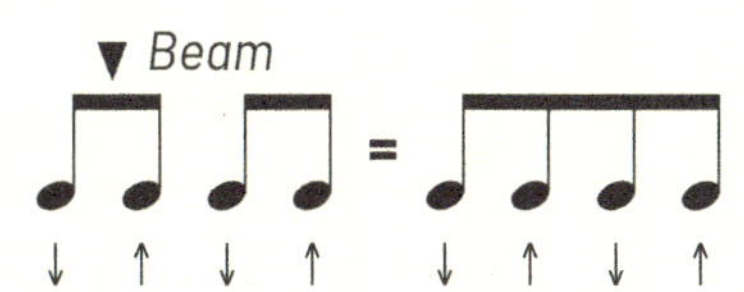

Tap your toe down on the number and up on the "&."

Teacher *Rhythm Raps* introduce new rhythms and meters. Notice the exercises that immediately follow the *Rhythm Raps* are in the same rhythm. This helps students combine their bowing, fingering, and rhythm reading skills. A suggested four-step teaching sequence for *Rhythm Raps*, as students tap their toes on the pulse, is as follows:

Step 1 – Shadow bow on rosin.
Step 2 – Bow rhythm in the air vertically, or through a tube attached to the string.
Step 3 – Bow rhythm on any open string.
Step 4 – Bow rhythm on a scale.
The piano accompaniment may be used with steps 1 and 2.

66. RHYTHM RAP *Shadow bow and count before playing.*

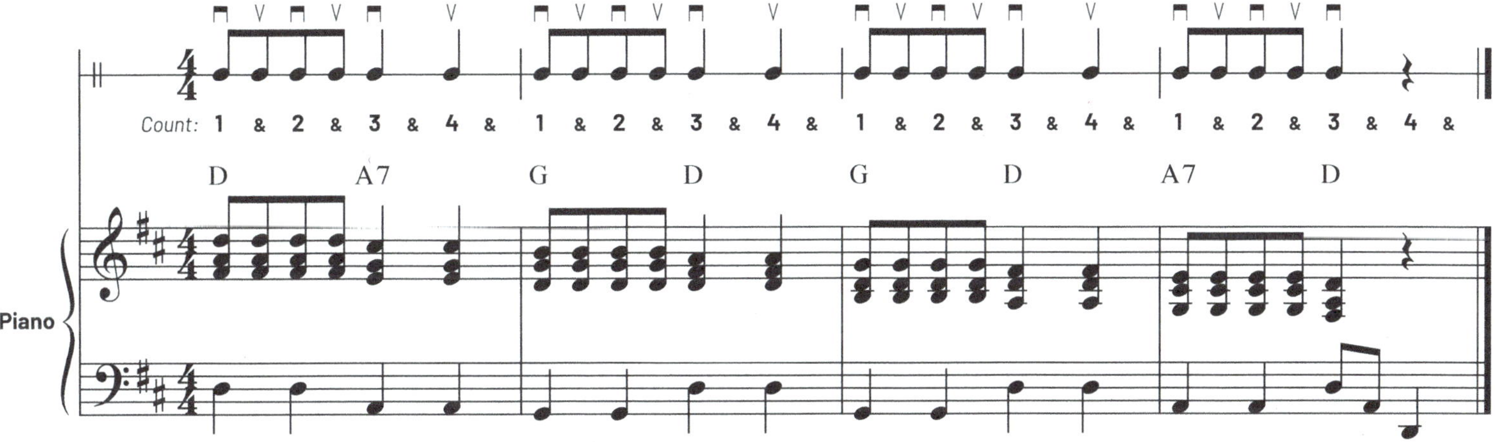

67. PEPPERONI PIZZA

68. RHYTHM RAP *Shadow bow and count before playing.*

Count: 1 & 2 & 3 & 4 & 1 & 2 & 3 & 4 & 1 & 2 & 3 & 4 & 1 & 2 & 3 & 4 &
D
Emi7/A
D/F♯
C
Dma7/A
Emi7/A
A7
D
Piano

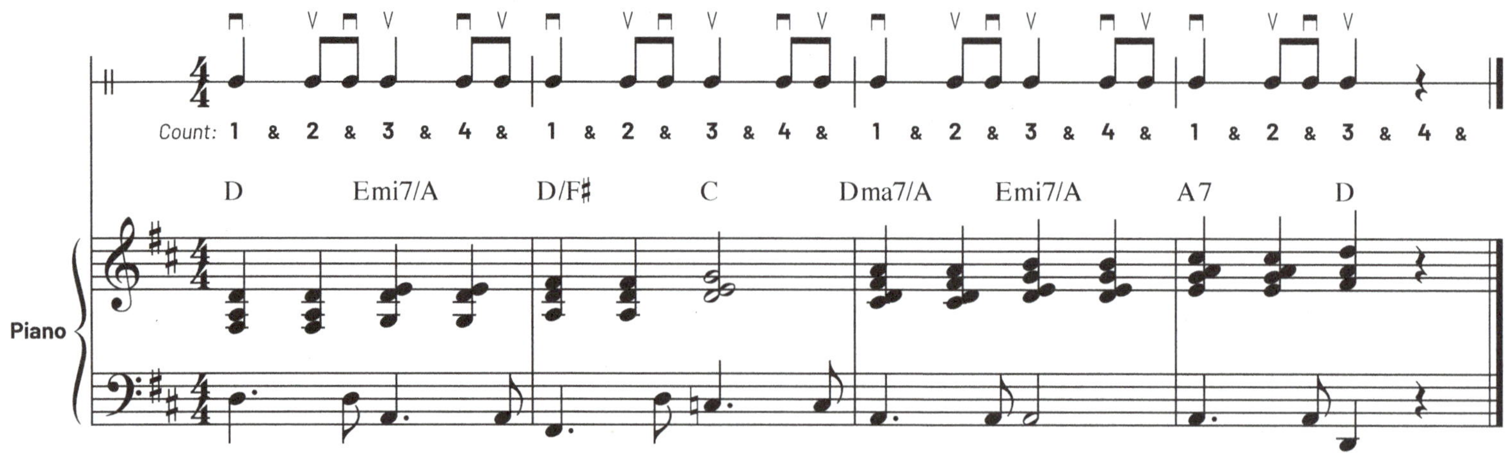

Piano part can be used to accompany shadow bowing and rhythm exercises.

69. D MAJOR SCALE UP

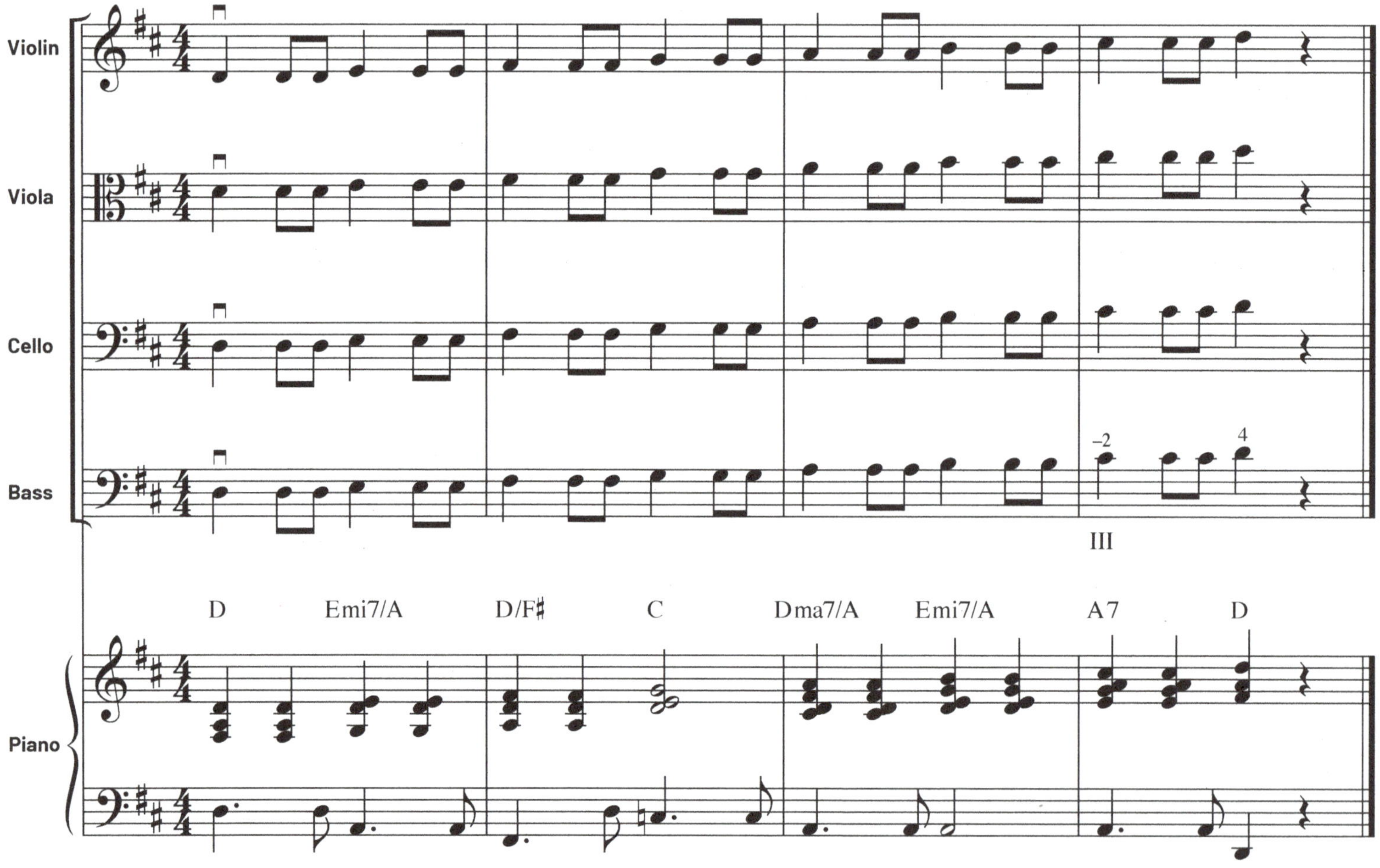

Violin
Viola
Cello
Bass
–2
4
III
D
Emi7/A
D/F♯
C
Dma7/A
Emi7/A
A7
D
Piano

Tempo Markings

Tempo is the speed of music. Tempo markings are usually written above the staff, in Italian.

Allegro – Fast tempo **Moderato** – Medium tempo **Andante** – Slower, walking tempo

Teacher The definition of tempo is presented on student book page 20. Only three different tempos are presented in Book 1, so that students may master their understanding.

70. HOT CROSS BUNS

Student books have repeats, not 1st and 2nd endings (until ex. 76).

Moderato

1. 2.

Violin

Viola

Cello

Bass

D A D D C D G A D C D D C D

Piano

71. AU CLAIRE DE LA LUNE

French Folk Song

Andante

Violin

Viola

Cello

Bass

D Emi/D D Emi/D D Emi/G A D Bmi Bmi/A G A G/B A/C♯ D

Piano

72. RHYTHM RAP *Shadow bow and count before playing.*

Count: 1 & 2 & 3 & 4 & 1 & 2 & 3 & 4 & 1 & 2 & 3 & 4 & 1 & 2 & 3 & 4 &

D A G D/F♯ D G G/B D/A D/F♯ E7 A7 D

Piano

1 & 2 & 3 & 4 & 1 & 2 & 3 & 4 & 1 & 2 & 3 & 4 & 1 & 2 & 3 & 4 &

Bmi F♯7 Bmi D7 G G♯o D/A G G♯o A7 D

Piano

73. BUCKEYE SALUTE

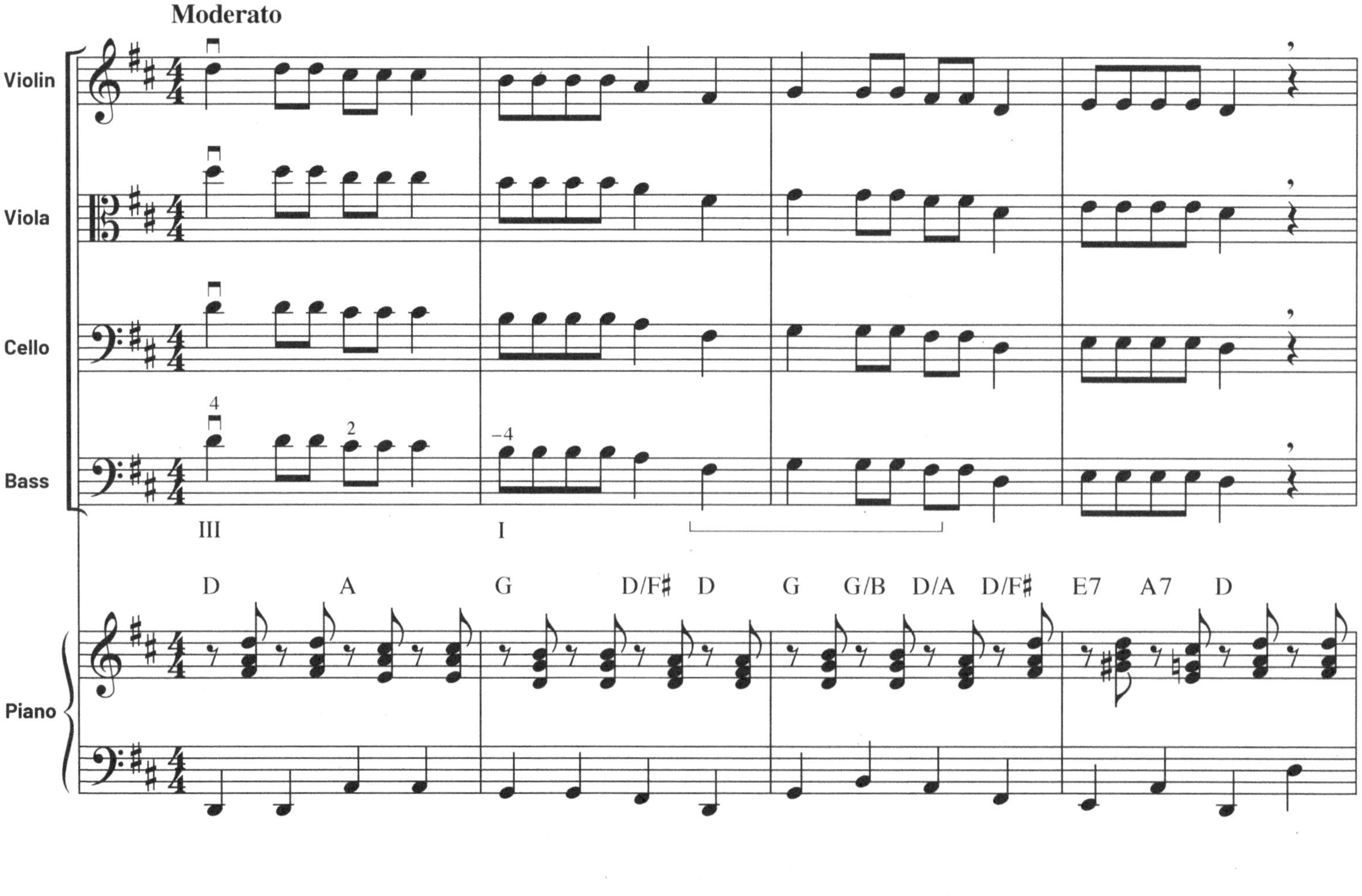

Moderato

Violin

Viola

Cello

Bass

4 2 −4

III I

D A G D/F♯ D G G/B D/A D/F♯ E7 A7 D

Piano

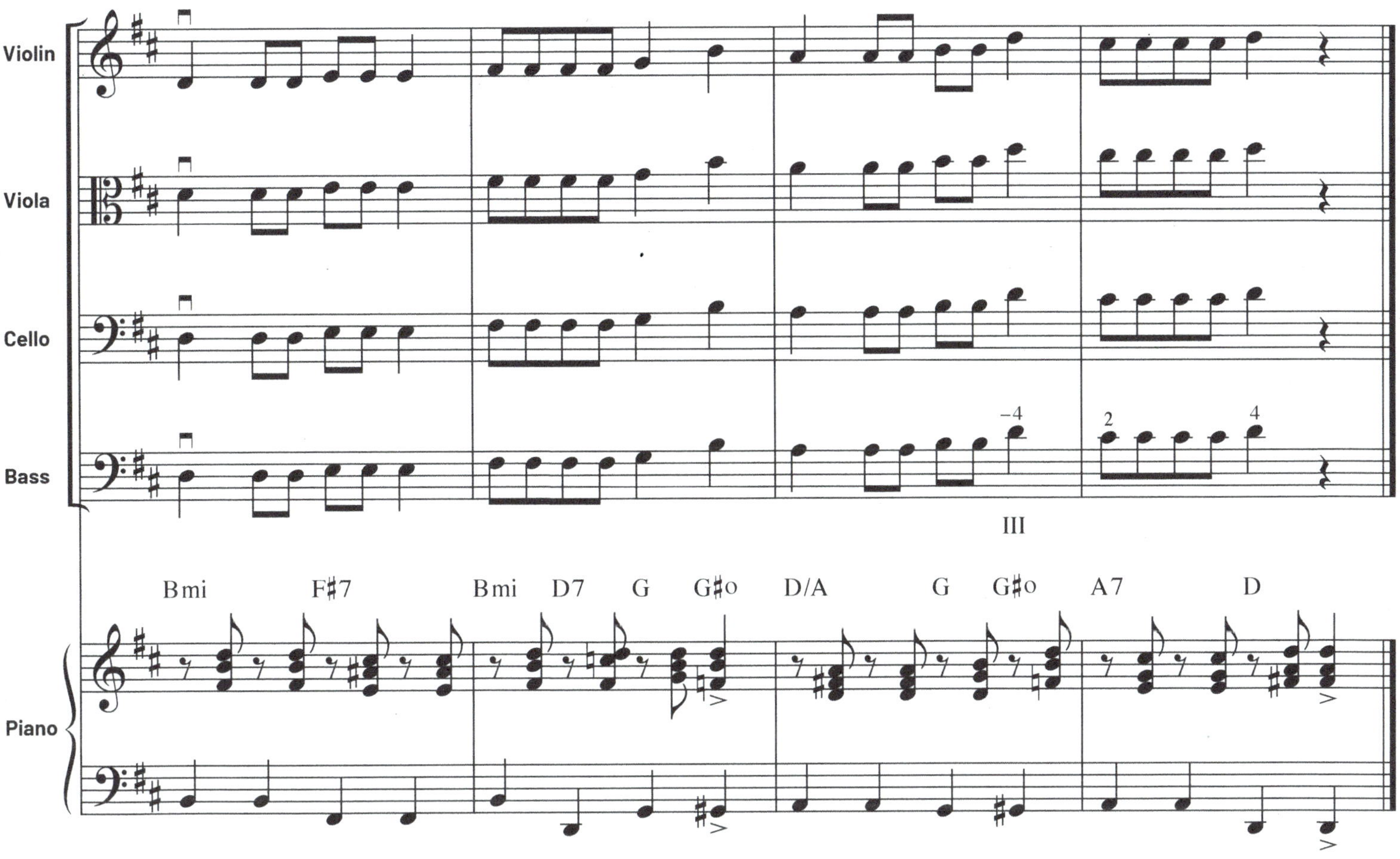

Violin
Viola
Cello
Bass
-4
2
4
III
Bmi F♯7 Bmi D7 G G♯o D/A G G♯o A7 D
Piano

Teacher Another way to help students feel a pulse is for them to conduct a meter pattern. Illustrations of meter conducting patterns are provided and can be practiced by students to develop their kinesthetic sense of pulse and consistent tempo. Please note that conducting patterns are for student use only. Teachers should be moving throughout class correcting students' playing position and posture, playing (modeling) for the students, and giving instruction. The $\frac{2}{4}$ time signature is introduced on student book page 21 and a sample 2-beat conducting pattern is shown.

$\frac{2}{4}$ Time Signature

= **2 beats** per measure
= **Quarter** note gets one beat

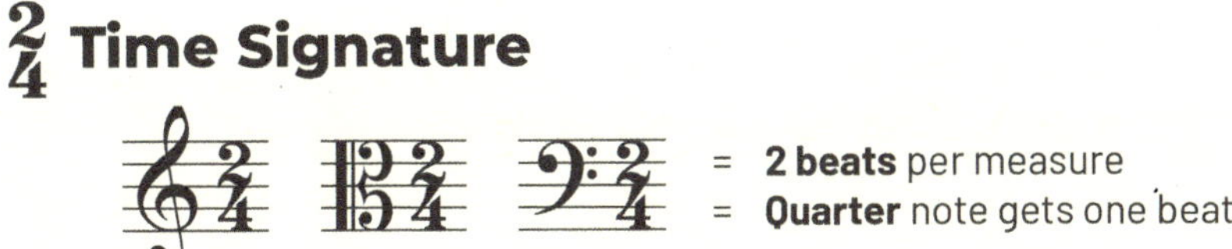

Conducting

Practice conducting this two-beat pattern.

1
2

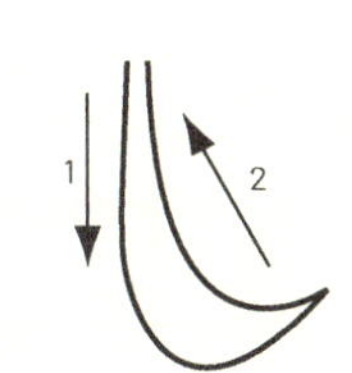

THEORY

74. RHYTHM RAP *Shadow bow and count before playing.*

Count: 1 & 2 & 1 & 2 & 1 & 2 & 1 & 2 & 1 & 2 & 1 & 2 & 1 & 2 & 1 & 2 &
Dsus D A/D G/D D Emi/A G/A Bmi7 A Dsus D
Piano

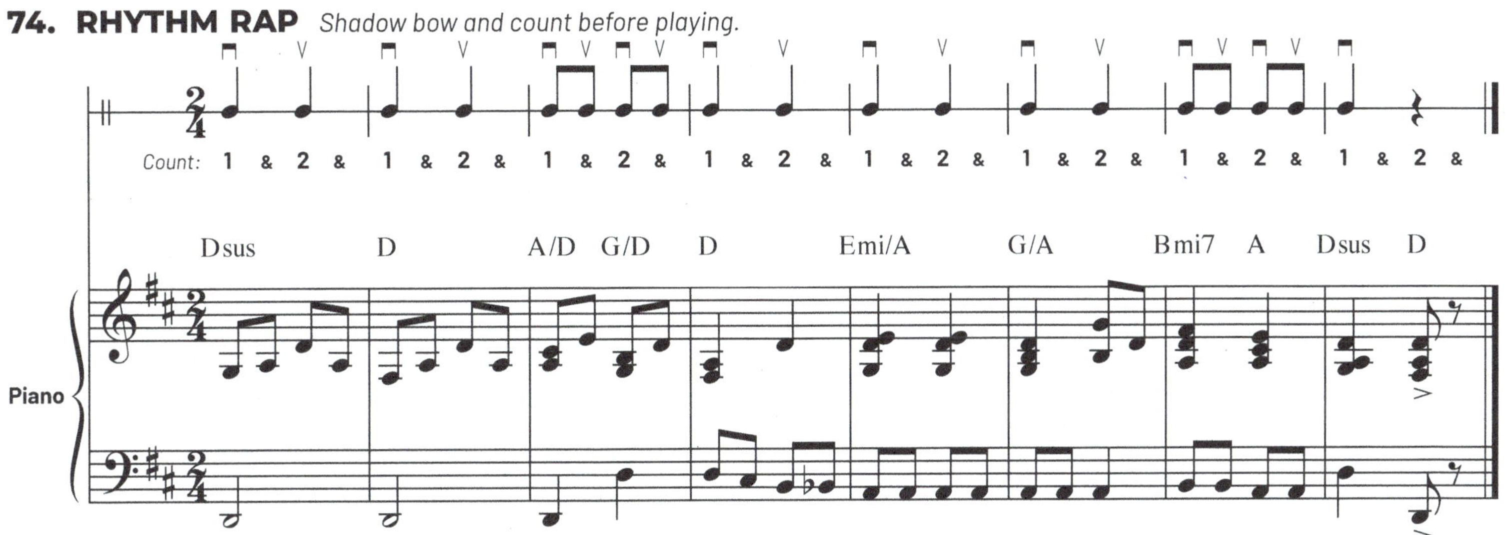

75. TWO BY TWO

Violin

Viola

Cello

Bass

Dsus D A/D G/D D Emi/A G/A Bmi7 A Dsus D

Piano

THEORY

1st & 2nd Endings

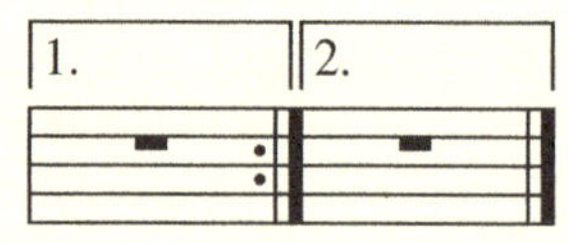

Play the 1st ending the 1st time through. Then, repeat the same section of music, skip the 1st ending, and play the 2nd ending.

Teacher The definition of 1st and 2nd endings is given on student book page 21. Present 1st and 2nd endings to students as they prepare to play exercise 76, an Essential Elements Quiz that includes this new musical element.

QUIZ OBJECTIVES – FOR PETE'S SAKE

- Playing correct bow markings
- Bowing parallel to the bridge
- String Levels
- Half steps and whole steps
- 1st and 2nd endings

Review Exercises:

68. *Rhythm Rap*
74. *Rhythm Rap*
75. *Two by Two*

76. ESSENTIAL ELEMENTS QUIZ – FOR PETE'S SAKE

Essential Elements for Strings Correlated Literature

Students will enjoy playing their own special part in string orchestra arrangements. The Explorer level of *Essential Elements for Strings* series is a collection of string orchestra arrangements that only use the rhythms, bowings, and notes that are introduced on pages student book page 1-21 (Teacher Manual pages 34-119). See your Hal Leonard dealer for the latest releases.

THEORY

Half Note

= 2 Beats

1 & 2 &

Half Rest

= 2 Silent Beats

1 & 2 &

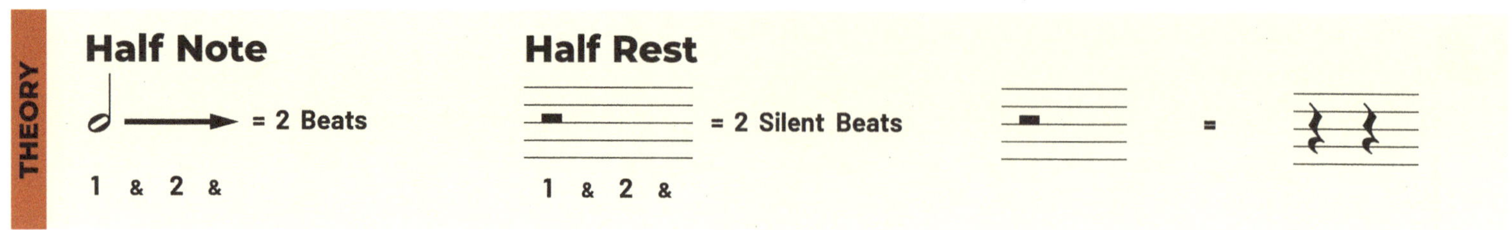

Teacher Use the suggested practice sequence for exercises 77-78 to introduce counting half notes. Be sure the students are subdividing while they are counting. The authors recommend that students count, tap, and clap each exercise before playing. You may have students shadow bow each exercise before playing as well.

Teacher When students begin to alternate bowing quarter notes and half notes, show students how the bow should travel slower during longer notes. Students can practice this skill by bowing in the air before playing on the string. You may also use a miles-per-hour analogy to help students understand different bow speeds, e.g. slower bows travel at lower miles-per-hour than faster bows.

77. RHYTHM RAP *Shadow bow and count before playing.*

Student books have repeats, not 1st and 2nd endings.

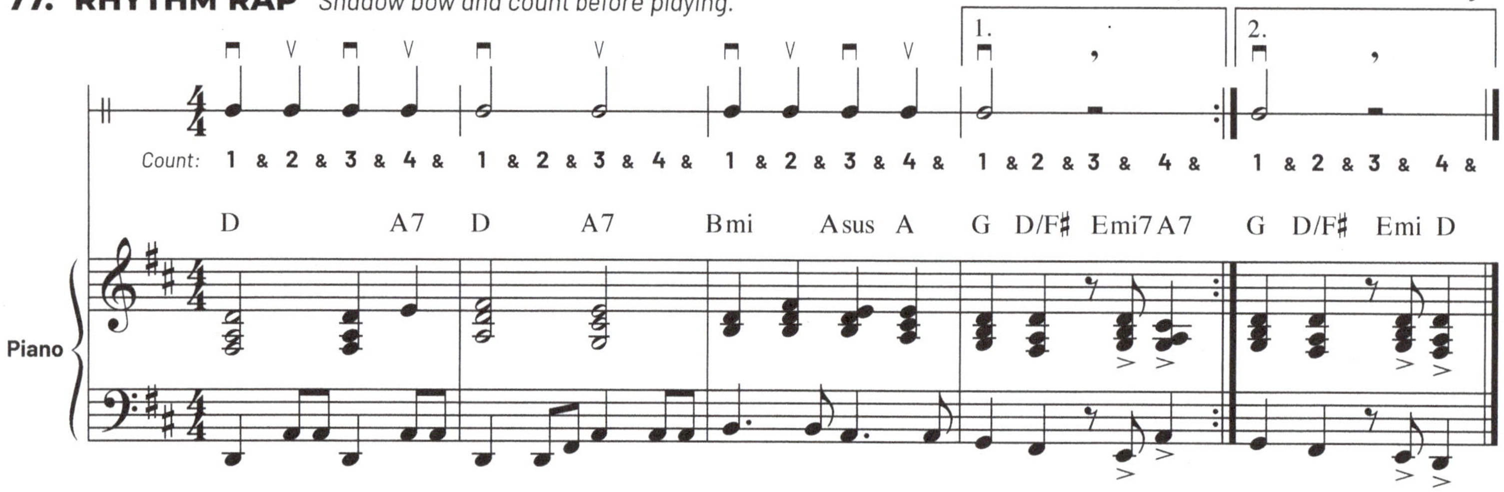
1.
2.
Count: 1 & 2 & 3 & 4 & 1 & 2 & 3 & 4 & 1 & 2 & 3 & 4 & 1 & 2 & 3 & 4 & 1 & 2 & 3 & 4 &
D A7 D A7 Bmi Asus A G D/F♯ Emi7 A7 G D/F♯ Emi D
Piano

78. AT PIERROT'S DOOR

Student books have repeats, not 1st and 2nd endings.

French Folk Song

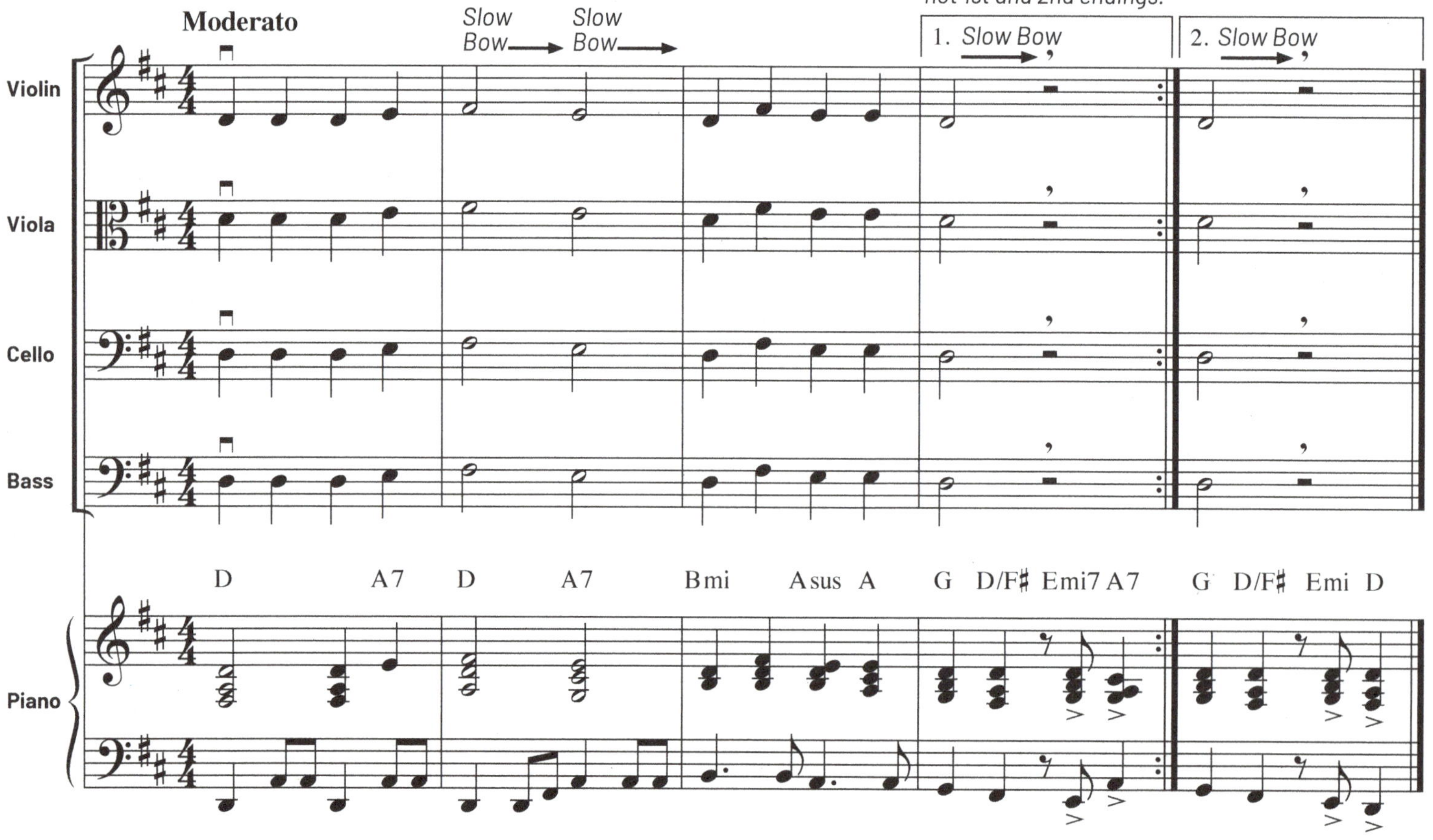
Moderato
Slow Bow
Slow Bow
1. Slow Bow
2. Slow Bow
Violin
Viola
Cello
Bass
D A7 D A7 Bmi Asus A G D/F♯ Emi7 A7 G D/F♯ Emi D
Piano

79. THE HALF COUNTS

80. GRANDPARENT'S DAY

THEORY

Repeat Signs

Repeat the section of music enclosed by the **repeat signs**. *(If 1st and 2nd endings are used, they are played as usual – but go back only to the first repeat sign, not to the beginning.)*

Teacher Have students point with their bows to the repeat signs and first and second endings in exercise 81. Show them other examples of music with repeats and 1st and 2nd endings. Ask students to explain how to play exercise 81 to check their understanding of repeat signs and 1st and 2nd endings.

81. MICHAEL ROW THE BOAT ASHORE

American Folk Song

Violin/ Viola It is important for students to develop their left hand fourth finger facility. The following exercises and melodies are designed to help students begin to develop their fourth finger playing skill. This is critical for successful playing in the future and should be reviewed frequently. Be sure students' left hands are balanced on the third finger to make playing with the fourth finger easier.

Use rote exercises such as tapping and sliding the fourth finger while other fingers are on the string to help prepare students to use the fourth finger in their playing.

Teacher Please note that exercise 82 involves pizzicato with the left hand, not right hand.

82. TEXAS TWO-STRING

Violin/Viola *Holding your violin/viola in shoulder position, pizz. this exercise with your left hand 4th finger. 4+ = 4th finger pizz.*
Cello/Bass *Pizz. this exercise with your left hand 4th finger. 4+ = 4th finger pizz.*

Looking for some more fun music to play?
See the inside front cover for instructions on accessing recent popular Bonus Songs.

Violin

4TH FINGER

Your **4th finger** is often used to match the pitch of the next highest open string, creating a smoother tone and fewer changes between the strings for bowing.

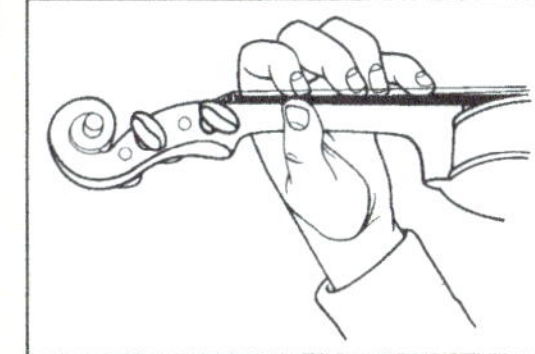

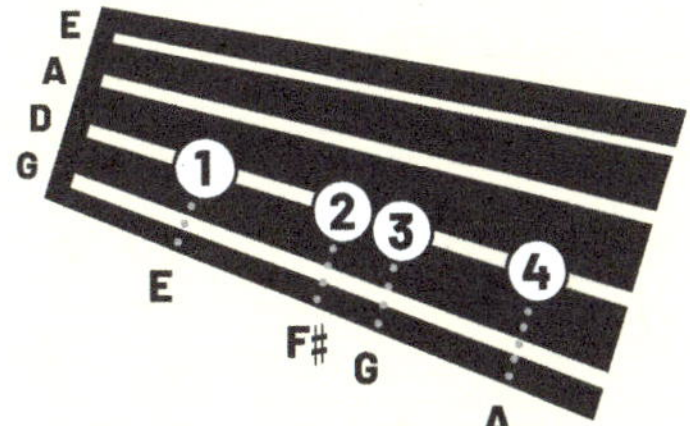

Viola

4TH FINGER

Your **4th finger** is often used to match the pitch of the next highest open string, creating a smoother tone and fewer changes between the strings for bowing.

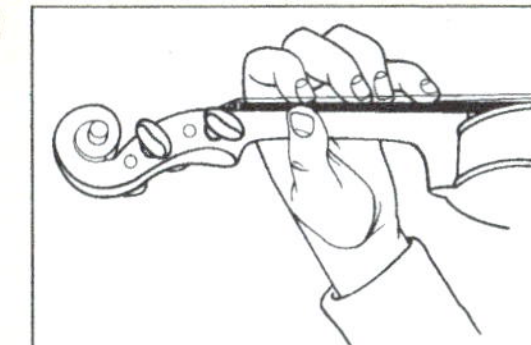

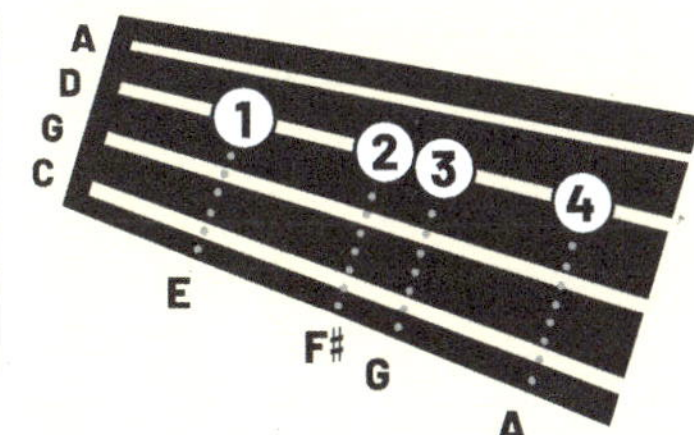

Bass

NEW NOTES

A is played with 4 fingers on the D string in third position (III).

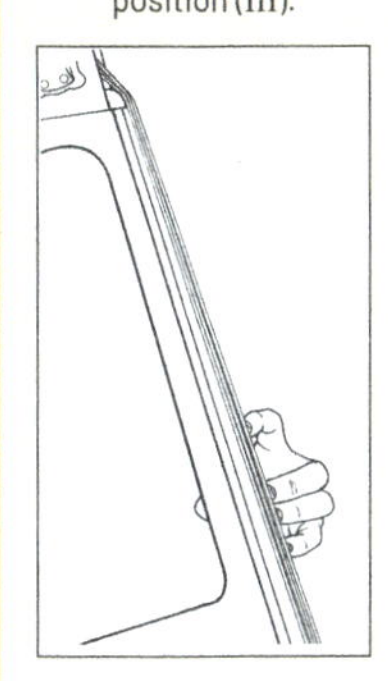

G is played with 1 finger on the D string in third position (III).

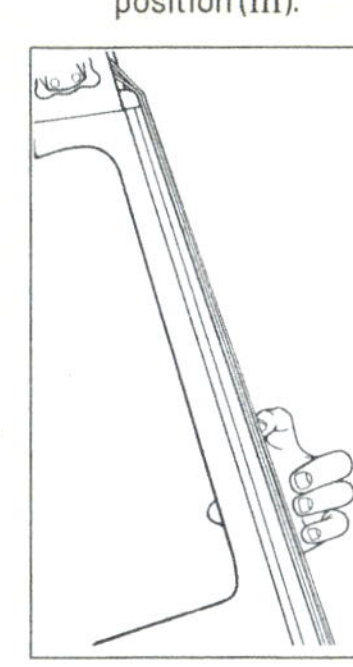

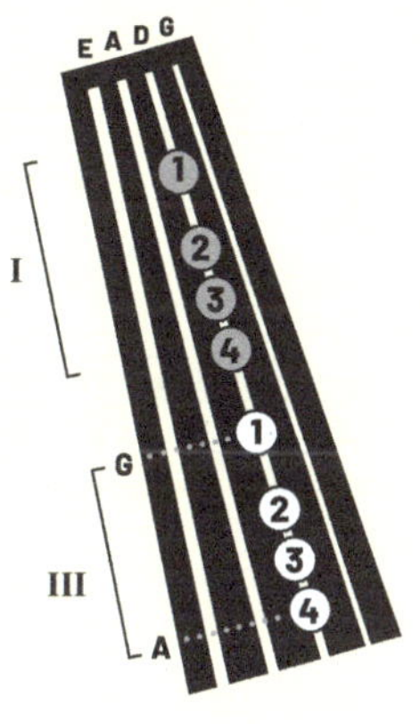

Bass New notes A and D in third position are introduced on student book page 23. First, have students only finger the pitches. Then, have them pizzicato the pitches. This teaching sequence will help prepare students to correctly bow the pitches.

Violin/ Viola Fourth finger on the D string is introduced on student book page 23. The fourth finger was prepared by left-hand pizzicato exercises on page 22. Be sure students hand shape is balanced on the third finger so that they can easily reach their fourth finger pitches.

Cello No new notes are presented. However, consider challenging your students by having them use II 1/2 position to play this page. Introduce this in exercise 83 by having them place their first finger on F♯, 2nd finger on G, and 4th finger on A. They stay in this position until measure 7 when they will need to slide their hand lightly back to first position to play E. Remember to tell your students to keep the second finger behind the thumb at all times. Let them discover how they can use this new position to play other lines on this page.

83. FOUR BY FOUR

Violin

Viola

Cello

Bass

III I

D G/D A(add9)/C♯ D D(add9)/A D G/A A7 D Gma7/A

Piano

Violin

Viola

Cello

Bass

III I

D G(add9)/B F♯mi/A D7 Gma9 G6 Emi9 A7 G/D D

Piano

84. 4TH FINGER MARATHON

85. HIGH FLYING

HISTORY

German composer **Ludwig van Beethoven** (1770–1827) was one of the world's greatest composers. He was completely deaf by 1802. Although he could not hear music like we do, he could "hear" it in his mind. The theme of his final *Symphony No. 9* is called "Ode To Joy," and was written to the text of a poem by Friedrich von Schiller. "Ode To Joy" was featured in concerts celebrating the reunification of Germany in 1990.

Teacher Familiarize students with the music of Beethoven by playing recorded examples of his music in class, especially the last movement of his Symphony No. 9 which includes the "Ode To Joy" theme.

QUIZ OBJECTIVES – ODE TO JOY

- Counting and playing quarter, eighth, and half notes in $\frac{4}{4}$ meter
- Changing bow speeds for different lengths of notes
- Violin/Viola fourth fingers

Review Exercises:

78. *At Pierrot's Door*
83. *Four by Four*
84. *Fourth Finger Marathon*
85. *High Flying*

86. ESSENTIAL ELEMENTS QUIZ – ODE TO JOY

Ludwig van Beethoven

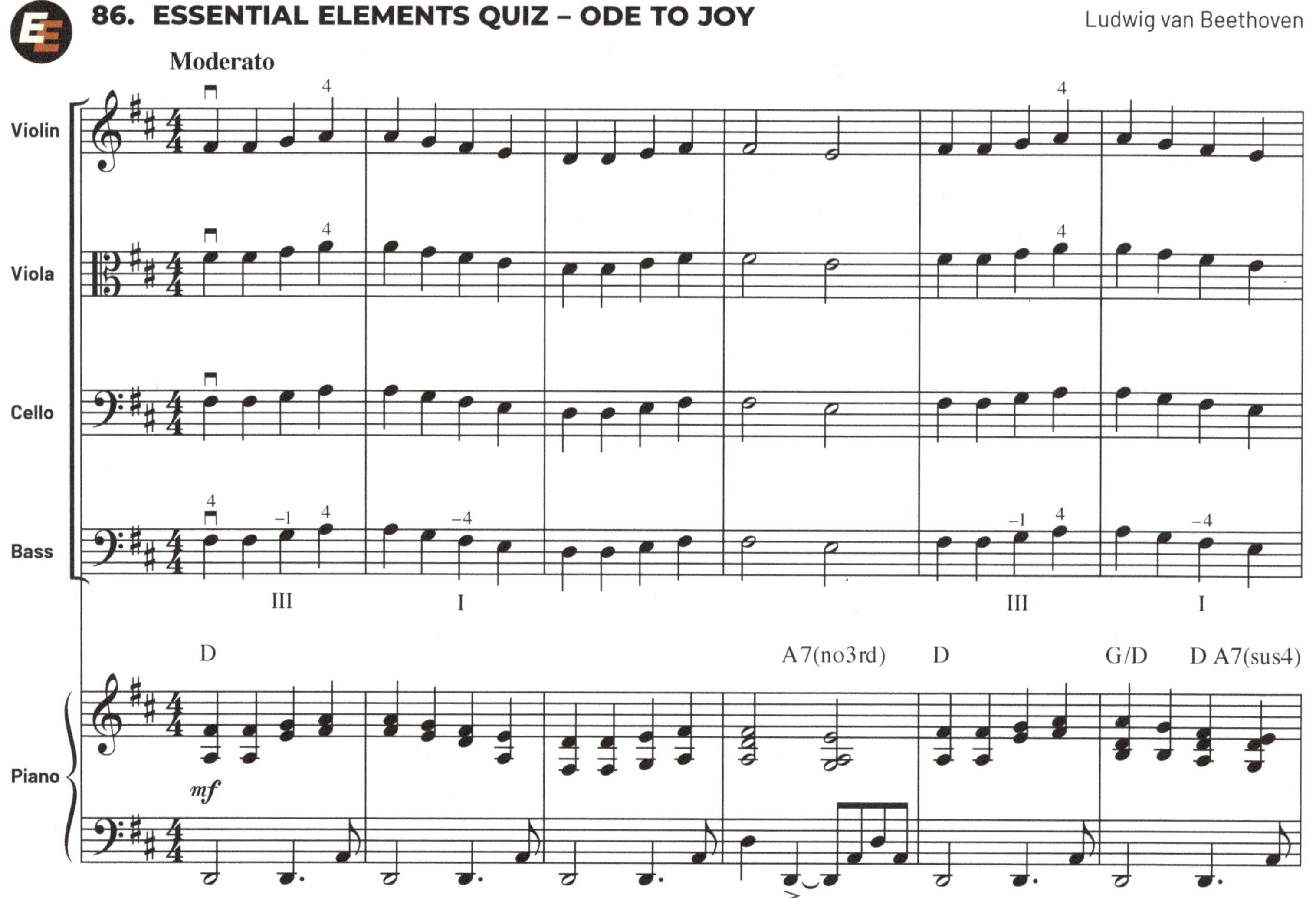

Violin
Viola
Cello
Bass
D Bmi Emi/G D A7sus A7 D A D/A A D/A A F♯7/A♯
Piano
Bmi E A D G/D D7 D7/G G D/G A7sus/G D/A D/C♯ A7(no3rd) D/F♯ A7sus A7 D

PERFORMANCE SPOTLIGHT

Teacher A PERFORMANCE SPOTLIGHT appears on student book pages 24 and 25. The purpose of these pages is to summarize some of the principal playing skills the students have learned. These pieces may be used in a special concert performance. You may wish to show the learning process through a progression of scales, rhythm studies, duets and rounds, and/or choose to showcase the orchestra arrangements. Different styles of music are included to provide a varied musical experience for both the audience and performers.

Discuss with students proper concert etiquette for both performers and audience members. Point out that performers must practice their music until it is mastered before performing. Performers must dress appropriately for the concert, and arrive on time. Once the music is ready for performance, the audience must respect the efforts of the performer by listening quietly and attentively.

Student ★ Good performers are on time with their instruments and music ready, dressed appropriately, and know their music well.

87. SCALE WARM-UP

Teacher Explain to students the organization of a round. Discuss with the class other examples of rounds common to American folk music, such as *Row, Row, Row Your Boat*.

88. FRÈRE JACQUES – Round *(When group A reaches ②, group B begins at ①)*

French Folk Song

Chord, Harmony

Two or more pitches sounding at the same time form a **chord** or **harmony**. Throughout this book, **A** = Melody and **B** = Harmony.

Teacher Review the definition of chords and harmony as presented. Show and demonstrate for students different examples of chords.

Boil 'Em Cabbage Down, exercise 89, is the first orchestra arrangement in this book. All arrangements can be played with many different combinations of instruments. For the best concert performance, violins should be divided between the A and B parts, and all other instruments should play part B.

89. BOIL 'EM CABBAGE DOWN – Orchestra Arrangement

American Fiddle Tune

Allegro

Violin A, B

Viola A, B

Cello A, B

Bass A, B (*pizz.*)

Piano

D A7/G D A7

5 ◄ Measure Number
Violin
A
B
Viola
A
B
Cello
A
B
Bass
A
B
5
D
A7/G
D
A7
D
Piano
90. ENGLISH ROUND
Andante
①
②
Repeat bar on last time
Violin
Viola
Cello
Bass
4
4
2
4
–1
–1
4
III
I
D
Emi/G
D
D
Emi/G
D
D
Emi/G
D
Emi/G
D
Emi/G
D
Piano

91. LIGHTLY ROW – Orchestra Arrangement

5
Violin
A
B
Viola
A
B
Cello
A
B
Bass
A
B
Piano
A
A7
D
D/F♯
D
A7
D
A
D
4
4
4
4

HISTORY

French composer **Jacques Offenbach** (1819–1880) was the originator of the **operetta** and played the cello. An **operetta** is a form of entertainment that combines several of the fine arts together: vocal and instrumental music, drama, dance, and visual arts. One of his most famous pieces is the "Can-Can" dance from *Orpheus And The Underworld*. This popular work was written in 1858, just three years before the start of the American Civil War (1861–1865).

Teacher Discuss the history and musical contributions of Jacques Offenbach as presented on student book page 25. Point out to students how European operettas are similar in some ways to today's American Broadway musicals. It is fun for students to find out that Offenbach, the famous composer of the *Can-Can*, was a cellist!

92. CAN-CAN – Orchestra Arrangement

Jacques Offenbach
Arr. John Higgins

Student ✔ What were the strong points of your performance?

Teacher The G string and the pitches C, B, and A are introduced for the violin, viola, and cello on student book page 26. C, B, and low G are introduced for the bass since the G string already was introduced on student book page 6.

The speed of the bow should be slower on the G string than on the D and A strings. Instruct students that the lower the string, the slower the bow must travel. In addition, the bow should travel closer to the bridge on lower strings, especially on the cello and bass.

Violin

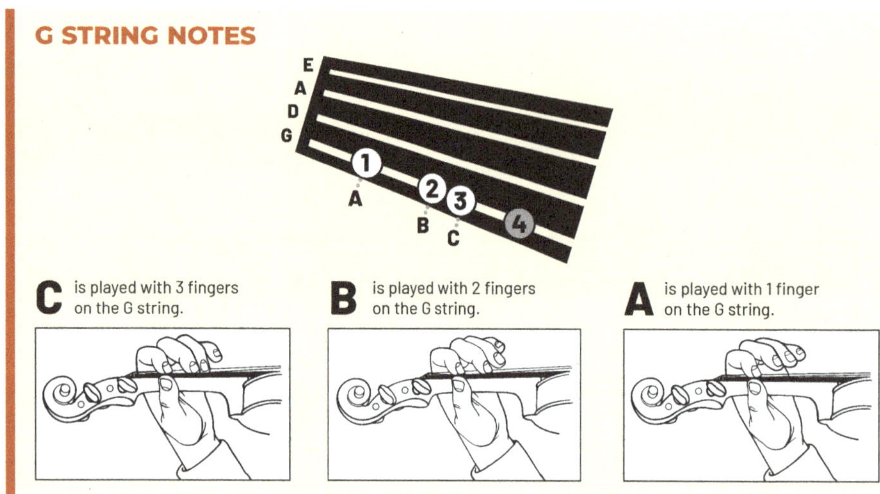

Viola

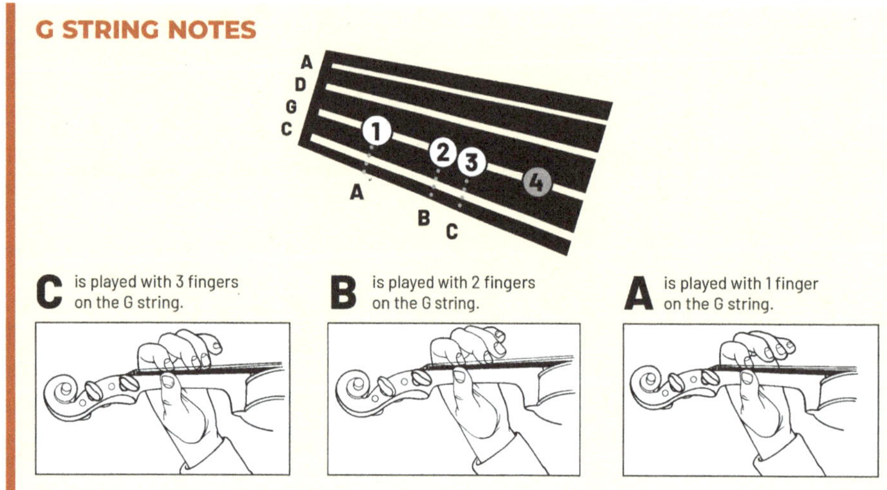

Cello

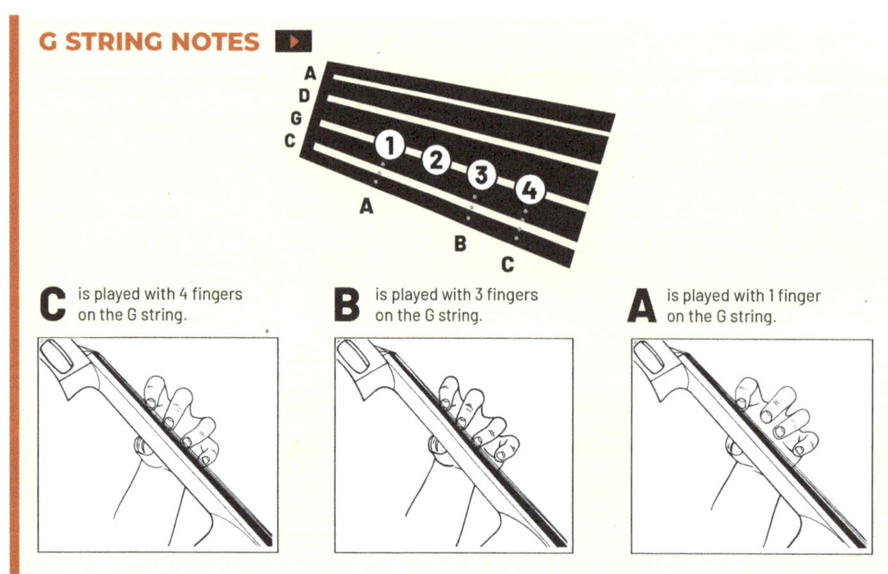

Bass

NEW NOTES – E AND A STRINGS

G is played with 2 fingers on the E string.

C is played with 2 fingers on the A string.

B is played with 1 finger on the A string.

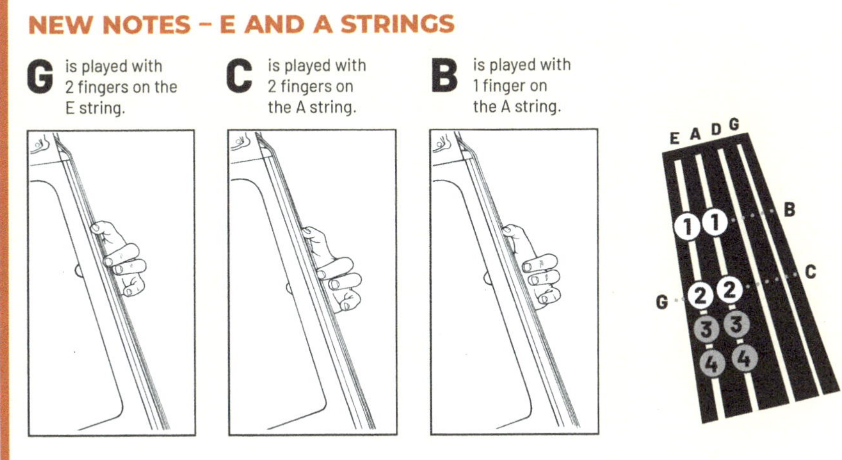

Listening Skills

Play what your teacher plays. Listen carefully.

1.

Teacher plays · Students echo · Teacher plays · Students echo · Teacher plays · Students echo

2.

Teacher plays · Students echo · Teacher plays · Students echo · Teacher plays · Students echo

3.

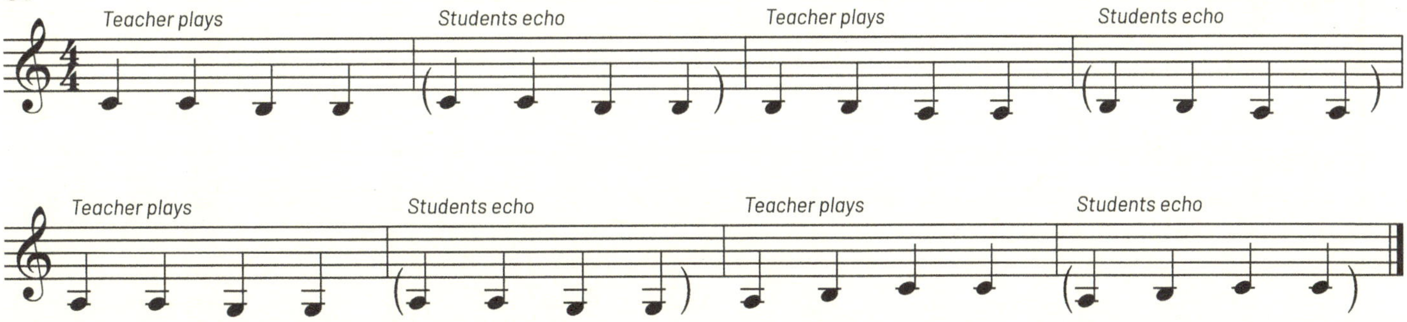

Teacher plays · Students echo · Teacher plays · Students echo

Teacher plays · Students echo · Teacher plays · Students echo

4.

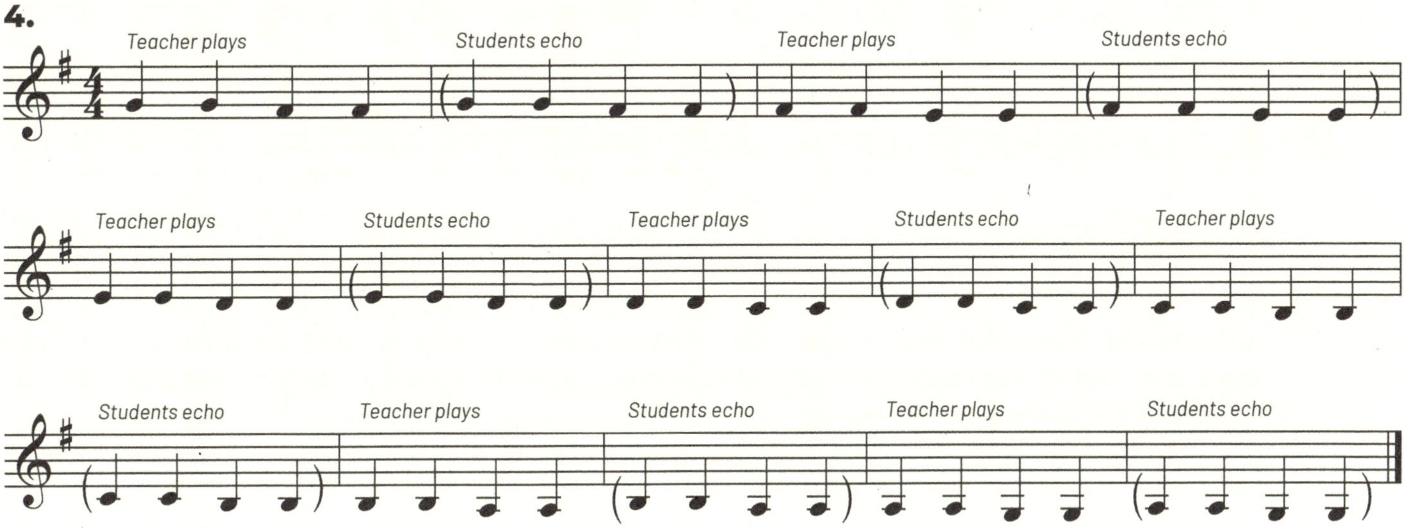

Teacher plays · Students echo · Teacher plays · Students echo

Teacher plays · Students echo · Teacher plays · Students echo · Teacher plays

Students echo · Teacher plays · Students echo · Teacher plays · Students echo

THEORY

Key Signature G MAJOR

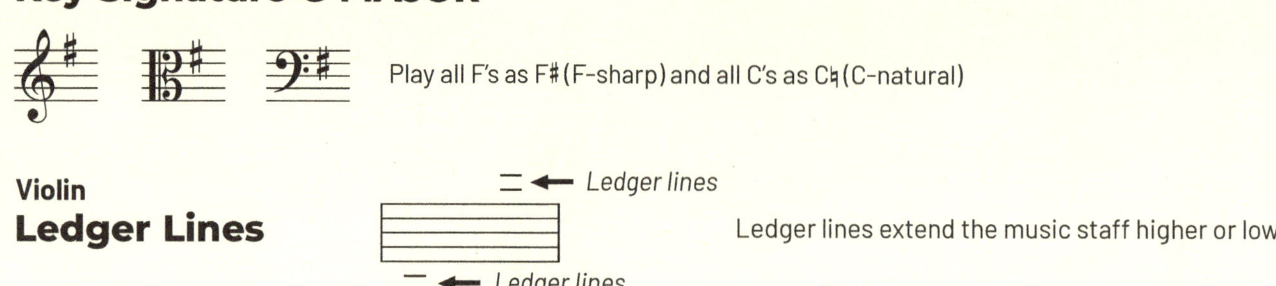

Play all F's as F♯ (F-sharp) and all C's as C♮ (C-natural)

Violin
Ledger Lines

Ledger lines extend the music staff higher or lower.

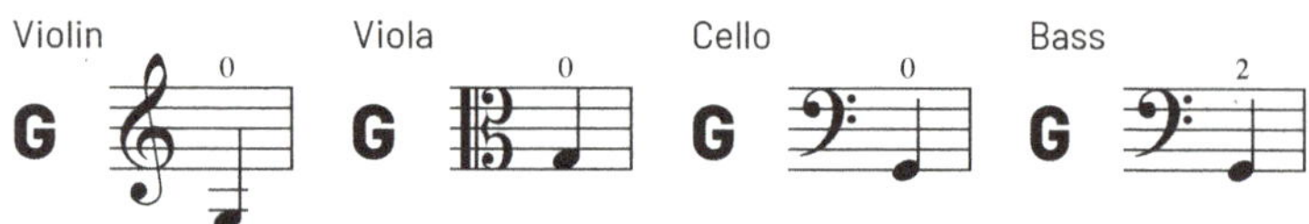

93. LET'S READ "G"

Play F♯'s and C♮'s in this key signature.

Violin
Viola
Cello
Bass
Piano

Gma7 C9 Gma7 C9 Gma7

Violin/ Viola When violin and viola students finger notes on the G string, their left elbow should be well under the instrument. If their arm is properly centered underneath the instrument, students should be able to see the side of their arm as they look through the C bout on the high string side of their instrument. Be aware that some students get confused and attempt to swing their arm underneath the instrument to try to see their elbow. However, only the side of the arm needs to be seen through the C bout.

Violin
C
Viola
C
Cello
C
Bass
C

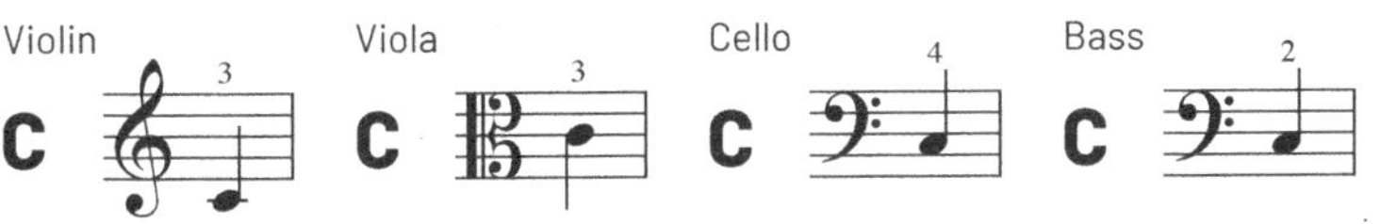

94. LET'S READ "C" (C-natural)

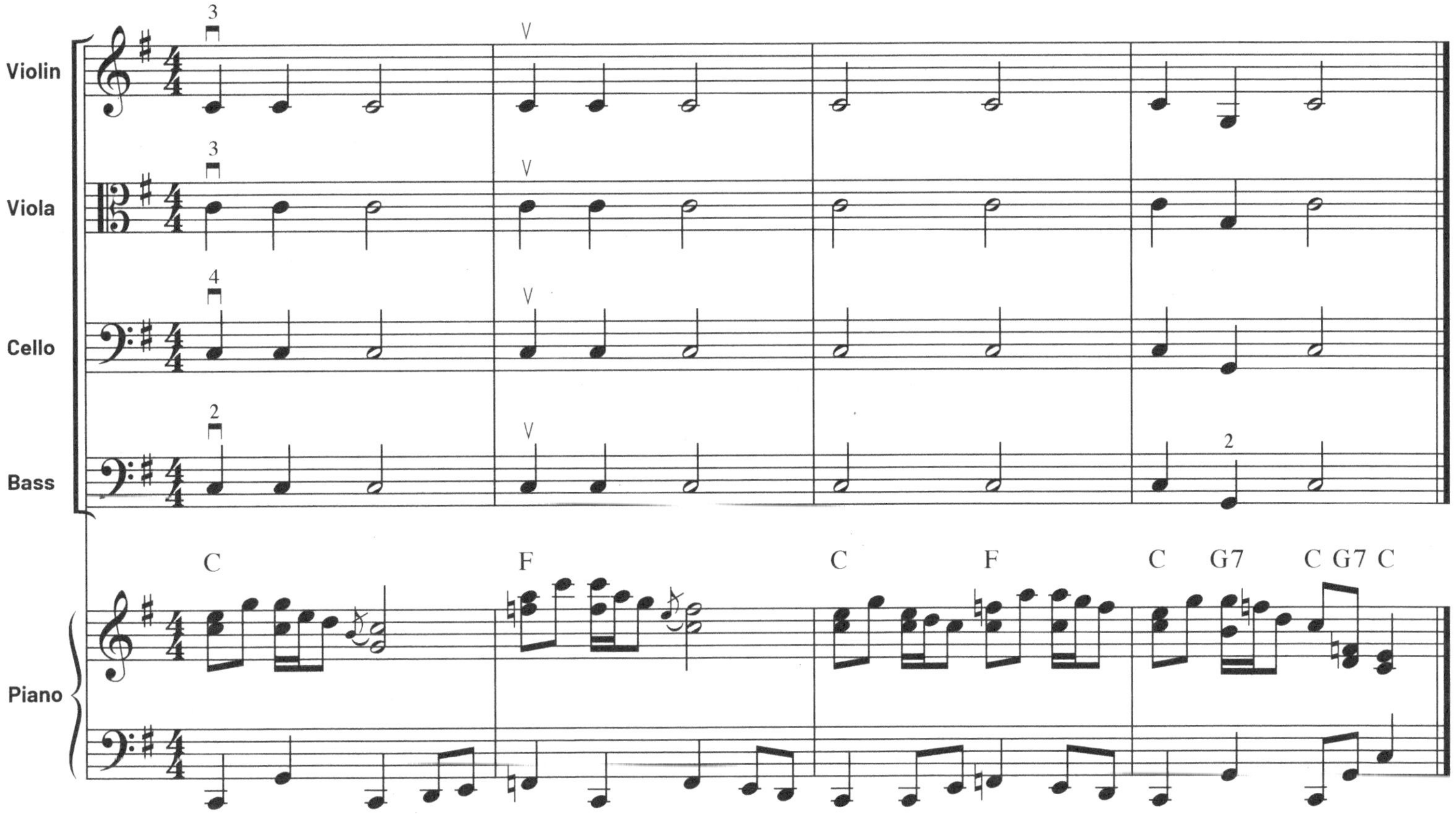

Violin
Viola
Cello
Bass
Piano
C
F
C F
C G7 C G7 C

Violin
B
Viola
B
Cello
B
Bass
B

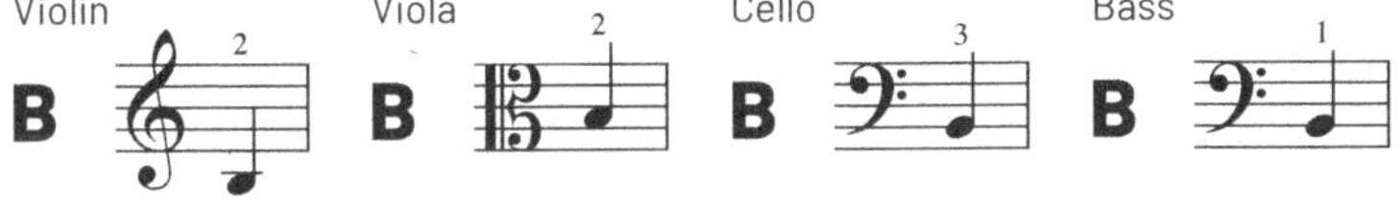

95. LET'S READ "B"

Violin
Viola
Cello
Bass
Piano
Emi
F Emi
F G C

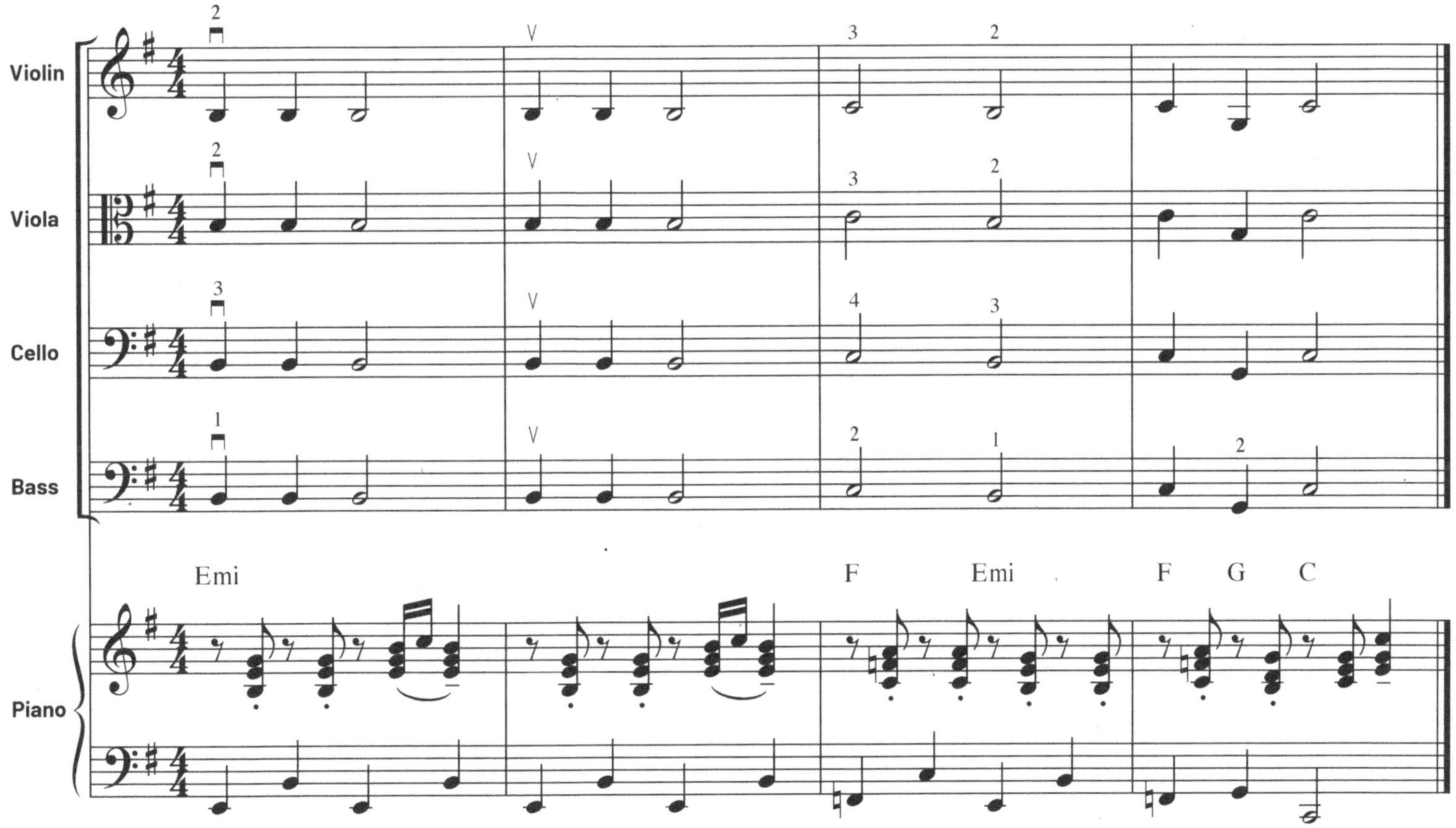

Violin
Viola

Be sure all violin and viola students are forming a square with their first finger on the fingerboard when playing "A" on the G string.

Violin A
Viola A
Cello A

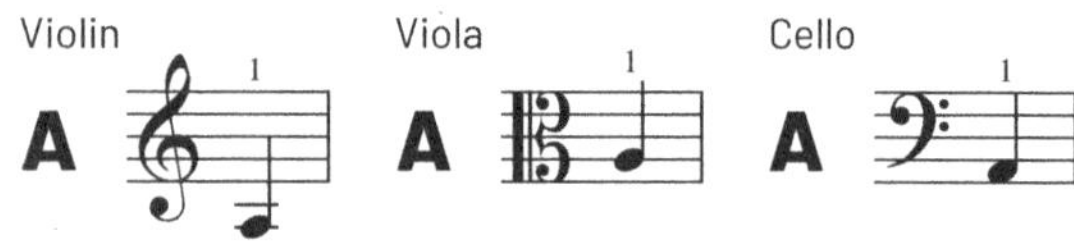

96. LET'S READ "A"

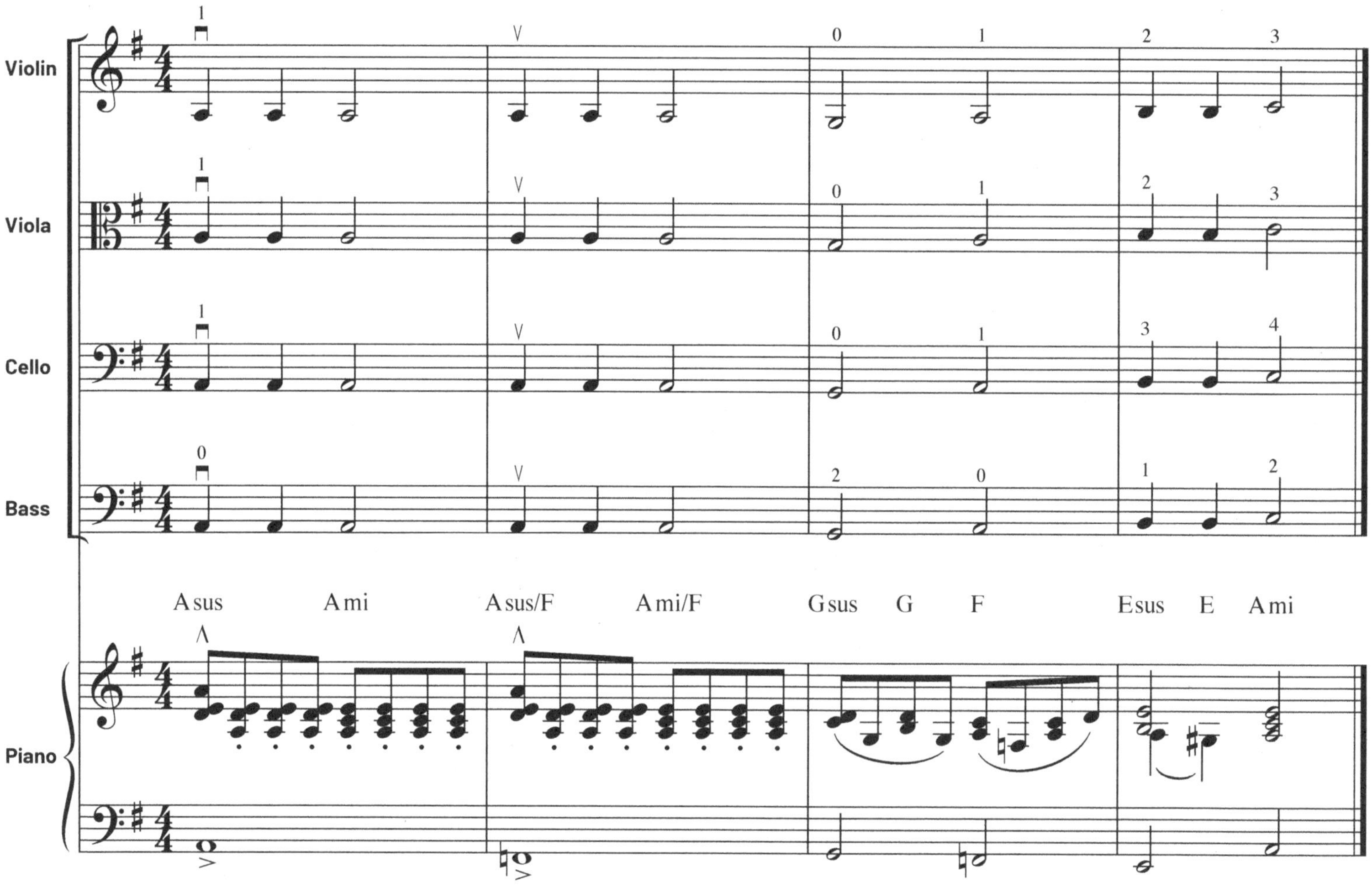
Violin
Viola
Cello
Bass
Piano
Asus
Ami
Asus/F
Ami/F
Gsus
G
F
Esus
E
Ami

97. WALKING AROUND *Name the notes before you play.*

Teacher Check that students have written the correct name of the notes in exercise 98 before playing.

98. G MAJOR SCALE *Write the note names before you play.*

Violin

Viola

Cello

Bass

2 0 1 2 0 1 4 0

G D/F♯ Emi7 Cmi/E♭ G/D C/D D7 G

Piano

Violin

Viola

Cello

Bass

C D/C Ami G/B Cmi/E♭ G/D Ami7/D D7 G

Piano

Violin/ Viola Fourth finger D on the G string is introduced in exercise 99. Have students compare their fingered D to their open D string for tuning. Be sure their left arm is centered underneath their instrument so that they may reach the fourth finger D on the G string.

99. FOURTH FINGER D

Time Signature
(Meter)

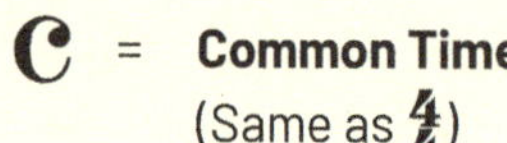

Conducting

Practice conducting this four-beat pattern.

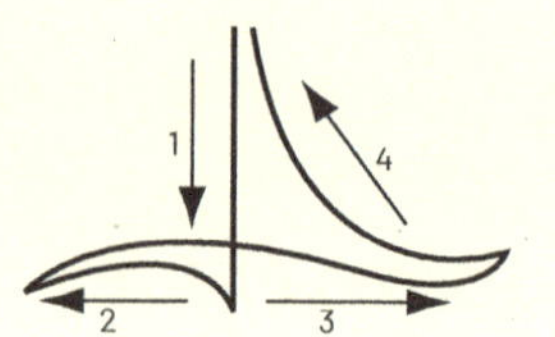

Teacher Have students practice the $\frac{4}{4}$ conducting pattern to reinforce their feeling and understanding of ***Common Time***.

100. LOW DOWN

Violin

Viola

Cello

Bass

G D7 G

Piano

Violin

Viola

Cello

Bass

G G/B C Ami7 D7 G

Piano

101. BAA BAA BLACK SHEEP

QUIZ OBJECTIVES – THIS OLD MAN

- G string notes
- Violin/Viola 4th finger D
- Counting quarter, eighth, and half notes in $\frac{4}{4}$ time

Review Exercises:

97. *Walking Around*
99. *Fourth Finger D*
100. *Low Down*
101. *Baa Baa Black Sheep*

102. ESSENTIAL ELEMENTS QUIZ – THIS OLD MAN

American Folk Song

Teacher $\frac{3}{4}$ meter and dotted half notes are introduced on student book page 28 in the familiar key of D Major. Newly learned skills will be combined for review and reinforcement on Skill Builder pages, such as the G Major Skill Builder on page 31.

THEORY

Time Signature
(Meter)

$\frac{3}{4}$ 3 = **3 beats** per measure; 4 = ♩ or 𝄽 note gets one beat

Conducting

Practice conducting this three-beat pattern.

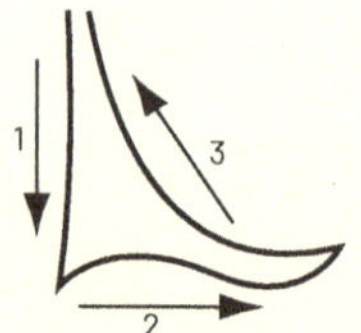

Dotted Half Note

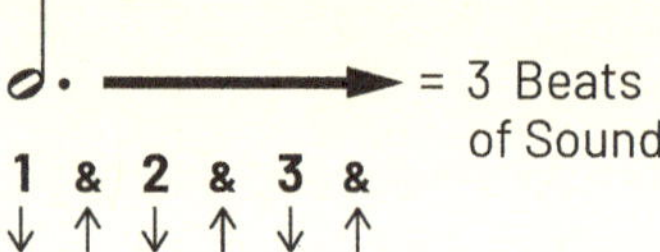

𝅗𝅥. ◄ **Dot**

A dot adds half the value of the note.

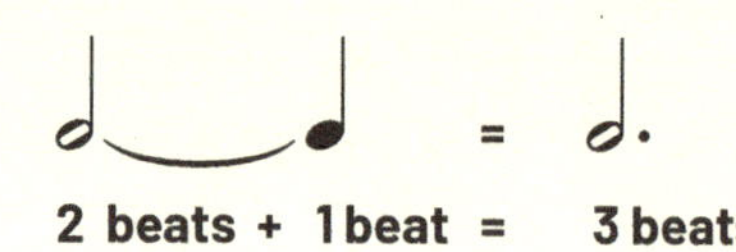

Teacher When students practice exercises on student book page 28 be sure that they count the dotted half notes carefully and move their bow slower while playing them. One suggested practice sequence is to follow the steps introduced for the previous Rhythm Raps (Teacher Manual page 113). As students are pulling their bows, they can count 1 & 2 & etc. for the rhythm while adjusting their bow speed and tapping their foot. Alternatively, they can describe the bow speed as they are bowing, using such phrases as:

- quarter note = "fast"
- half note = "slow bow"
- dotted half note = "real slow bow"
- whole note = "real, real slow bow"

103. RHYTHM RAP *Shadow bow and count before playing.*

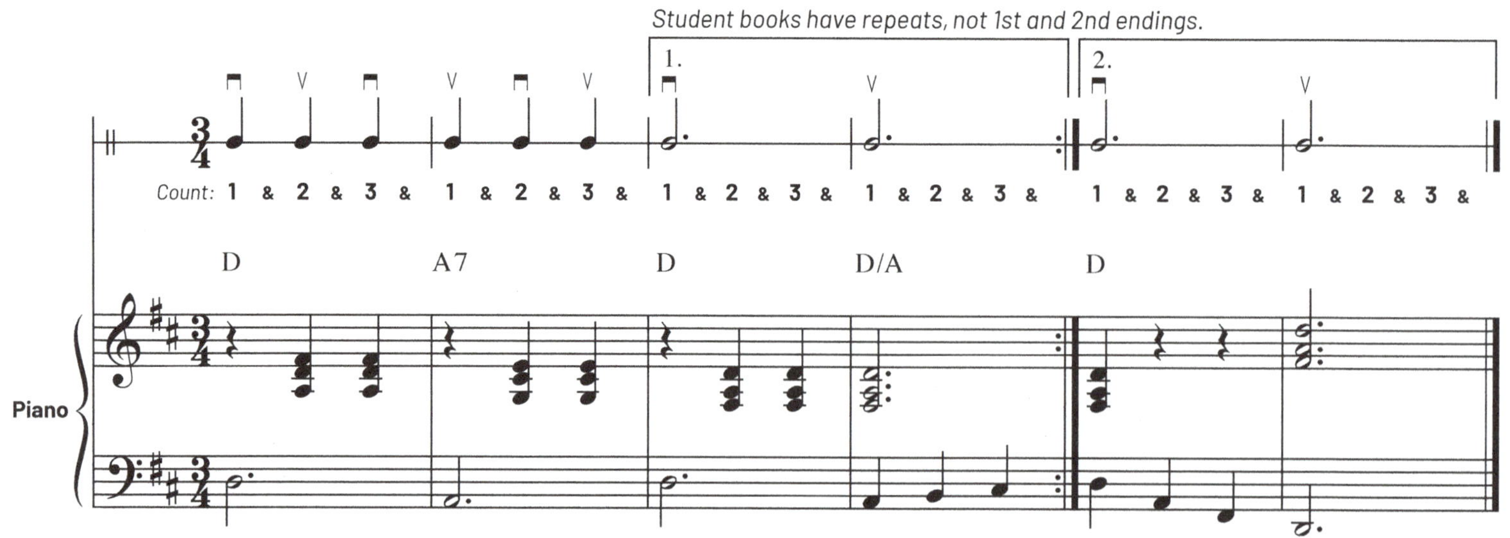

104. COUNTING THREES

Student books have repeats, not 1st and 2nd endings.

105. D MAJOR SCALE IN THREES

Bass In *French Folk Song*, basses should play B in measure 3 with the first finger. Students may either shift their hand back to B in second and a half position, or they may pivot their hand on their thumb back to B. Remind students that the thumb slides with the hand as a unit when shifting. Instruct them that when pivoting, the thumb does not slide along the neck of the instrument, but pivots on the pad of the thumb.

Bass

New Position – II½ (Second and a half position – first finger on B.)

106. FRENCH FOLK SONG

French Folk Song

Violin
Viola
Cello
Bass
Piano
III
I
Emi/A D/A G/A
A Bmi A/C♯
D A/D Emi7
D/F♯ Emi7 D
A7sus A7
G D

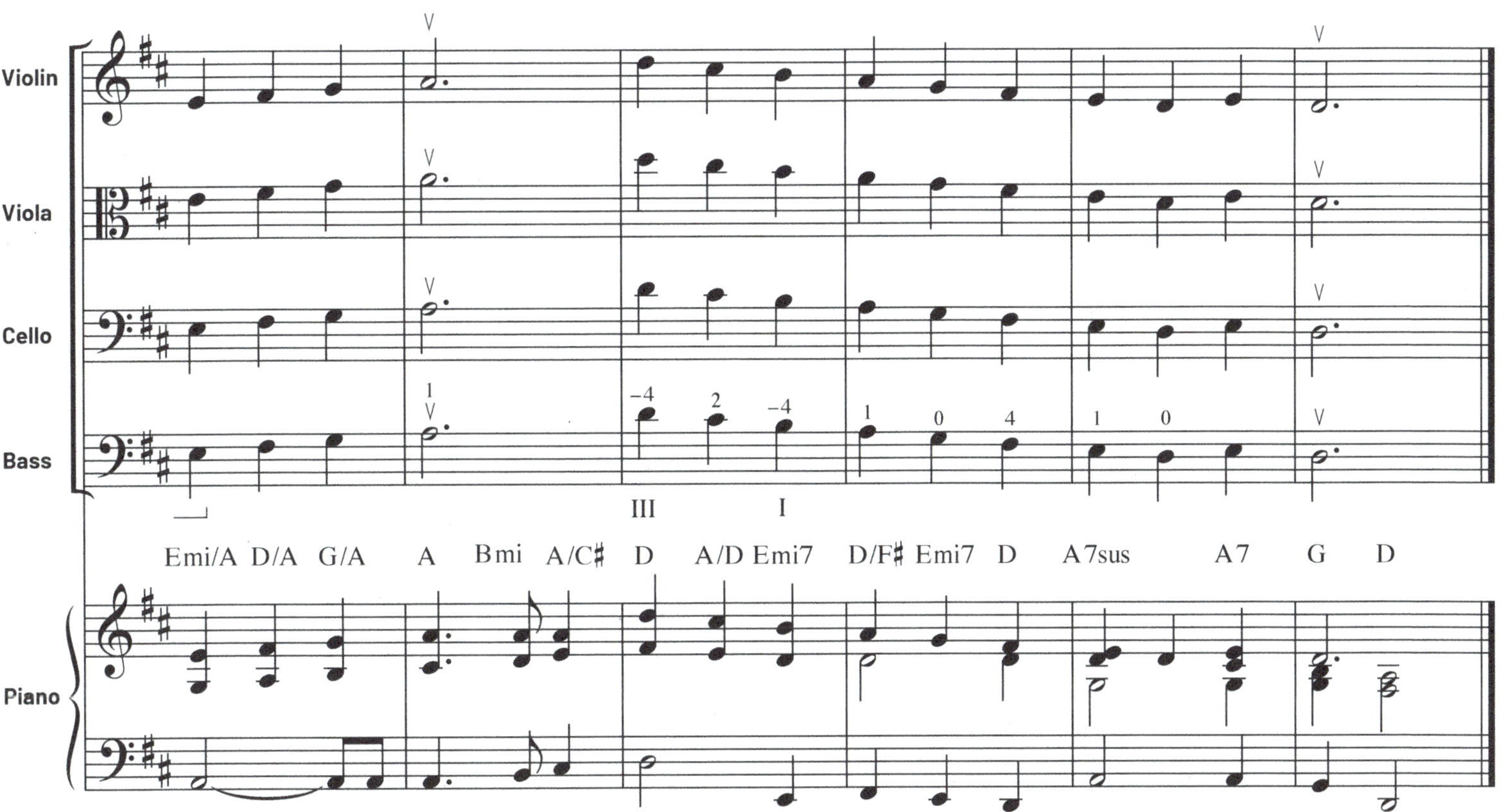

QUIZ OBJECTIVES – SAILOR'S SONG

- $\frac{3}{4}$ time signature
- Counting dotted half notes
- Changing bow speeds for different note lengths

Review Exercises:

104. *Counting Threes*
105. *D Scale in Threes*
106. *French Folk Song*

107. ESSENTIAL ELEMENTS QUIZ – SAILOR'S SONG

English Sea Song

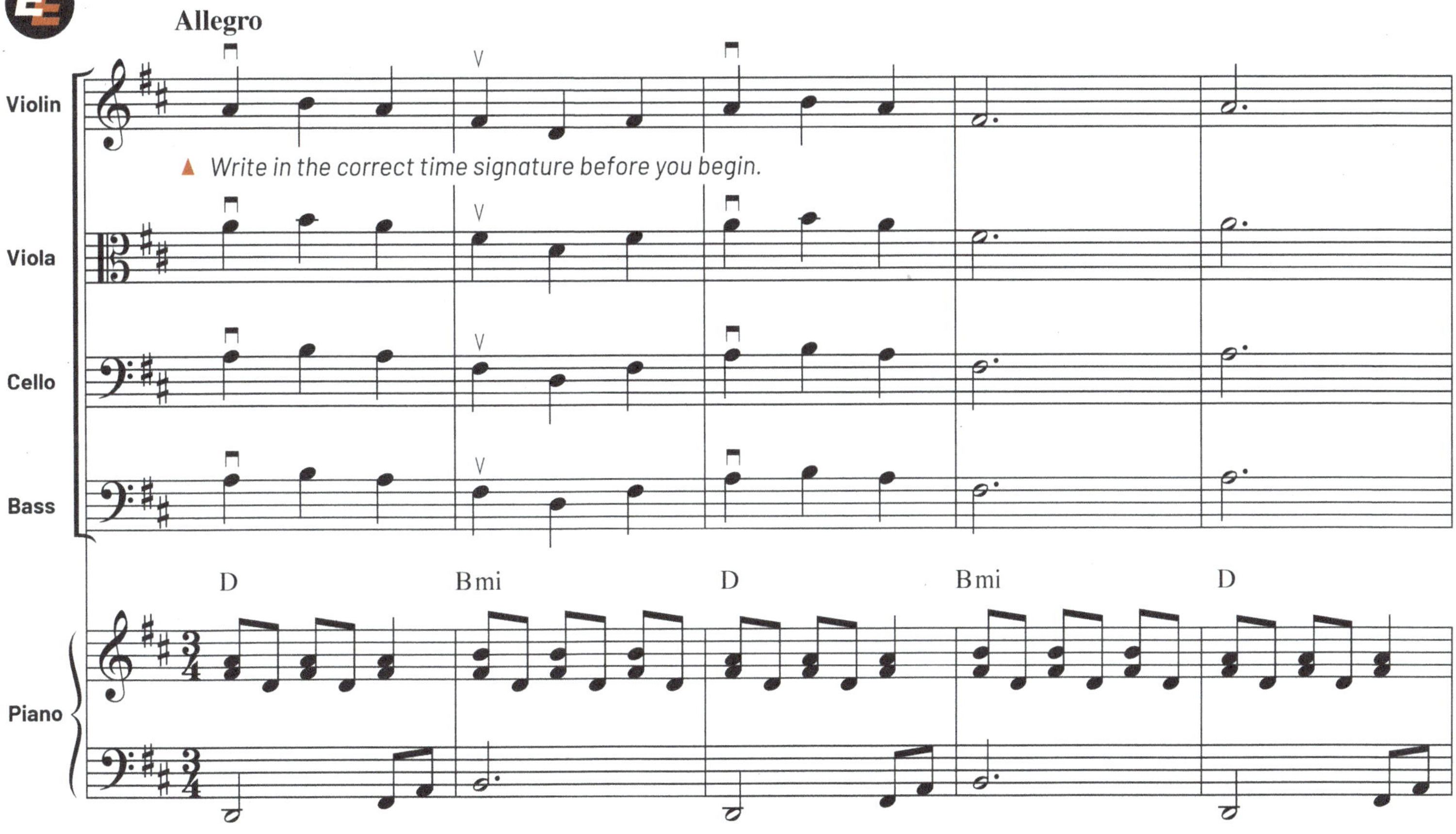
Allegro
Violin
▲ Write in the correct time signature before you begin.
Viola
Cello
Bass
Piano
D
Bmi
D
Bmi
D

Violin

Viola

Cello

Bass

B7 Emi A Emi7 A7

Piano

Violin

Viola

Cello

Bass

Emi7 A7 D

Piano

Tie 

A **tie** is a curved line that connects notes of the **same** pitch.
Play a single note for the combined counts of the tied notes.

♩‿♩ = 2 beats

THEORY

Teacher Ties and slurs are presented on student book page 29. Discuss with students the difference between a tie and a slur.

108. FIT TO BE TIED

Violin
Viola
Cello
Bass

D Asus D/F♯ G D/F♯ G Asus A

Piano

Violin
Viola
Cello
Bass

D/F♯ G D/A Asus Gsus G Asus A Dsus D

Piano

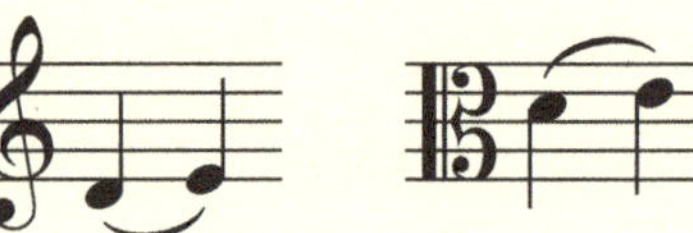

A **slur** is a curved line that connects two or more **different** pitches. Play slurred notes together in the same bow stroke.

Teacher To help prepare to learn slurring, have students trill while pulling their bow in one direction. Incorporate slurred examples in their listening skill echoes. Also, consider adding slurs to the D major scale and to previously learned pieces. Another effective way to introduce slurring is to have students practice bowing two detached notes in the same direction, eventually eliminating the bow stop between the pitches, e.g.

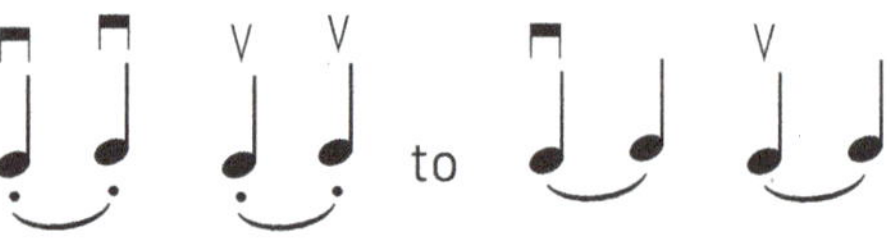

109. STOP AND GO

Violin

Viola

Cello

Bass

Piano

B♭ C/B♭ D Gmi Ami7 D

Violin

Viola

Cello

Bass

Piano

D Emi/D D Emi/D D Gmi Ami7 D

110. SLURRING ALONG

111. SMOOTH SAILING

Violin

Viola

Cello

Bass

D A G D A Bmi E9 Asus A

Piano

Violin

Viola

Cello

Bass

D D/F♯ G E/G♯ G/A D

Piano

112. D MAJOR SLURS

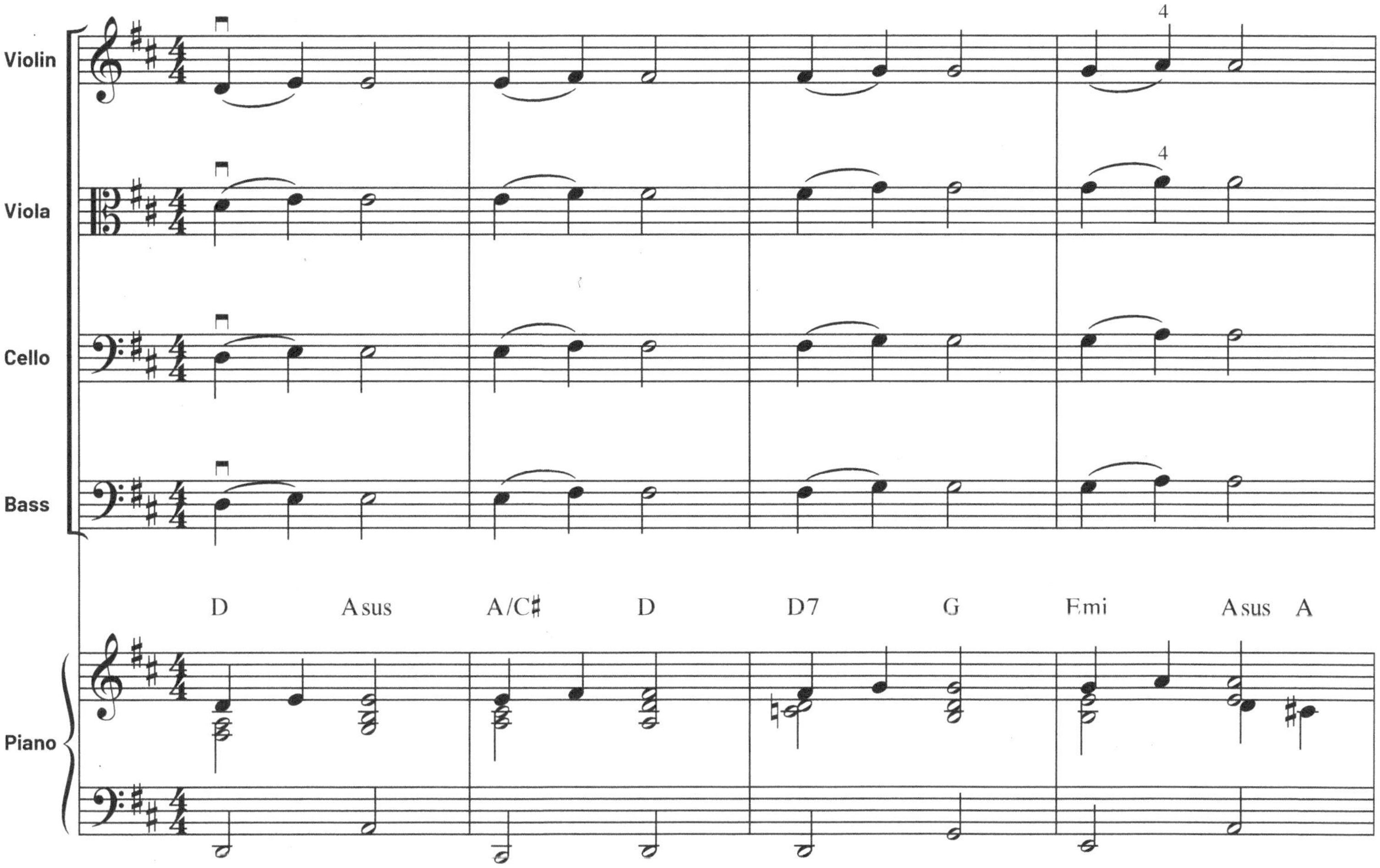

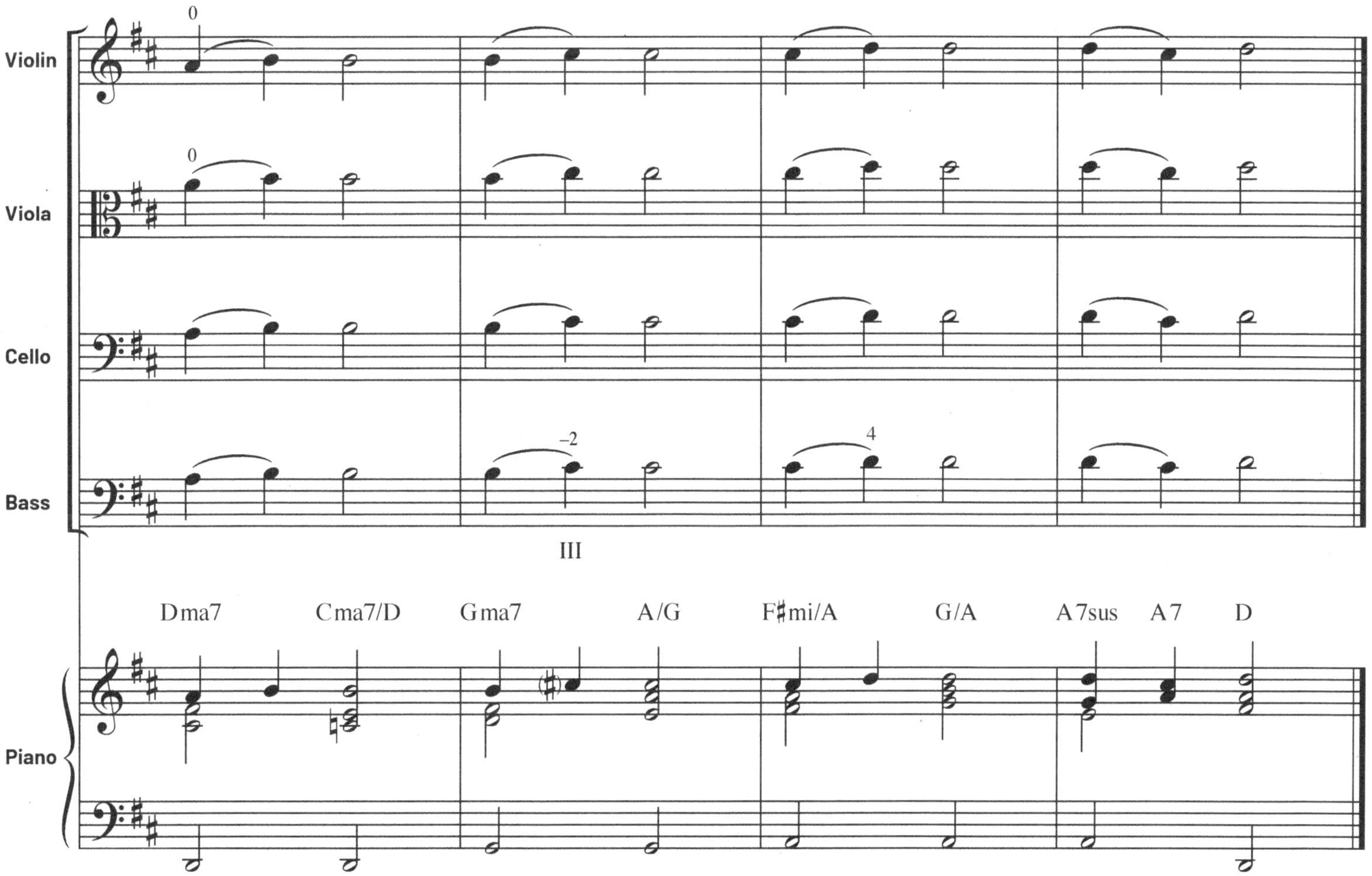

Violin
Viola
Cello
Bass
Piano

4 4 4

D Asus A/C♯ D D7 G Emi Asus A

0 0 –2 4 III

Dma7 Cma7/D Gma7 A/G F♯mi/A G/A A7sus A7 D

Teacher Tell students that their string crossings should be smooth. Show them that in slurred string crossings their bow should follow the natural curvature of their instrument's bridge. Check to see if their right arm and bow hand are changing levels when changing strings.

113. CROSSING STRINGS

Violin

Viola

Cello

Bass

D9 D9/F♯ G13 A9 D9 D9/F♯ G13 A7 D9 N.C.

Piano

114. GLIDING BOWS

Violin

Viola

Cello

Bass

Bmi7 B♭ma7 Asus A D(add9) F♯mi7 G6 Asus Gmi Ami D

Piano

115. UPSIDE DOWN

Upbeat

A note (or notes) that appears before the first full measure is called an **upbeat** (or **pickup**). The remaining beats are found in the last measure.

Teacher Read the definition of upbeat presented on student book page 30. Upbeats are sometimes called pick-up notes.

116. SONG FOR MARIA

Andante

Violin

▲ *Upbeat*

Viola

Cello

Bass

D D/F♯ G A7 D Emi/G F♯mi7 G A7 D

Piano

Where is beat 4? ▼

Violin

Viola

Cello

Bass

D D/F♯ G A7 Bmi Emi/G D/A A7sus A7 D

Piano

HISTORY

Latin American music combines the folk music from South and Central America, the Caribbean Islands, African, Spanish, and Portuguese cultures. Melodies often feature a lively accompaniment by drums, maracas, and claves. Latin American styles have become part of jazz, classical, and rock music.

THEORY

D.C. al Fine

Play until you see the **D.C. al Fine**. Then go back to the beginning and play until you see **Fine** (*fee'- nay*). **D.C.** is the abbreviation for **Da Capo**, the Italian term for "return to the beginning." **Fine** is the Italian word for "the finish."

Teacher Play recorded examples of Latin, Caribbean, African, Spanish, and Portuguese music to familiarize students with these musical styles.

117. BANANA BOAT SONG

Caribbean Folk Song

118. FIROLIRALERA – Orchestra Arrangement

Mexican Folk Song
Arr. John Higgins

Violin
A
B
Viola
A
B
Cello
A
B
Bass
A
B
Piano
D
A7
D

Violin
A
B
4
Tie
Viola
A
B
4
Cello
A
B
Bass
A
B
Piano
G
D/A
A7
D

SKILL BUILDERS – G Major

Teacher The purpose of EE SKILL BUILDERS is to summarize and reinforce playing skills that have been recently learned. The exercises are in sequential order of playing difficulty. Students should master each of the exercises in the EE SKILL BUILDERS before proceeding to the next one.

120.

121.
Violin
Viola
Cello
Bass
Piano
G G7 C G D7 G
122.
Violin
Viola
Cello
Bass
Piano
G C C/D D7 Emi Ami G/B C6 G/D C/E D7/F♯ G

123.
Violin
Viola
Cello
Bass
Slur three
G
Bmi7
C
D7
Emi7
D/C
C
Bmi7
Ami7
D6
D7
G
Piano
124.
Violin
Viola
Cello
Bass
Emi
Bmi
Ami
Emi
C
D7
C
D7
G
Piano

Far Eastern music comes from Malaysia, Indonesia, China and other areas. Historians believe the first orchestras, known as **gamelans**, existed in this region as early as the 1st century B.C. Today's gamelans include rebabs (spiked fiddles), gongs, xylophones, and a wide variety of percussion instruments.

HISTORY

125. JINGLI NONA

Far Eastern Folk Song

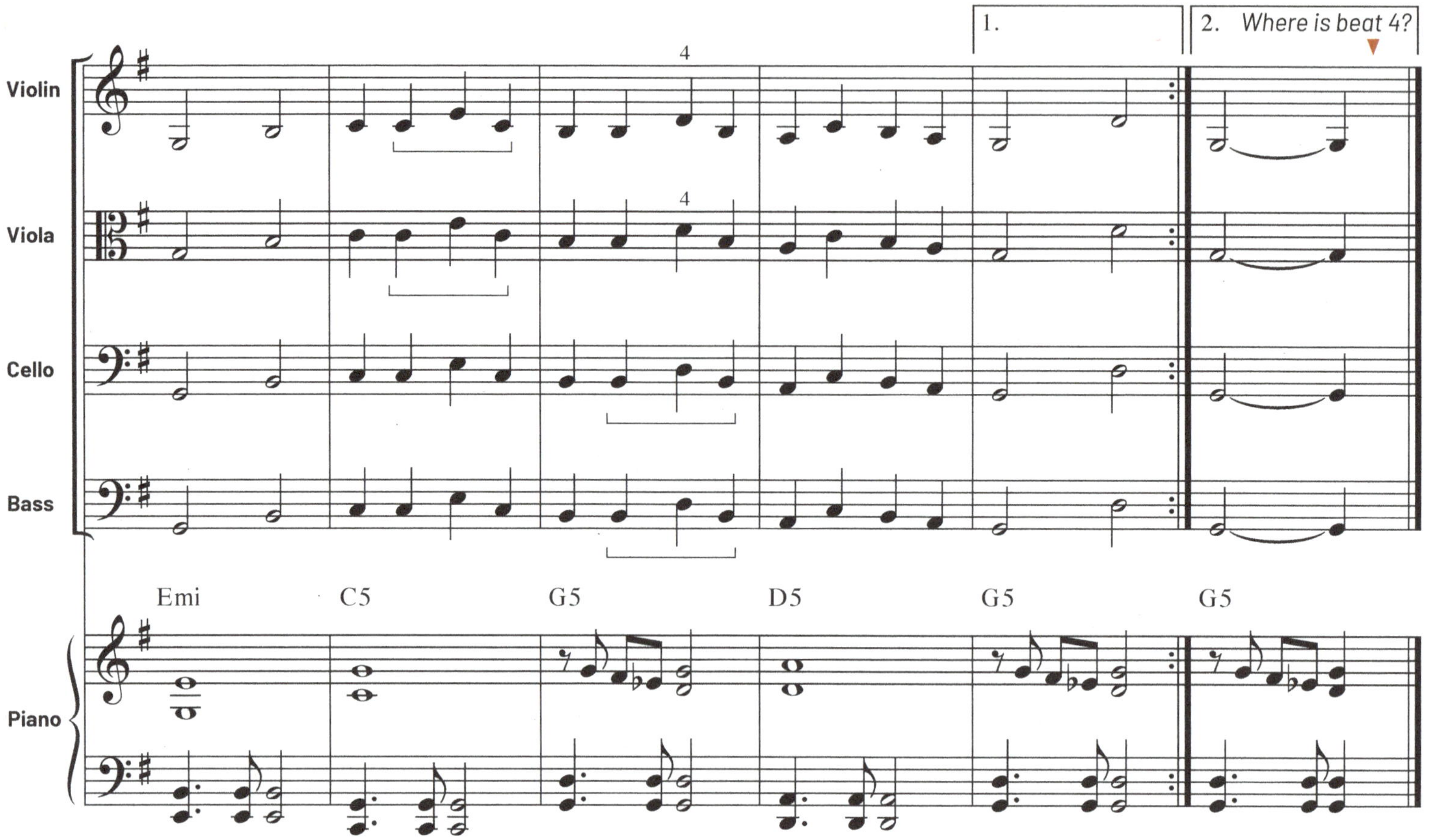

1.
2. Where is beat 4?
Violin
4
Viola
4
Cello
Bass
Emi
C5
G5
D5
G5
G5
Piano

Teacher F♮ and C♮ are introduced on student book pages 32 and 33. To help prepare students to finger F♮, which requires a new finger pattern for the violin and viola, have students tap their second finger while keeping their other fingers on the string. Also, have them slide their second finger back and forth between their first and third fingers, while keeping all of their fingers on the string. Both of these rote exercises help develop finger flexibility and independence of fingers. In addition, prepare and reinforce student aural learning of F♮ by incorporating the following *Listening Skills* echo patterns for students.

Violin/ Viola

NEW FINGER PATTERN

Low 2nd Finger

Step 1
Shape your left hand as shown. Be certain your palm faces you. Notice your 2nd finger lightly touches your 1st finger.

1
2
3
4

Step 2
Bring your hand to the fingerboard. Your 1st and 2nd fingers touch. There is a space between your 2nd and 3rd fingers, and between your 3rd and 4th fingers.

Violin

F
is played with low 2nd finger on the D string.

E
A
D
G
1
2
3
4
E
F

Viola

F
is played with low 2nd finger on the D string.

A
D
G
C
1
2
3
4
E
F

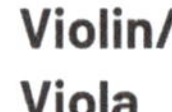

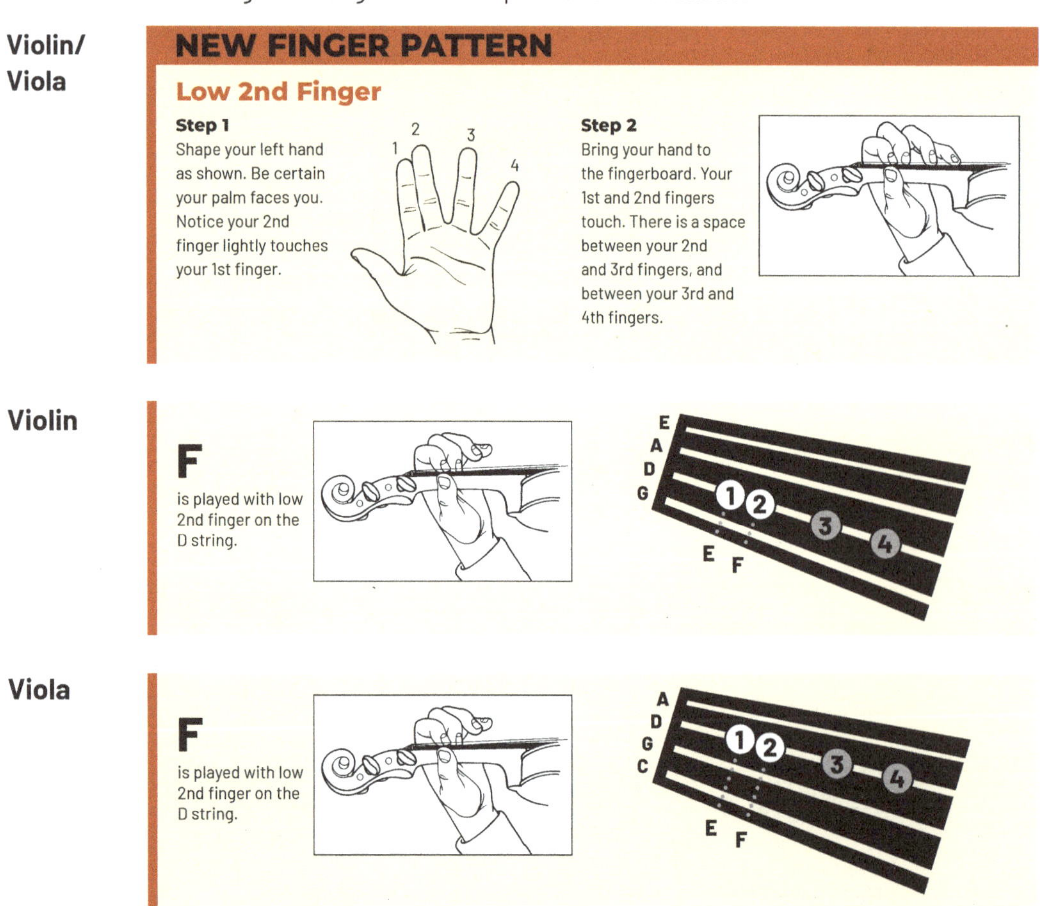

Cello

Second Finger on the D String

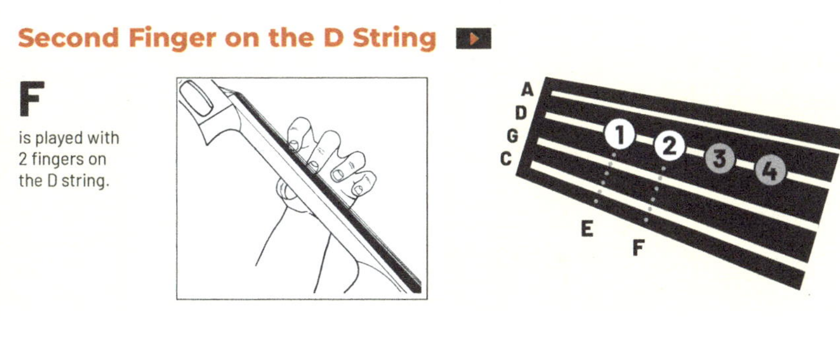

F

is played with 2 fingers on the D string.

Bass

SECOND FINGER ON THE D STRING

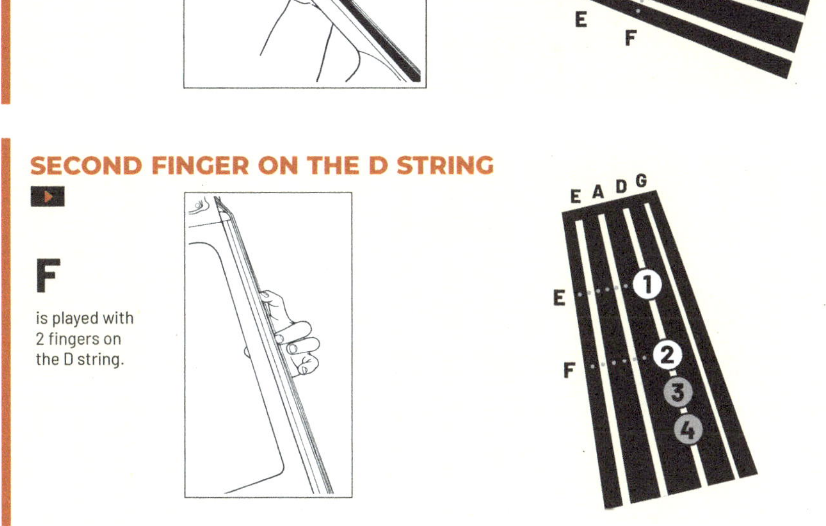

F

is played with 2 fingers on the D string.

Listening Skills

Play what your teacher plays. Listen carefully.

1.

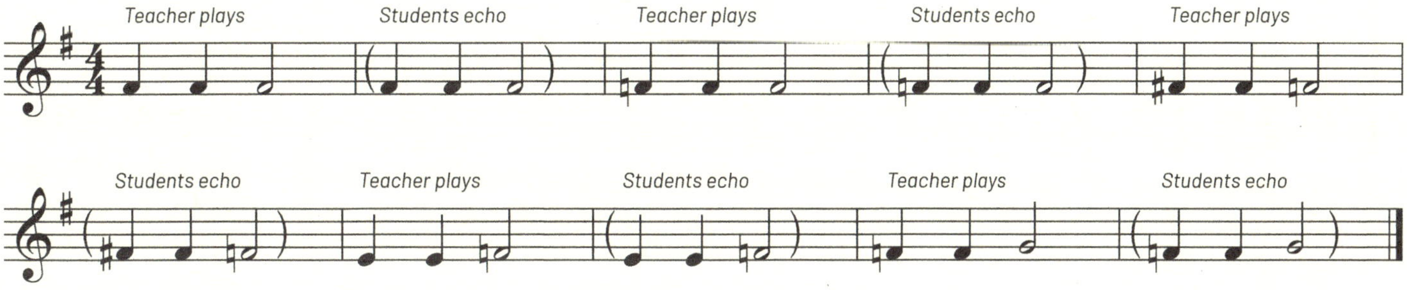

Teacher plays — *Students echo* — *Teacher plays* — *Students echo* — *Teacher plays*

Students echo — *Teacher plays* — *Students echo* — *Teacher plays* — *Students echo*

2.

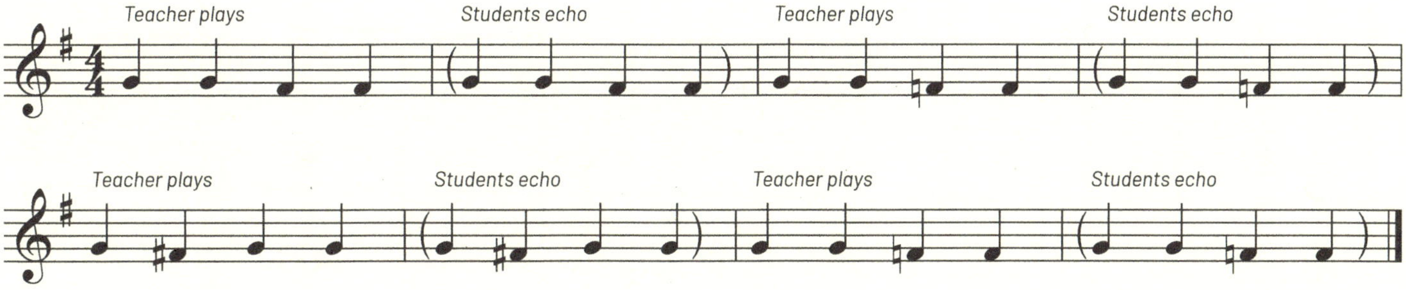

Teacher plays — *Students echo* — *Teacher plays* — *Students echo*

Teacher plays — *Students echo* — *Teacher plays* — *Students echo*

3.

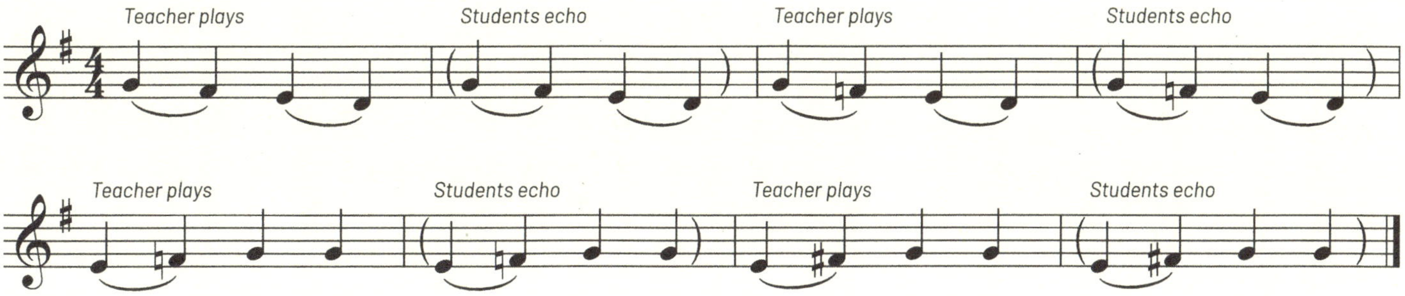

Teacher plays — *Students echo* — *Teacher plays* — *Students echo*

Teacher plays — *Students echo* — *Teacher plays* — *Students echo*

THEORY

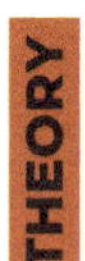

Natural ♮

A **natural** sign cancels out a flat (♭) or a sharp (♯) and remains in effect for the entire measure.

Violin

F
= Low
2nd
finger

Viola

F
= Low
2nd
finger

Cello

F
2

Bass

F
2

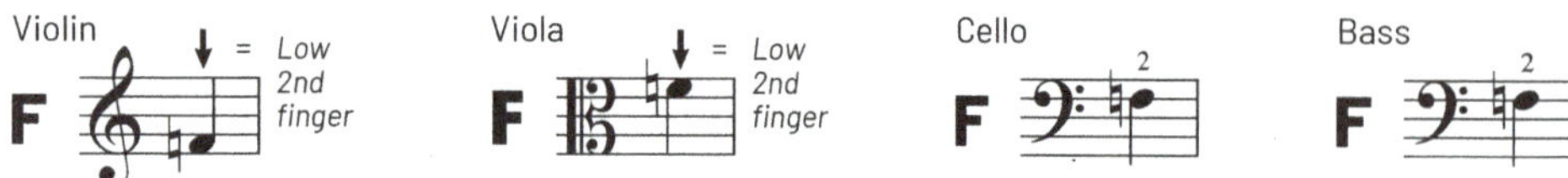

Teacher Review with students the definition of a natural sign as presented on student book page 32.

126. LET'S READ "F" (F-natural)

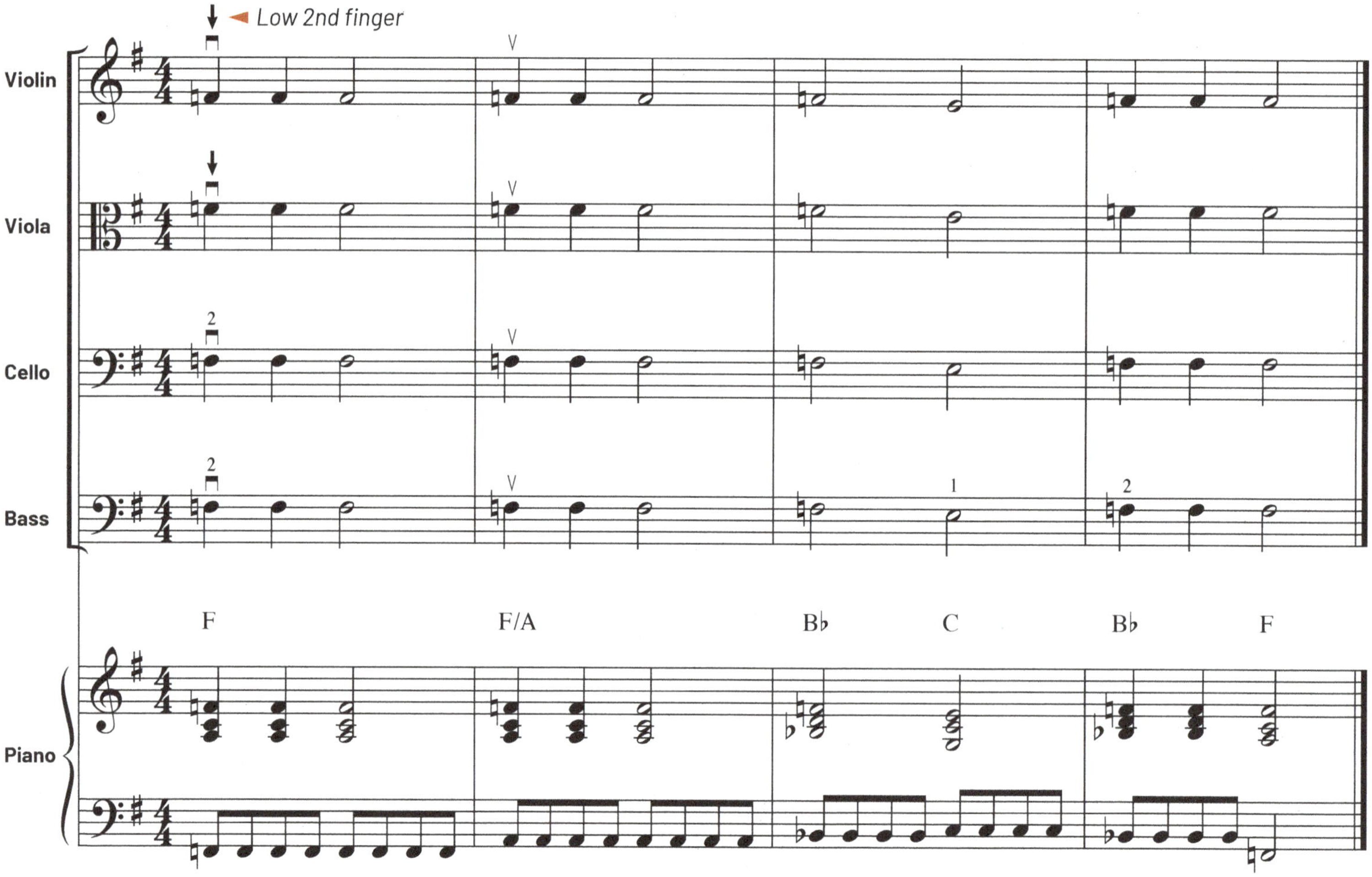

Low 2nd finger
Violin
Viola
Cello
Bass
Piano
F
F/A
B♭
C
B♭
F

THEORY

Half Step
Whole Step

A **half step** is the smallest distance between two notes.

A **whole step** is two half steps combined.

Teacher Read and discuss the definitions of half and whole steps found on student book page 32. Present some rote listening-skill echoes to students that incorporate both half and whole steps. Also, have students mark the half steps in exercises 128, 129, and 132 to reinforce their understanding of half and whole steps.

127. HALF-STEPPIN' AND WHOLE STEPPIN'

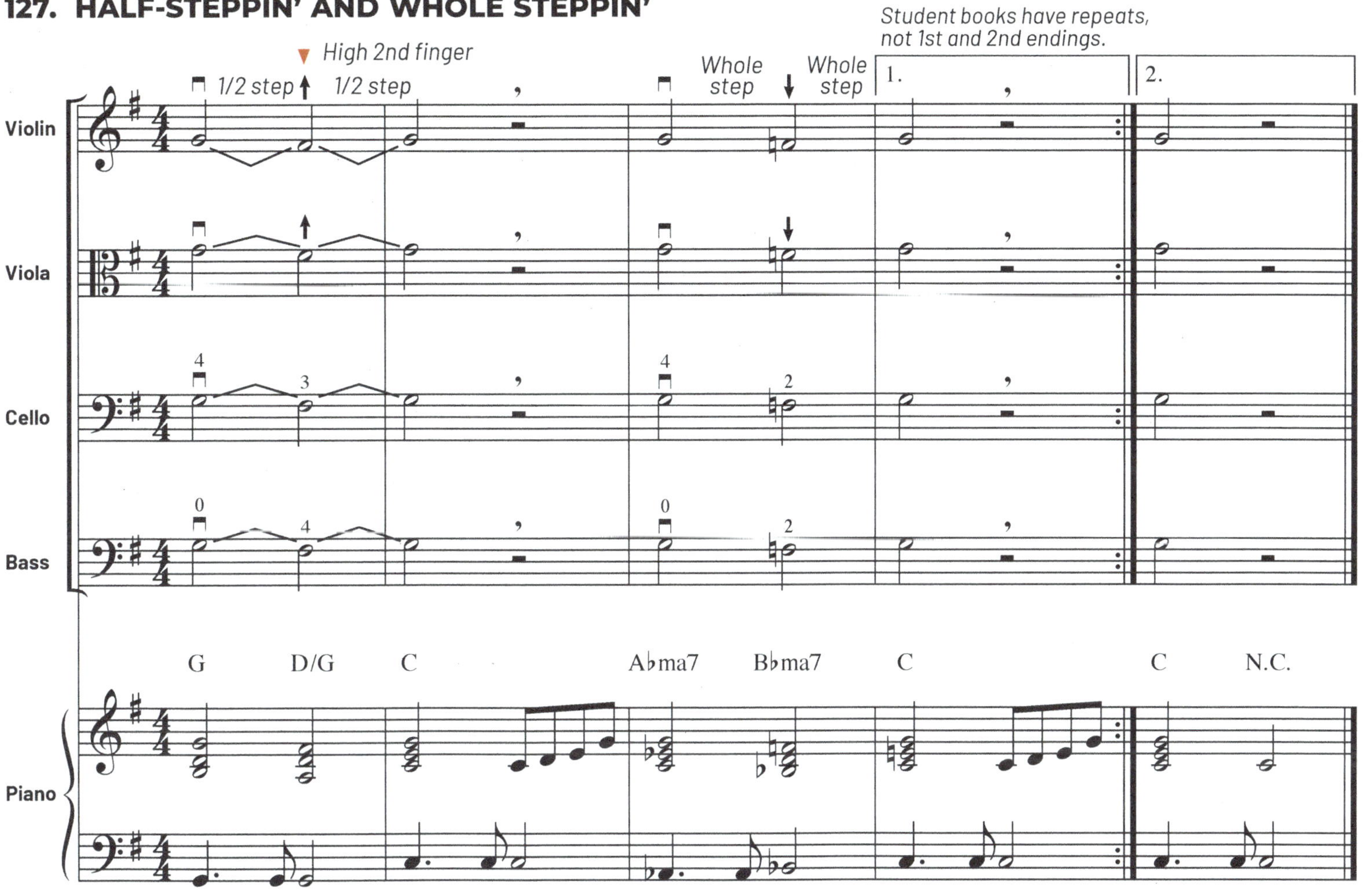

128. SPY GUY

Violin
Viola
Cello
Bass
Piano
Gmi
D/F♯
B♭/F
D/F♯
Gmi
D/F♯
D
Cmi/E♭
C
Gmi
D/F♯
B♭/F
C/E
B♭/F
B♭/D
D/F♯
D
Gmi

129. MINOR DETAILS

Violin

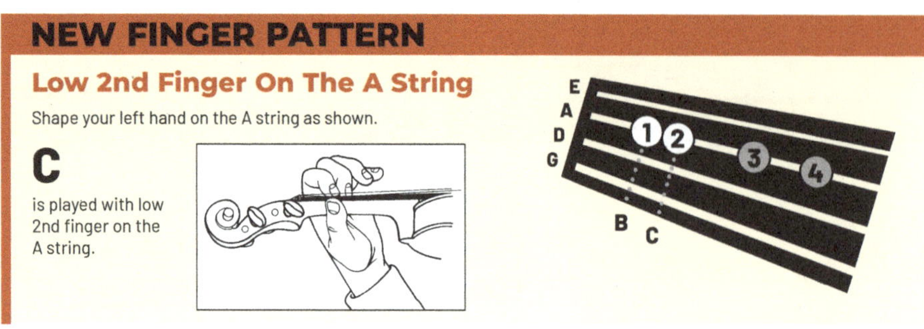

Viola

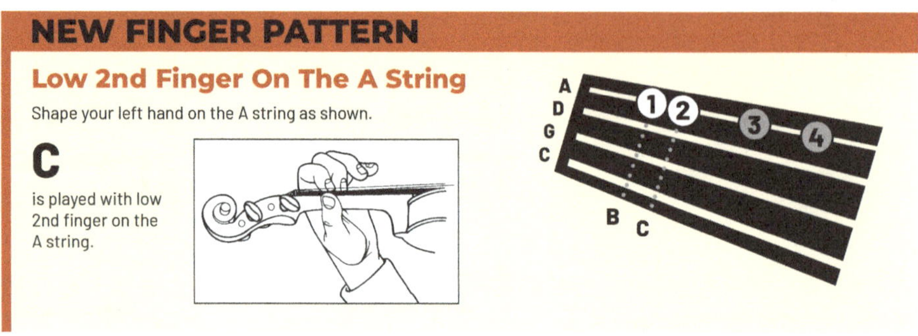

Cello

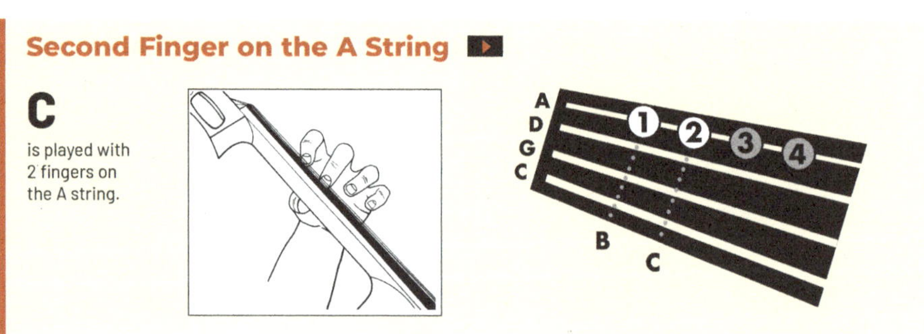

Bass

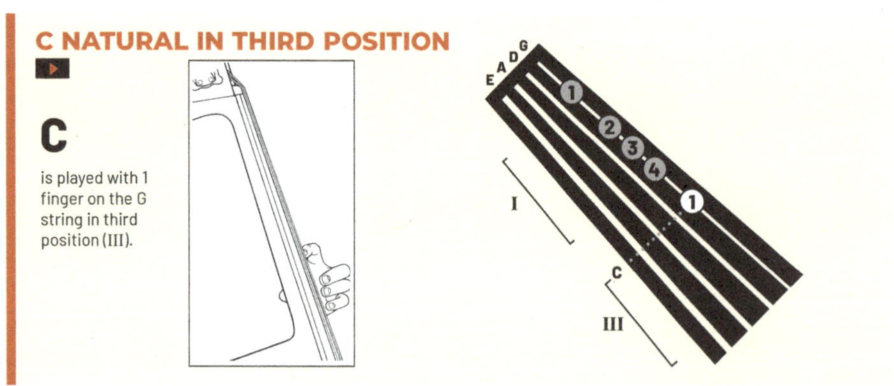

Listening Skills
Play what your teacher plays. Listen carefully.
1.
Teacher plays
Students echo
Teacher plays
Students echo
Teacher plays
Students echo
Teacher plays
Students echo
Teacher plays
Students echo
2.
Teacher plays
Students echo
Teacher plays
Students echo
Teacher plays
Students echo
Teacher plays
Students echo
Teacher plays
Students echo
3.
Teacher plays
Students echo
Teacher plays
Students echo
Teacher plays
Students echo
Teacher plays
Students echo
Teacher plays
Students echo
Teacher plays
Students echo
Violin
C
Viola
C
Cello
C
Bass
C
III
130. LET'S READ "C" (C-natural)
Violin
Viola
Cello
Bass
III
Piano
C5
C5
F5
C5
G5
F5
C5

131. HALF STEP AND WHOLE STEP REVIEW

Student books have repeats, not 1st and 2nd endings.

THEORY

Chromatics

Chromatic notes are altered with sharps, flats, and naturals.
A chromatic pattern is two or more notes in a sequence of half steps.

132. CHROMATIC MOVES

Violin
Viola
Cello
Bass
II 1/2
III
G7 F♯7 F7 E7 A♭7 A7 D7
Piano

133. THE STETSON SPECIAL

Violin
Viola
Cello
Bass
III
II 1/2 III
I
G D7 G G D7 G G D7 G C D7 G
Piano

134. BLUEBIRD'S SONG

Texas Folk Song

Essential Elements for Strings Correlated Literature

Students will enjoy playing their own special part in string orchestra arrangements. The Explorer level of *Essential Elements for Strings* series is a collection of string orchestra arrangements that only use the rhythms, bowings, and notes that are introduced on pages student book page 1-33 (Teacher Manual pages 39-182). See your Hal Leonard dealer for the latest releases.

THEORY

Key Signature C MAJOR

All notes are naturals.

THEORY

Bass **New Position – II**

(2nd finger on B, 4th finger on C.)

Teacher Student book page 34 introduces the key of C major. A one-octave C major scale is presented, along with three melodies in C Major. This involves introducing second-finger B and fourth-finger C in second position on the double bass.

135. C MAJOR SCALE – Round

Violin ① ② 1/2 step 1/2 1/2
Viola
Cello
Bass II
Piano C(add9) G7sus C(add9) G7sus C(add9) G7sus C(add9) G7sus

Violin 1/2
Viola
Cello
Bass I
Piano C(add9) G7sus C(add9) G7sus C(add9) G7sus Repeat to accompany round C(add9) G7sus

Duet A composition with two different parts, played together.

136. SPLIT DECISION – Duet

A
Violin
B
A
Viola
B
A
Cello
B
–2
4
A
II
Bass
–2
4
B
II
C/G
Ami
F
G
F/C
C
Piano

137. OAK HOLLOW

Moderato

Violin

Viola

Cello

Bass

C G7sus C F Dmi F/G Gsus G

Piano

Violin

Viola

Cello

Bass

1 4 −4 −1

II I

C Emi Ami Ami/G F♯mi7(♭5) C/G Ami7 F6/G G6 C

Piano

138. A-TISKET, A-TASKET

HISTORY

In the second half of the 1800s many composers tried to express the spirit of their own country by writing music with a distinct national flavor. Listen to the music of Russian composers such as Borodin, Tchaikovsky, and Rimsky-Korsakov. They often used folk songs and dance rhythms to convey their nationalism. Describe the sounds you hear.

Teacher Discuss the concept of nationalistic music. Play recordings of music by Russian composers, Borodin, Tchaikovsky and Rimsky-Korsakov. Discuss how their music is often nationalistic. Introduce recordings of other nationalistic compositions such as *Finlandia* by Sibelius and *The Moldau* by Smetana.

QUIZ OBJECTIVES – RUSSIAN FOLK TUNE

- F natural
- C natural
- Violin/Viola 4th finger
- Andante tempo

Review Exercises:

129. *Minor Details*
133. *The Stetson Special*
135. *C Major Scale*
137. *Oak Hollow*

139. ESSENTIAL ELEMENTS QUIZ – RUSSIAN FOLK TUNE

Russian Folk Song

Violin
Viola
Cello
Bass
Piano
4
4
F
C
G7
C
G/B
F/A
C/G
G7
C

Alert This page mixes finger patterns. Watch for low 2nd finger (C♮) and high 2nd finger (F♯).

Teacher Student book page 35 reinforces students' knowledge of the notes F♮ and C♮ by contrasting them with F♯ and C♯ within melodies. Have students play C♮ and C♯ and F♮ and F♯ as a review in listening-skill rote echoes before beginning to practice the melodies on this page.

140. BINGO

18th Century English Game Song

Allegro *Student books repeat to the upbeat before measure 1.*

Violin

Viola

Cello

Bass

Piano

D7 G C G D7 G C D7

Student books have repeats, not 1st and 2nd endings.

Where is beat 2? ▼

Violin

Viola

Cello

Bass

Piano

G Emi A7 D7 G C G N.C. G

English composer **Thomas Tallis** (1505-1585) served as royal court composer during the reigns of Henry VIII, Edward VI, Mary, and Elizabeth I. Composers and artists during this era wanted to recreate the artistic and scientific glories of ancient Greece and Rome. The great artist Michelangelo painted the Sistine Chapel during Tallis' lifetime. **Rounds** and **canons** were popular forms of music during the early 16th century. Divide into groups, and play or sing the *Tallis Canon* as a 4-part round.

HISTORY

Teacher Have students use note names or solfeggio to sing the *Tallis Canon.*

141. TALLIS CANON – Round

Thomas Tallis

Theme and Variations

Theme and Variations is a musical form where a theme, or melody, is followed by different versions of the same theme.

Teacher Contrast the differences between the musical forms of Rounds and Theme and Variations as students prepare to play exercise 142.

In exercise 142 students are given the opportunity to compose their own variation on the melody Skip to My Lou. Specify musical parameters to help them compose their variation. For example, suggest sample rhythms or slurring that they can use.

142. VARIATIONS ON A FAMILIAR SONG

Moderato

Violin
Viola
Cello
Bass

III I III

G D7/F♯

Piano

Violin
Viola
Cello
Bass

I III I

G D7/F♯ G Gsus G

Piano

Variation 1
Violin
Viola
Cello
Bass
Piano
III
I
III
G
G/B
G/D
G/B
D/F♯
D
D7/F♯
I
III
I
G
G/B
G/D
G7/B
Ami/C Ami
G/D
D7
G

Teacher Teach students Exercise 143 *The Birthday Song* as printed. Students will notice that the typical two-eighth note pick up is missing from the traditional *Happy Birthday* melody. Have them add this rhythm when performing as a part of their creativity development.

Student *Now play the line again and create your own rhythm.*

Teacher Student book page 36 introduces C string pitches to viola and cello students. Once learned, the cellos and violas will be prepared to play two-octave C major scales on their instruments. Be sure to incorporate listening-skill rote echoes in your teaching to help develop students' aural understanding of C string pitches.

It is important for the violas and cellos to have enough time in class to develop skill playing on their C string. Even though the following exercises are a review of previously learned pitches for the violin and bass, students must understand the importance of being patient while their classmates learn new notes. To help, a message about the importance of team work in the orchestra and special note and story writing exercises are provided in violin and bass student books.

Introduce C string pitches through listening exercises. Violin and bass students echo the pitches on their instruments in different octaves.

Viola

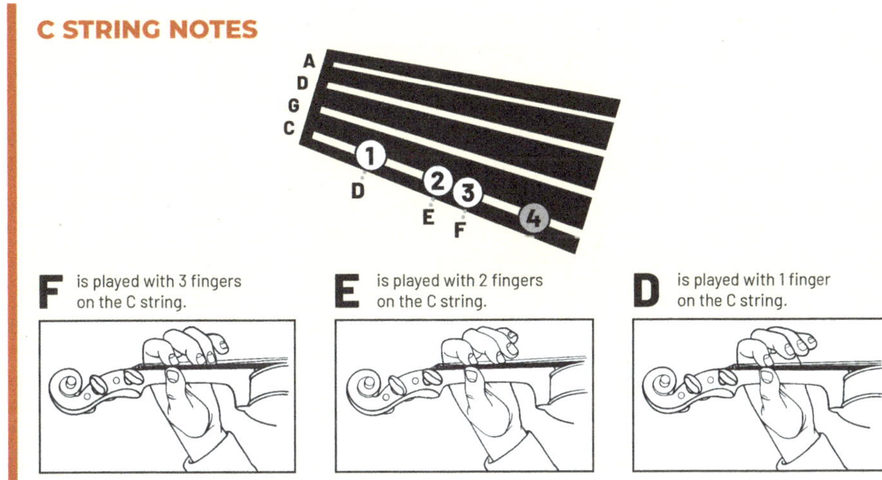

Cello

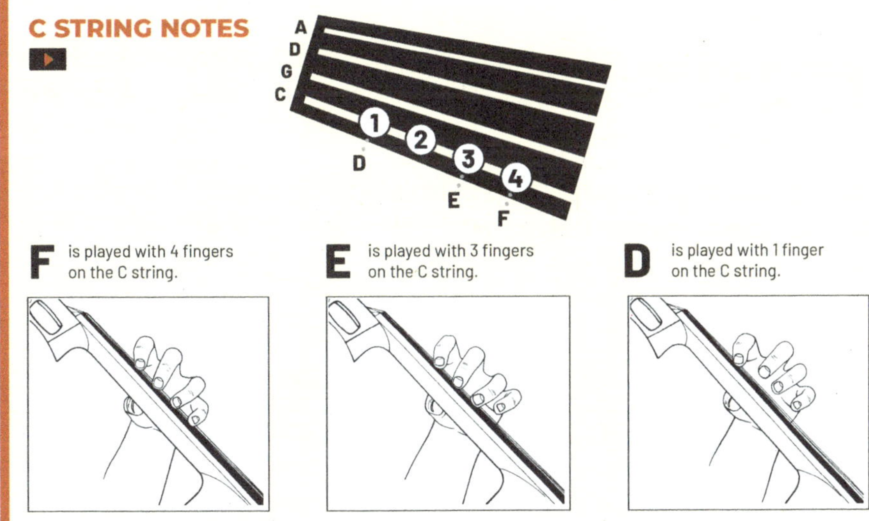

Violin

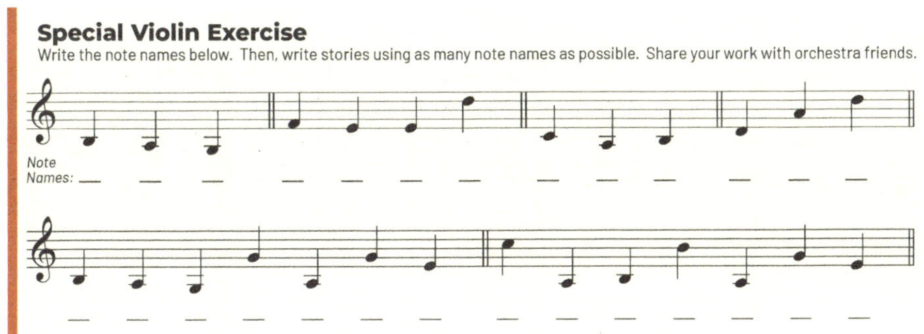

Bass

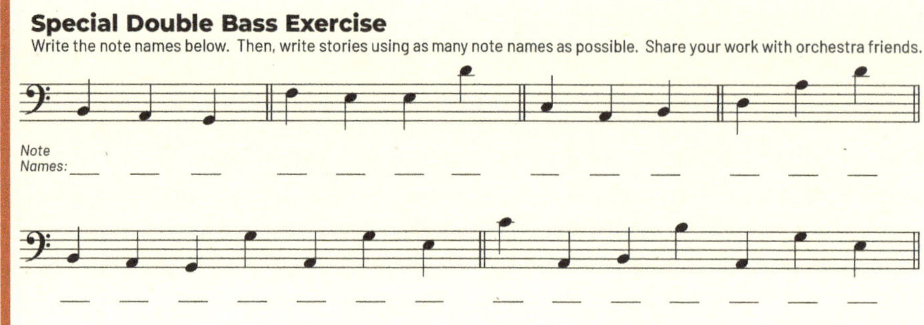

Violin/Bass

Team Work

Great musicians give encouragement to their fellow performers. Viola and cello players will now learn new challenging notes. The success of your orchestra depends on everyone's talent and patience. Play your best as these sections advance their musical technique.

Listening Skills

Play what your teacher plays. Listen carefully.

1.

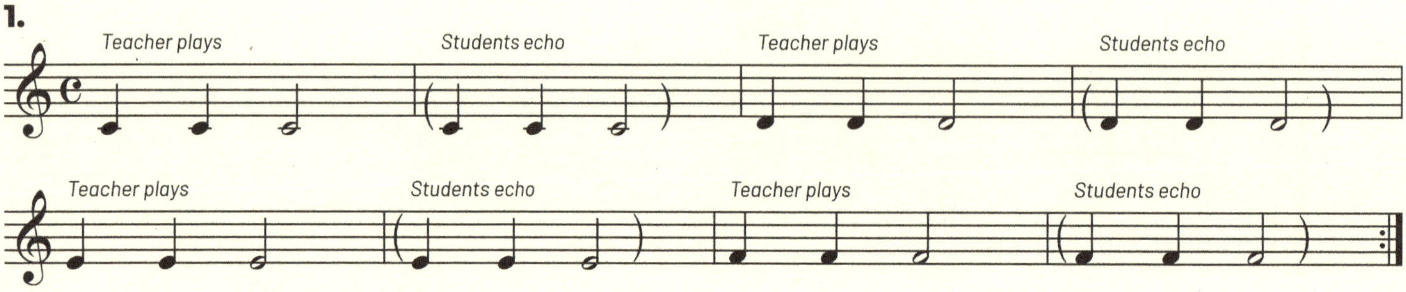

Teacher plays — *Students echo* — *Teacher plays* — *Students echo*

Teacher plays — *Students echo* — *Teacher plays* — *Students echo*

2.

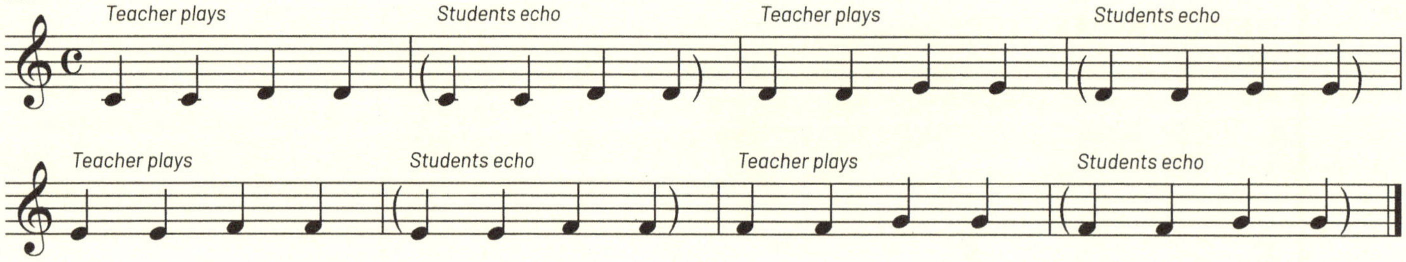

Teacher plays — *Students echo* — *Teacher plays* — *Students echo*

Teacher plays — *Students echo* — *Teacher plays* — *Students echo*

3.

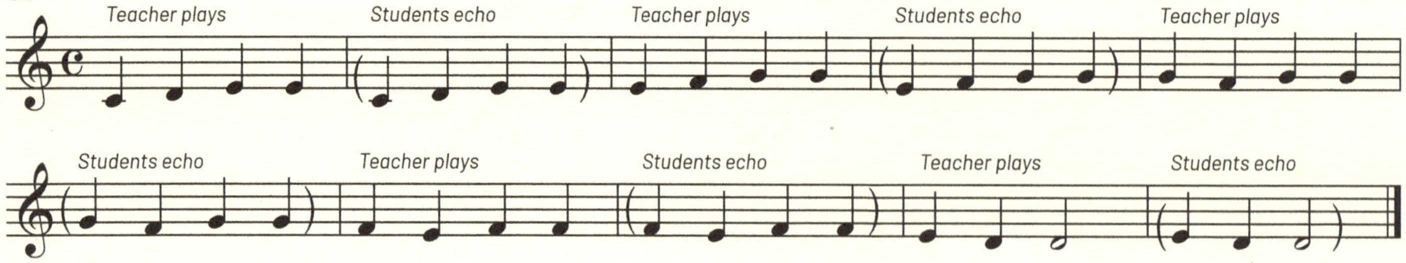

Teacher plays — *Students echo* — *Teacher plays* — *Students echo* — *Teacher plays*

Students echo — *Teacher plays* — *Students echo* — *Teacher plays* — *Students echo*

4.

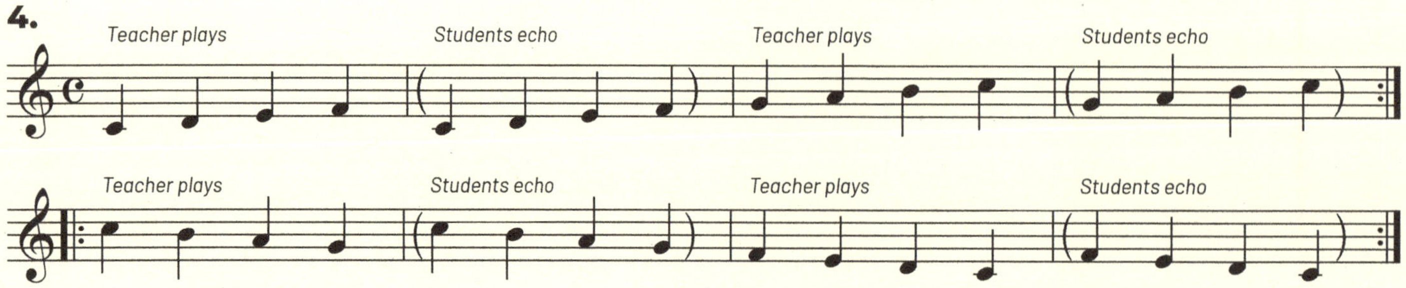

Teacher plays — *Students echo* — *Teacher plays* — *Students echo*

Teacher plays — *Students echo* — *Teacher plays* — *Students echo*

Viola
C

Cello
C

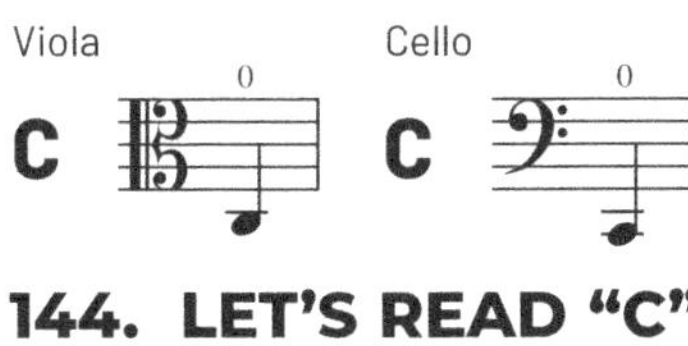

144. LET'S READ "C"

Violin
Viola
Cello
Bass
Piano
Cmi
F/C
C7(no3rd)
F/C
Cmi F/C Cmi

Viola
F

Cello
F

145. LET'S READ "F"

Violin
Viola
Cello
Bass
Piano
F B♭ F
B♭ F
F/A B♭ B°
F/C C7 F

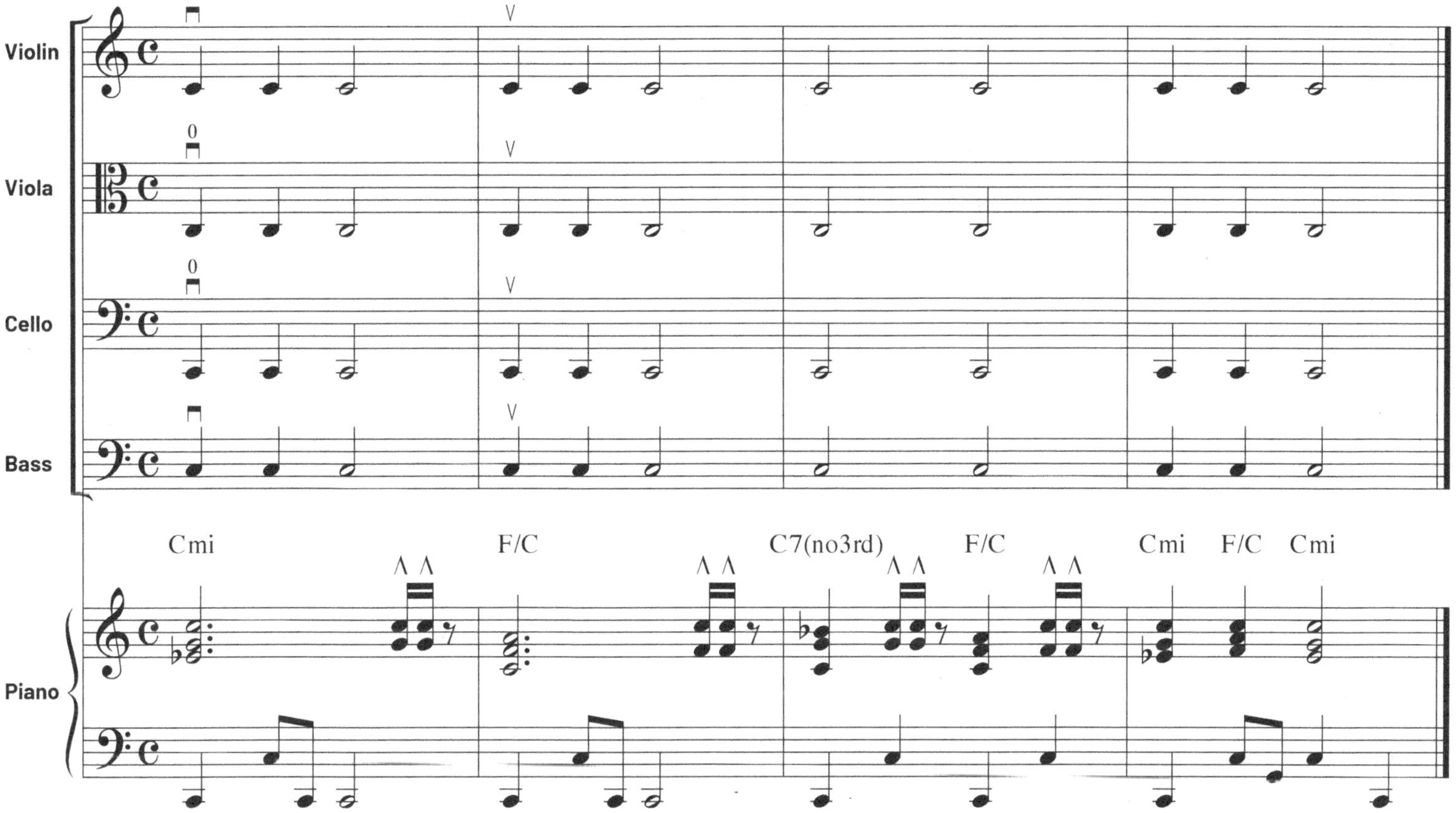

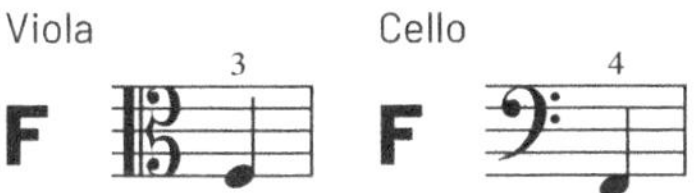

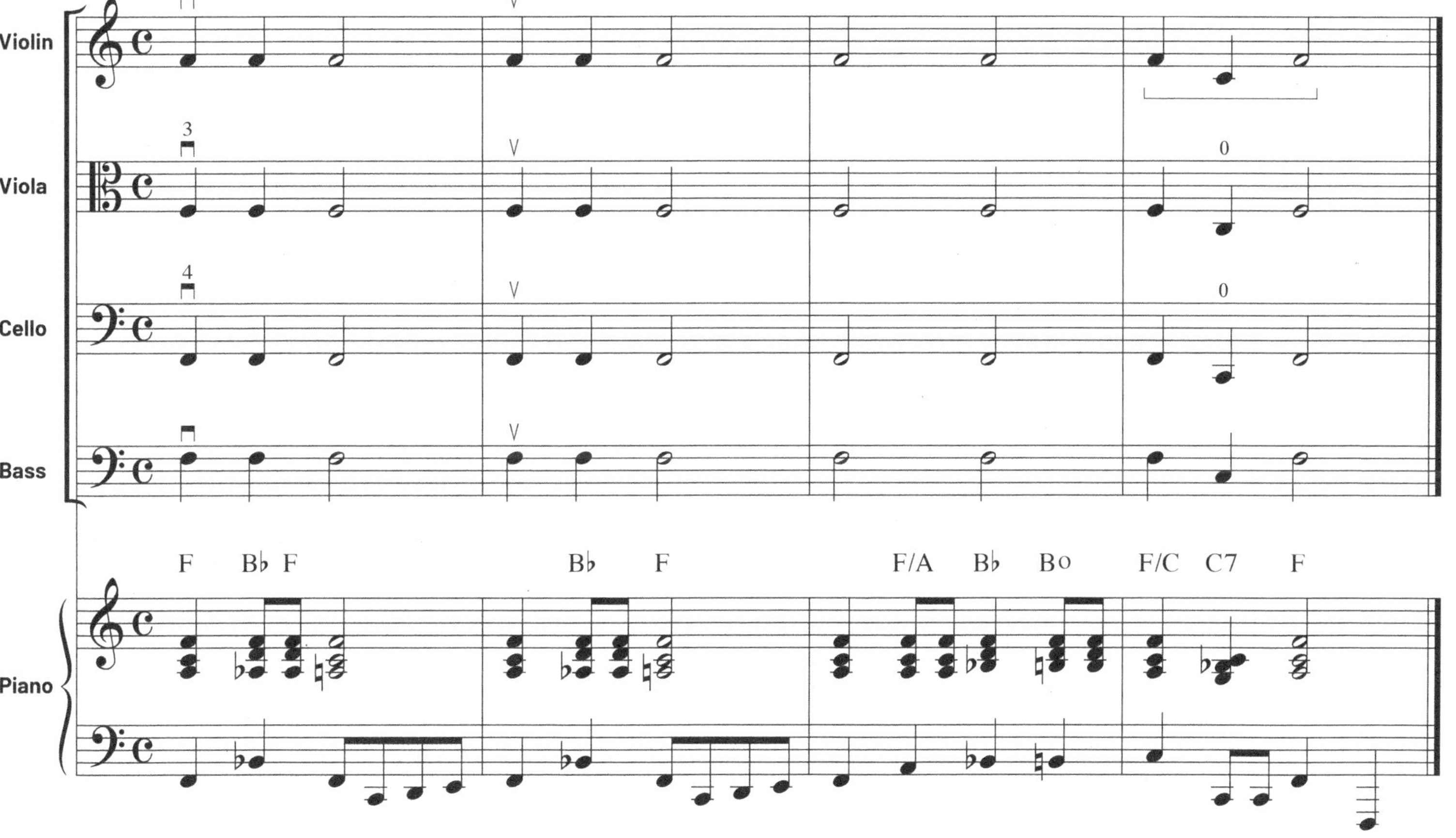

Viola

E

Cello

E

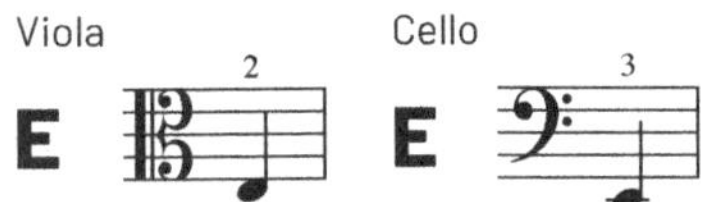

146. LET'S READ "E"

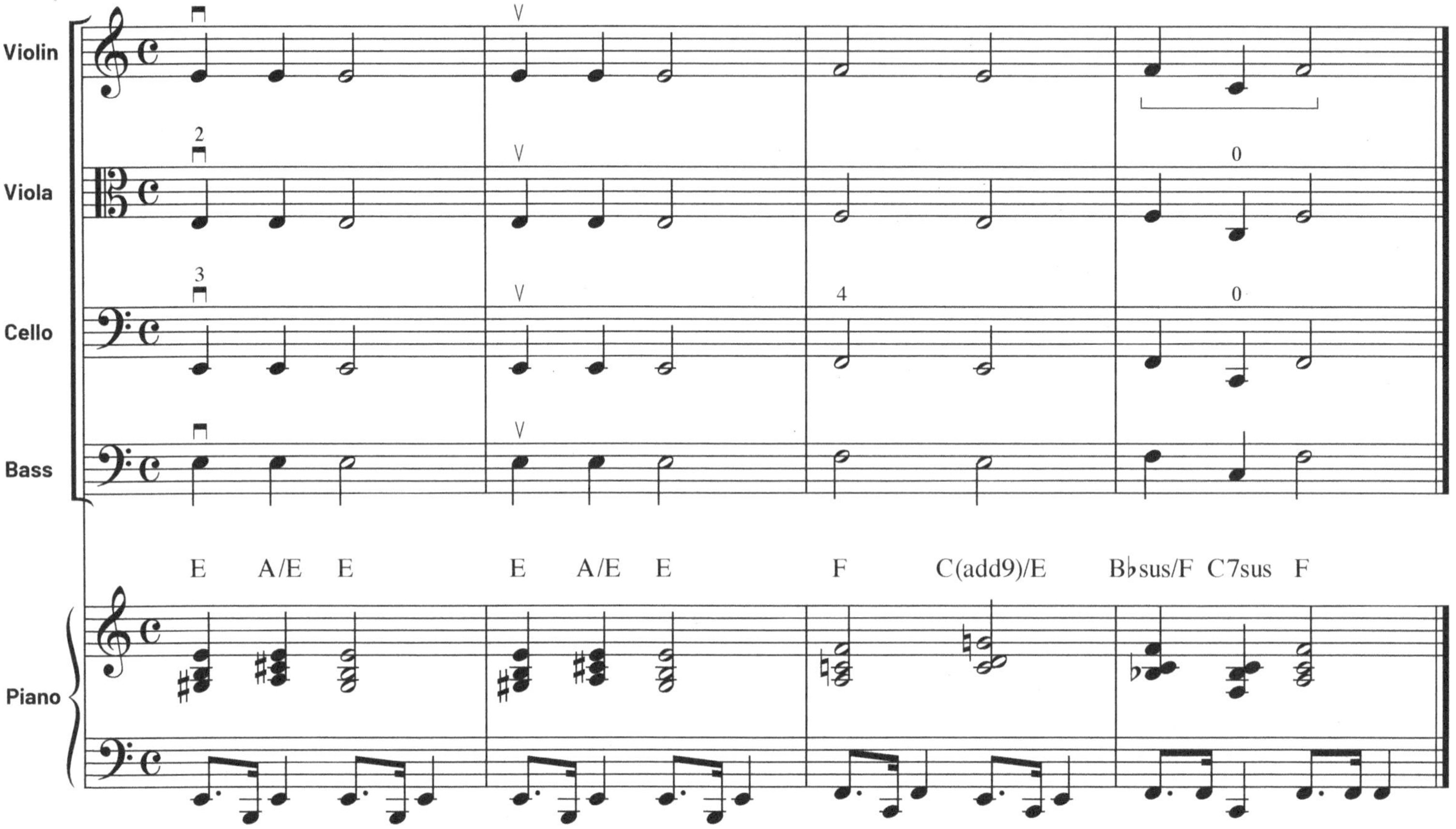
Violin
Viola
Cello
Bass
E A/E E
E A/E E
F C(add9)/E
B♭sus/F C7sus F
Piano

Viola

D 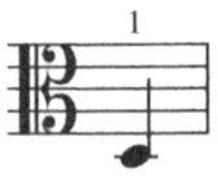

Cello

D 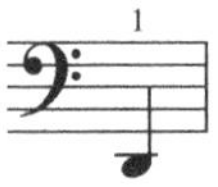

147. LET'S READ "D"

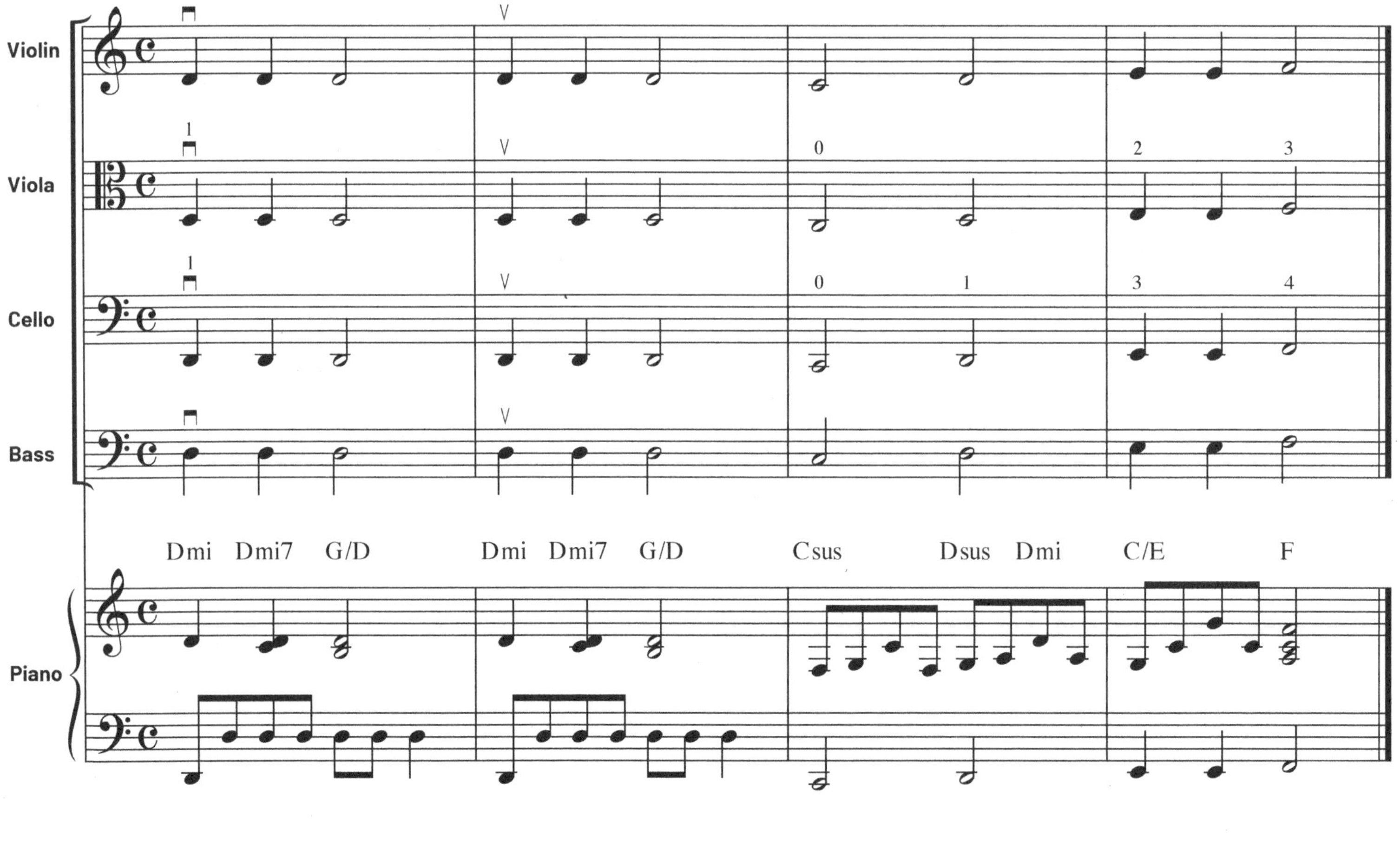
Violin
Viola
Cello
Bass
Dmi Dmi7 G/D
Dmi Dmi7 G/D
Csus Dsus Dmi
C/E F
Piano

148. SIDE BY SIDE *Name the notes before you play.*

149. C MAJOR SCALE

Violin
Viola
Cello
Bass

4 2 −1

II I

C G/B F/A Emi/G F C/G Dmi7 G7 C

Piano

Violin
Viola
Cello
Bass

−2 4

II

C Csus/D C/E Fmi/A♭ C/G F/G G7 C

Piano

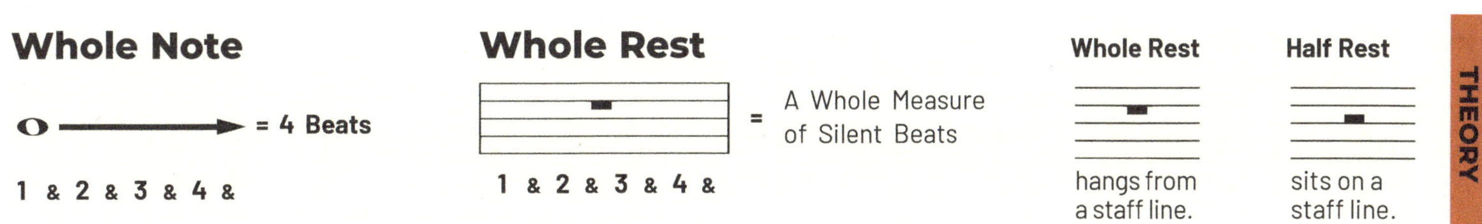

THEORY

Whole Note

= 4 Beats

1 & 2 & 3 & 4 &

Whole Rest

= A Whole Measure of Silent Beats

1 & 2 & 3 & 4 &

Whole Rest

hangs from a staff line.

Half Rest

sits on a staff line.

Teacher Practice with students the *Rhythm Rap*, exercise 150, using the suggested practice techniques from previous *Rhythm Raps*. Remind students that they must pull their bows very slowly and count carefully when playing whole notes. Emphasize the difference in placement on the staff of a whole rest and a half rest.

150. RHYTHM RAP *Shadow bow and count before playing.*

Count: 1 & 2 & 3 & 4 & 1 & 2 & 3 & 4 & 1 & 2 & 3 & 4 & 1 & 2 & 3 & 4 & 1 & 2 & 3 & 4 & 1 & 2 & 3 & 4 &
Dmi
A/C♯
B♭
F/A
C
F
Piano

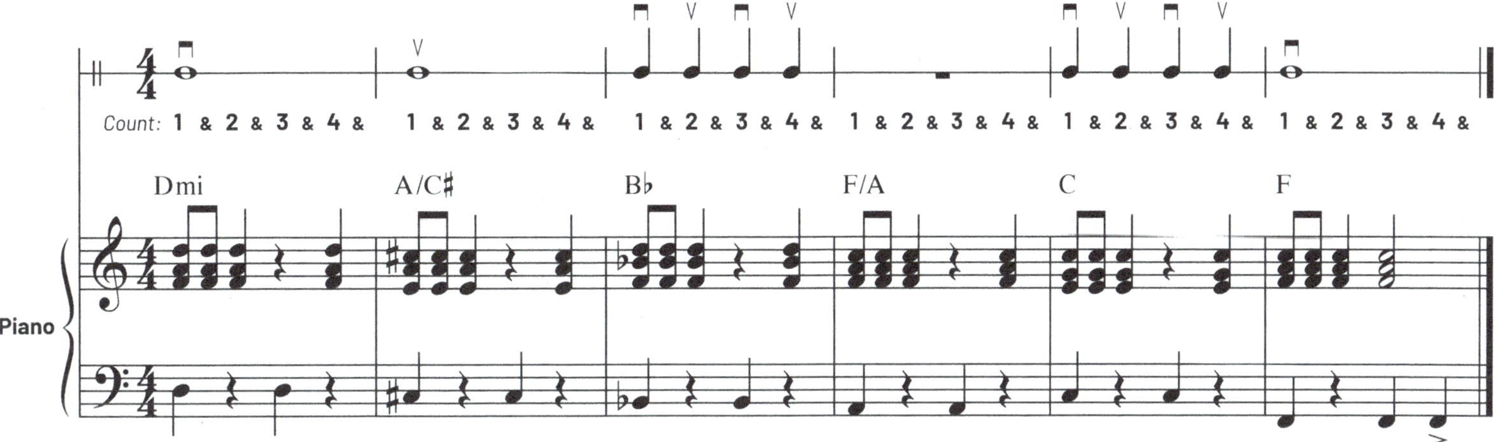

151. SLOW BOWS

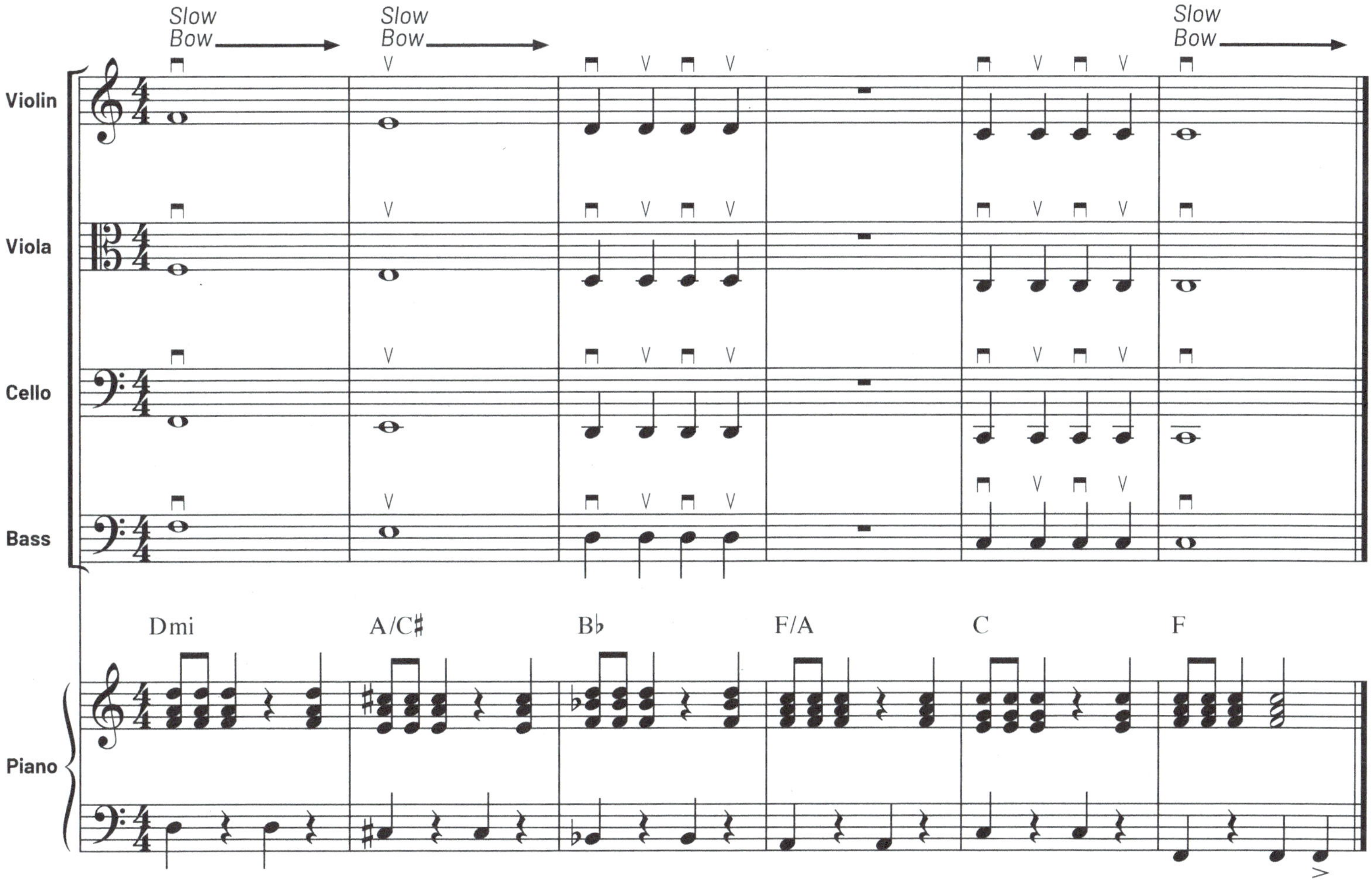

Slow Bow
Slow Bow
Slow Bow
Violin
Viola
Cello
Bass
Dmi
A/C♯
B♭
F/A
C
F
Piano

152. LONG, LONG AGO

T. H. Baily

THEORY

Arpeggio

An **arpeggio** is a chord whose pitches are played one at a time.
Your first arpeggio uses the 1st, 3rd, 5th, and 8th steps from the C major scale.

Teacher Discuss the definition of arpeggio. Practice the arpeggio in the last four measures before playing the entire exercise.

153. C MAJOR SCALE AND ARPEGGIO

154. LISTEN TO OUR SECTIONS

Violin Viola Cello Bass Vln. Vla. Cello Bass All

Violin

Viola

Cello

Bass

N.C. G7 C

Piano

155. MONDAY'S MELODY

Traditional Folk Song

Moderato

Violin

Viola

4

Cello

Bass

4 1 4 1 –1 –2 0

III I

C F C F D7 G

Piano

Fine
Violin
Viola
Cello
Bass
0
4
1
4
1
–1
–2
III
I
C
F
C
F
C
A mi
D7
G7
C
Piano
D.C. al Fine
Violin
Viola
Cello
Bass
–1
1
4
1
4
1
1
1
4
1
4
1
III
F
C
F
C
F
C
A7
D7
G
Piano

Teacher The E string and the pitches A, G, and F♯ are introduced for violin on student book page 38. Fourth finger E on the A string is introduced on the viola. No new notes for the cello are introduced, while the E string and F♯ are introduced for the bass. Special writing exercises are provided for the viola and cello.

Violin

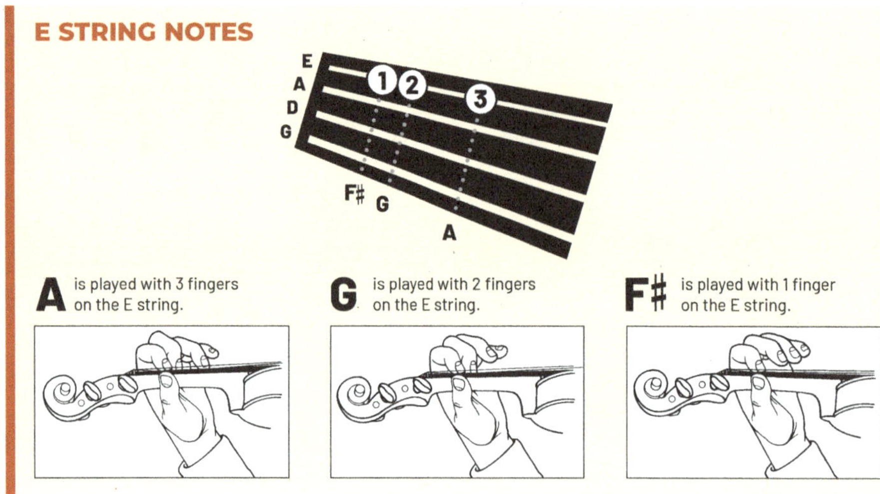

Viola

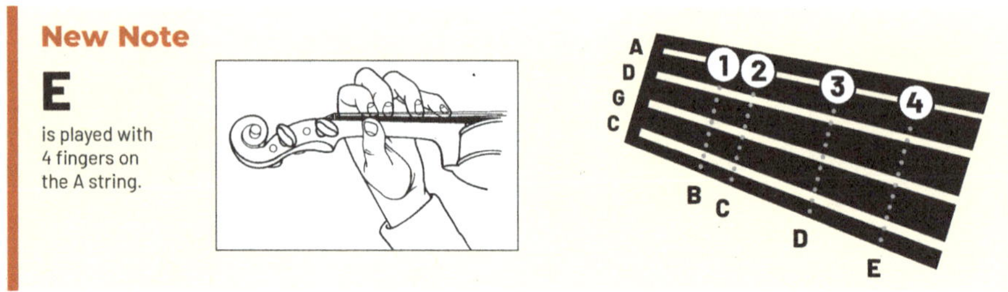

Cello

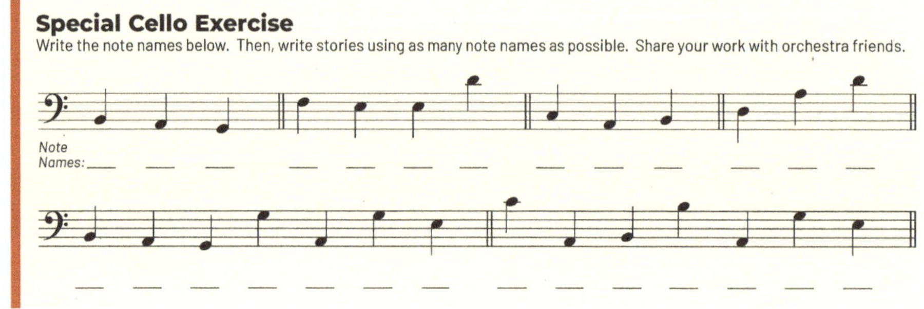

Bass

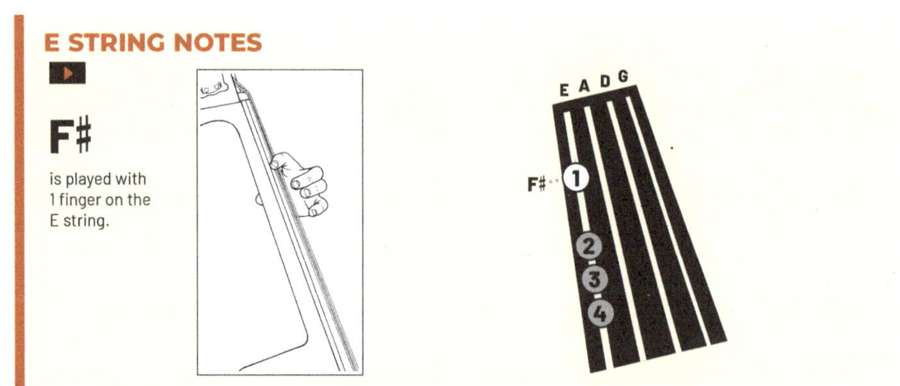

Viola/Cello

Team Work

Great musicians give encouragement to their fellow performers. Violin and bass players will now learn new challenging notes. The success of your orchestra depends on everyone's talent and patience. Play your best as these sections advance their musical technique.

Teacher Play the following Listening Skills patterns to begin introducing the new notes to students. Remember that the patterns may be played on any instrument.

Listening Skills

Play what your teacher plays. Listen carefully.

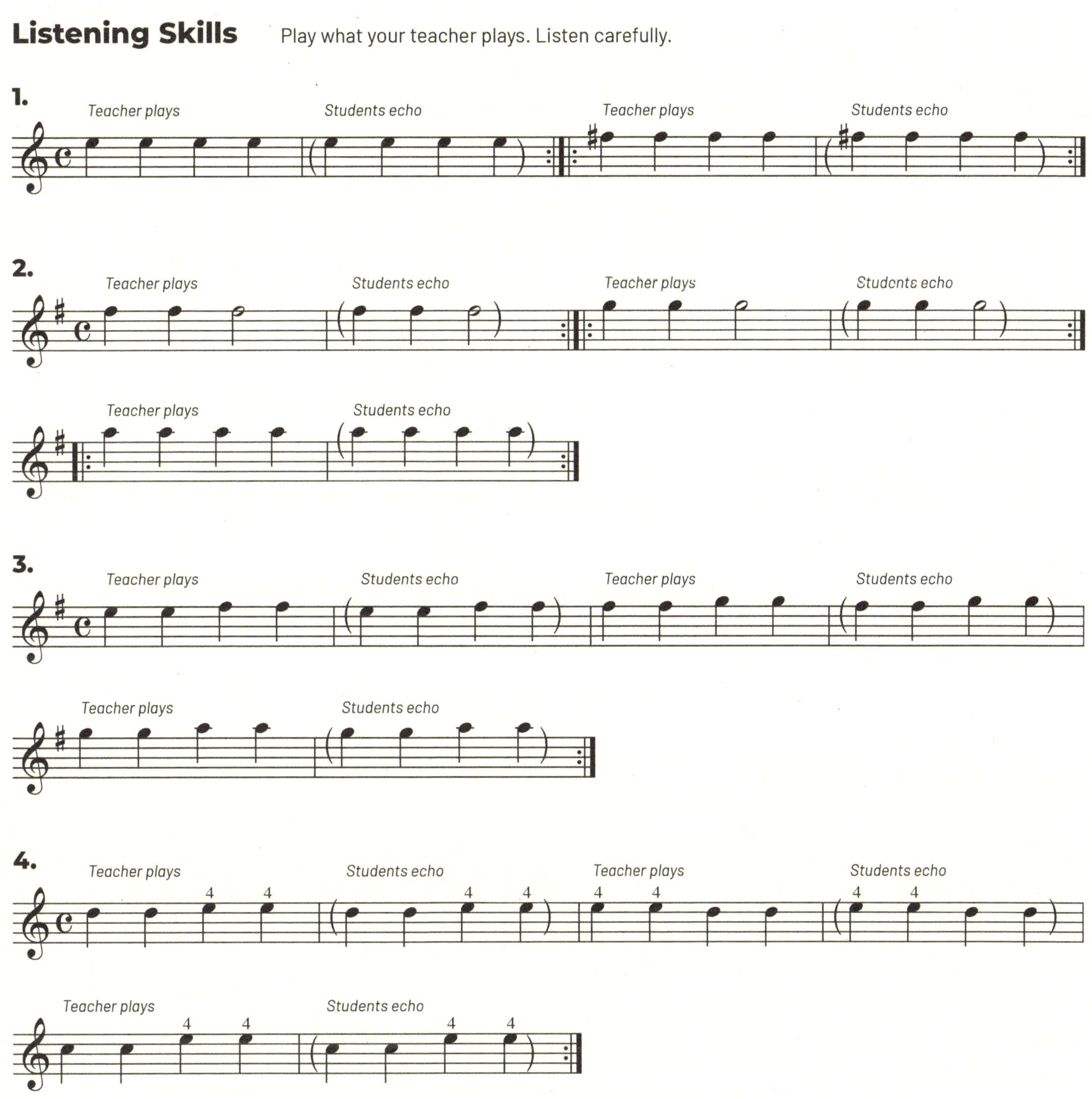

Violin
Viola
Bass
E
E
E

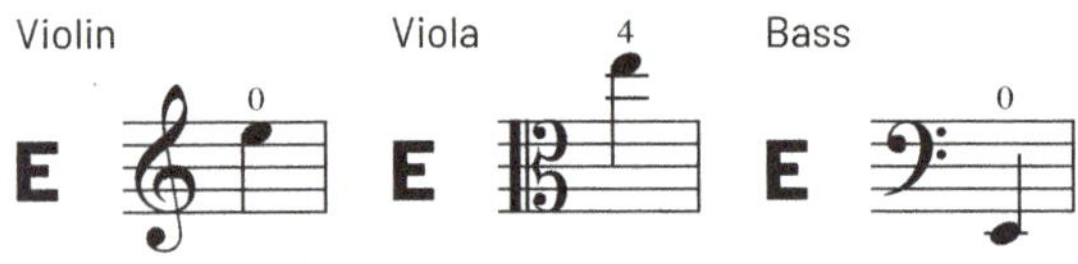

156. LET'S READ "E"

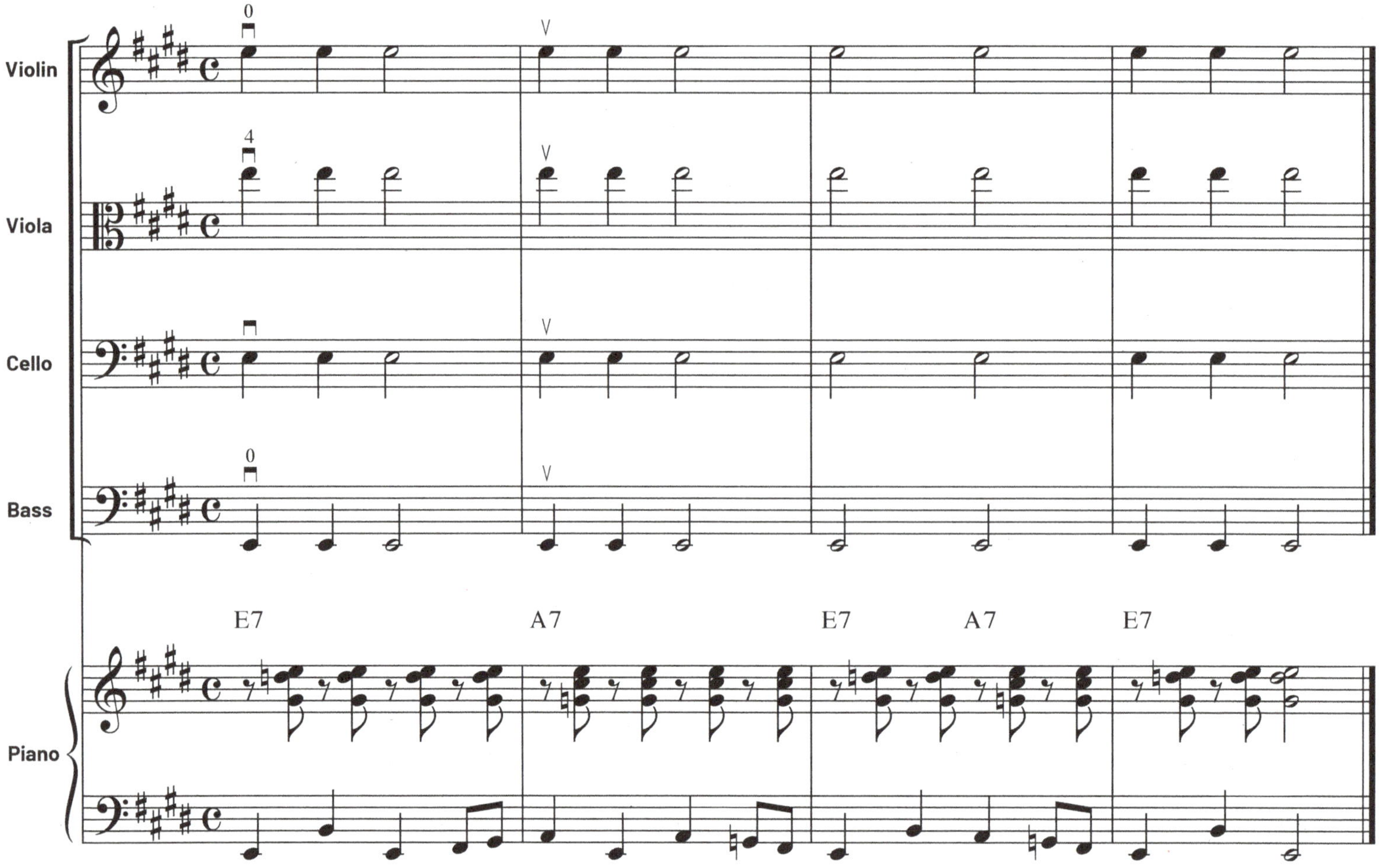
Violin
Viola
Cello
Bass
Piano
E7
A7
E7
A7
E7

Viola

Special Viola Exercise

Write the note names below. Then, write stories using as many note names as possible. Share your work with orchestra friends.

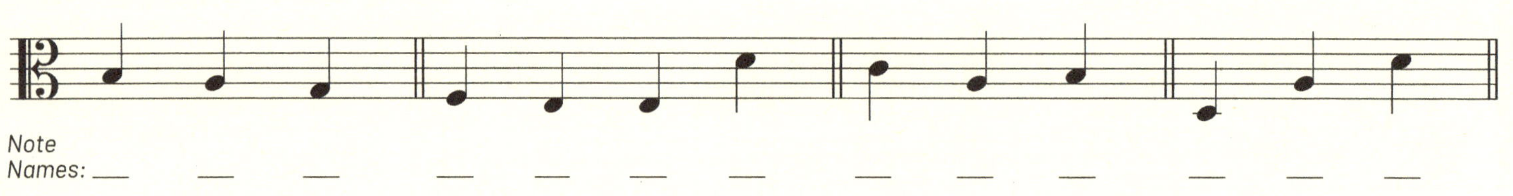

Note Names: ___ ___ ___ ___ ___ ___ ___ ___ ___ ___ ___ ___ ___

Viola

Team Work

Great musicians give encouragement to their fellow performers. Viola and bass players will now learn new challenging notes. The success of your orchestra depends on everyone's talent and patience. Play your best as these sections advance their musical technique.

Violin

A

3

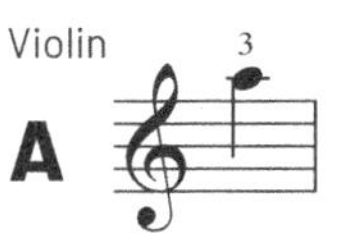

157. LET'S READ "A"

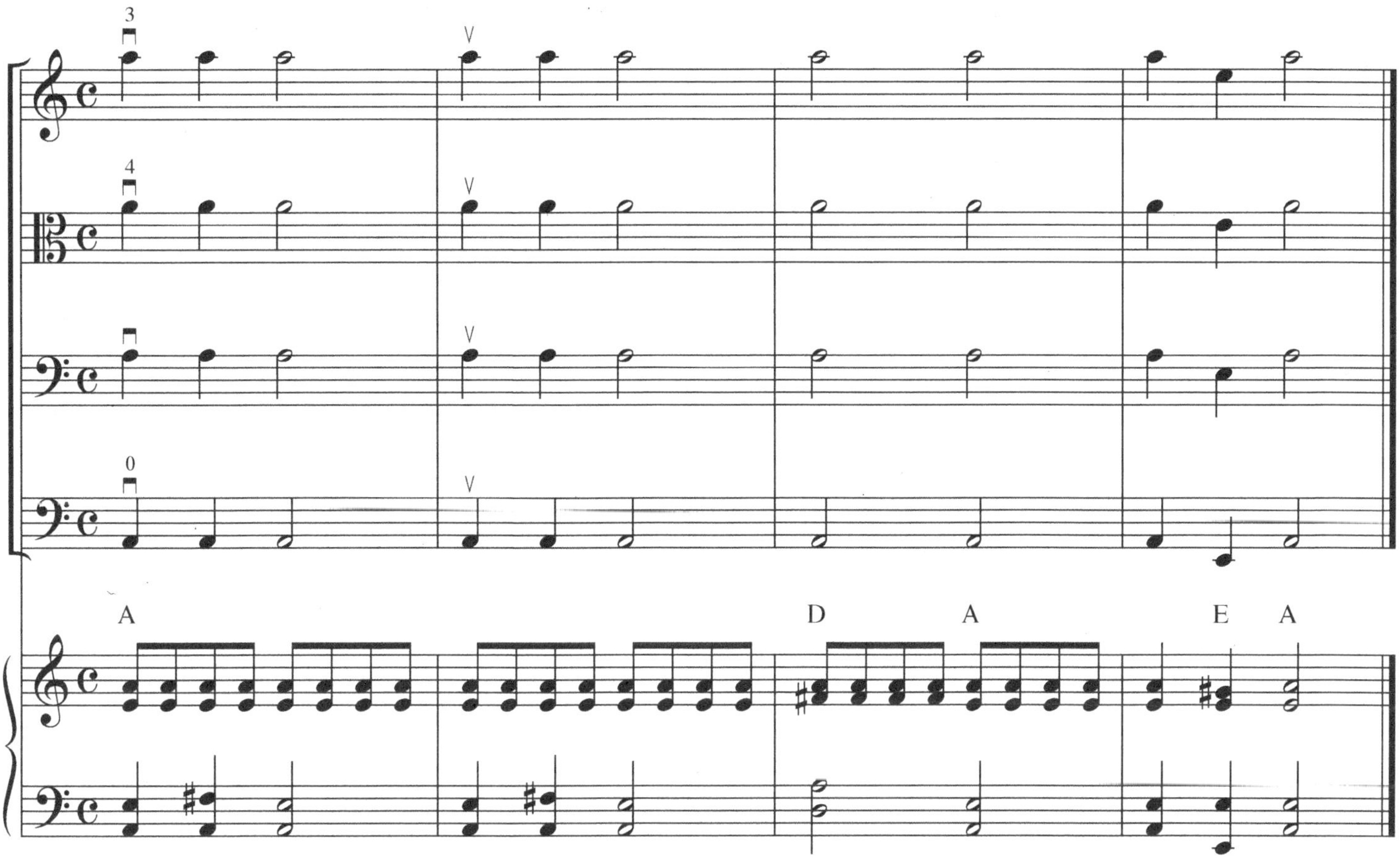
Violin
Viola
Cello
Bass
Piano
3
4
0
A
D
A
E
A

Violin

G

2

158. LET'S READ "G"

Violin
Viola
Cello
Bass
Piano
2
2
G5
F/G
G
F/G
G

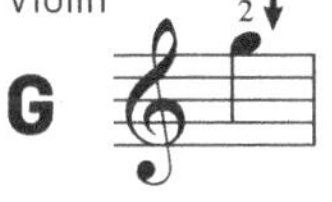

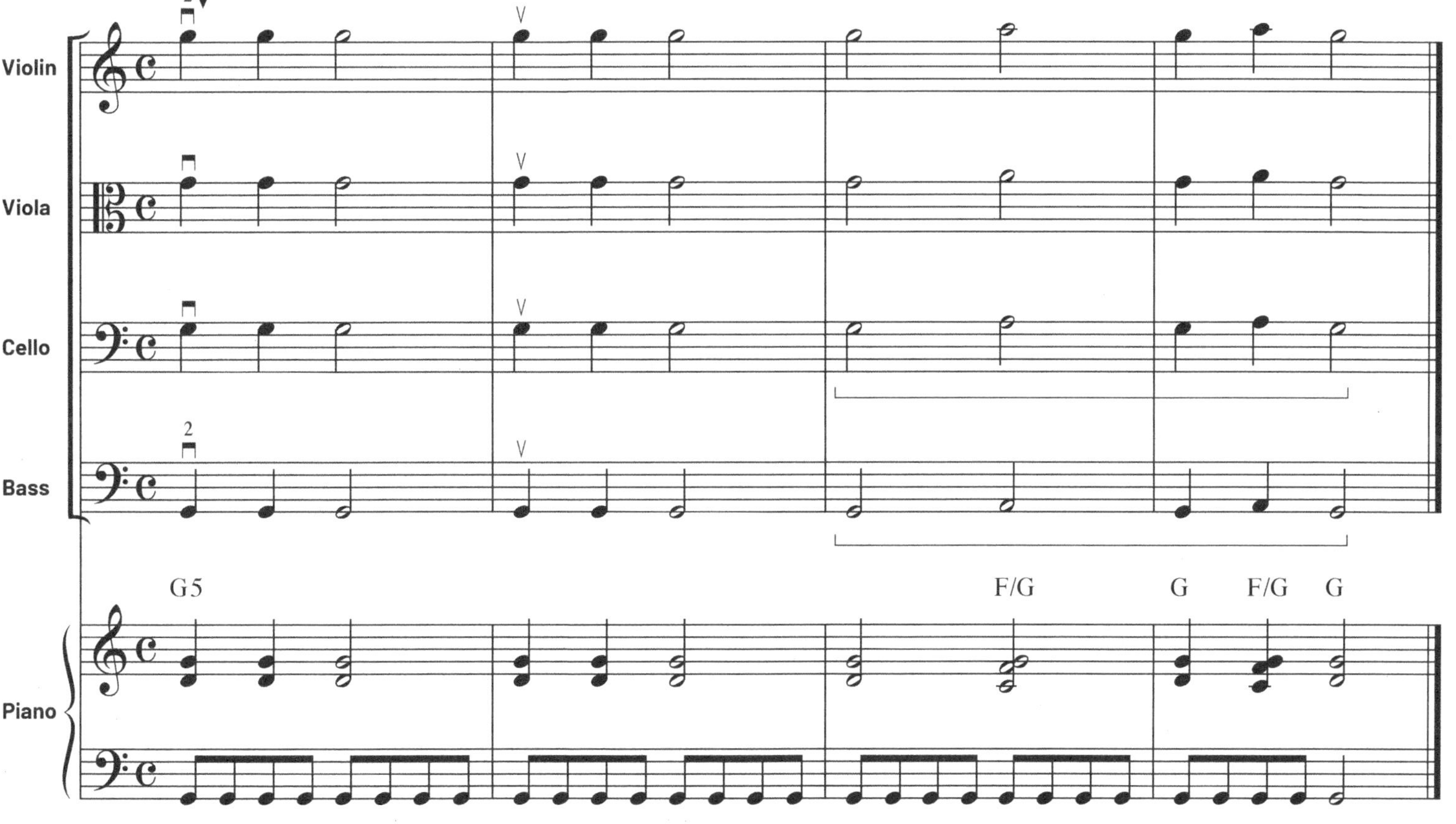

Violin
F♯
1

Bass
F♯
1

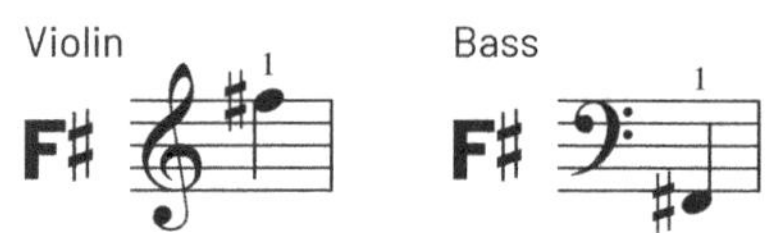

159. LET'S READ "F♯" (F-sharp)

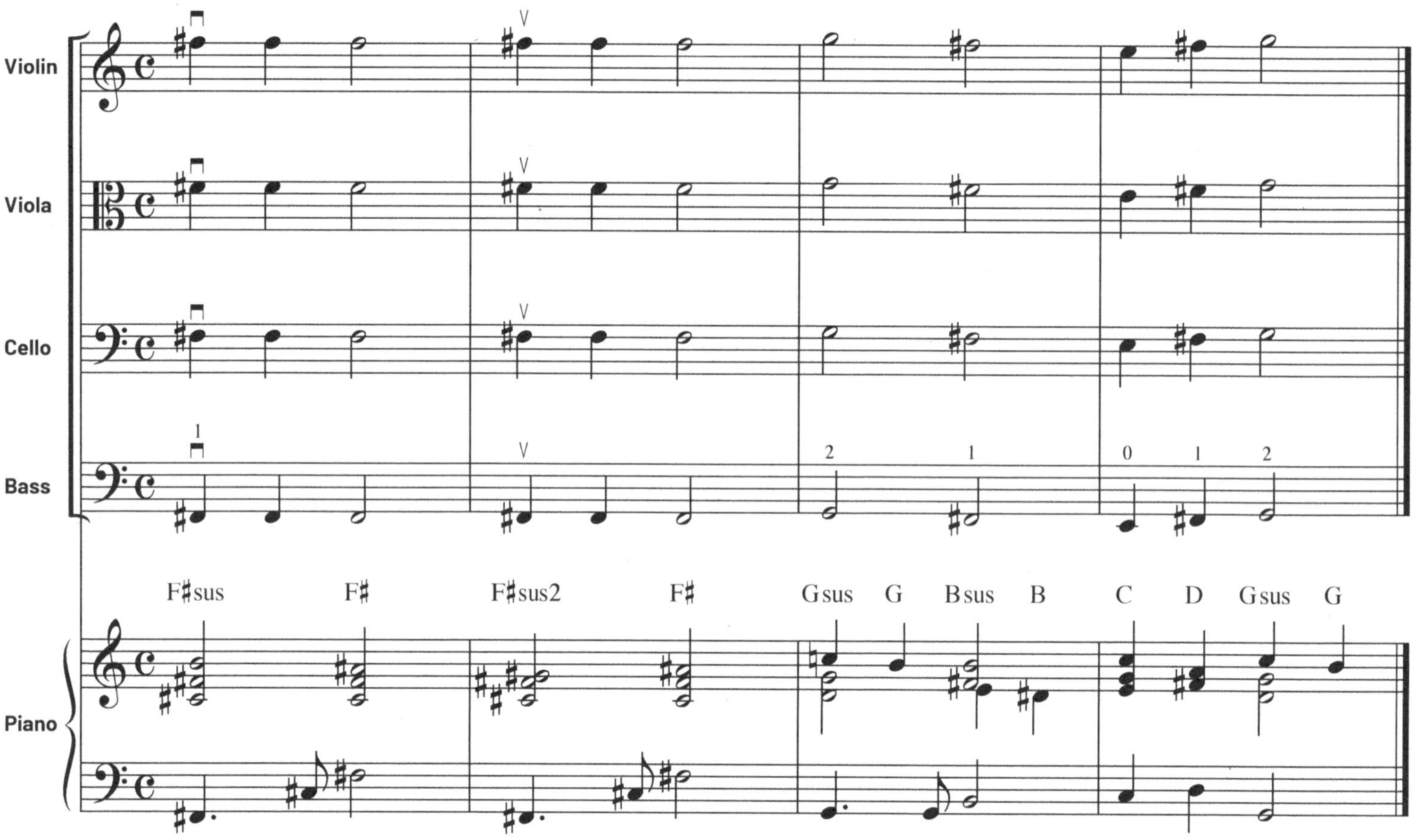
Violin
Viola
Cello
Bass
1
2 1
0 1 2
F♯sus F♯ F♯sus2 F♯ Gsus G Bsus B C D Gsus G
Piano

160. MOVING ALONG *Name the notes before you play.*

161. G MAJOR SCALE

Violin
Viola
Cello
Bass

2 0 1 2 0 1 4 0

G D G F G C D G

Piano

Violin
Viola
Cello
Bass

G B7 C G C G F D G

Piano

162. SHEPHERD'S HEY
English Folk Song
Moderato
Violin
Viola
Cello
Bass
Piano
D5 Emi/D D Dsus A7 D5 D5/C G/B G/B♭ D/A A7sus D
163. BIG ROCK CANDY MOUNTAIN
American Folk Song
Allegro
1.
A7 D A7 D A7 D A7 D A7

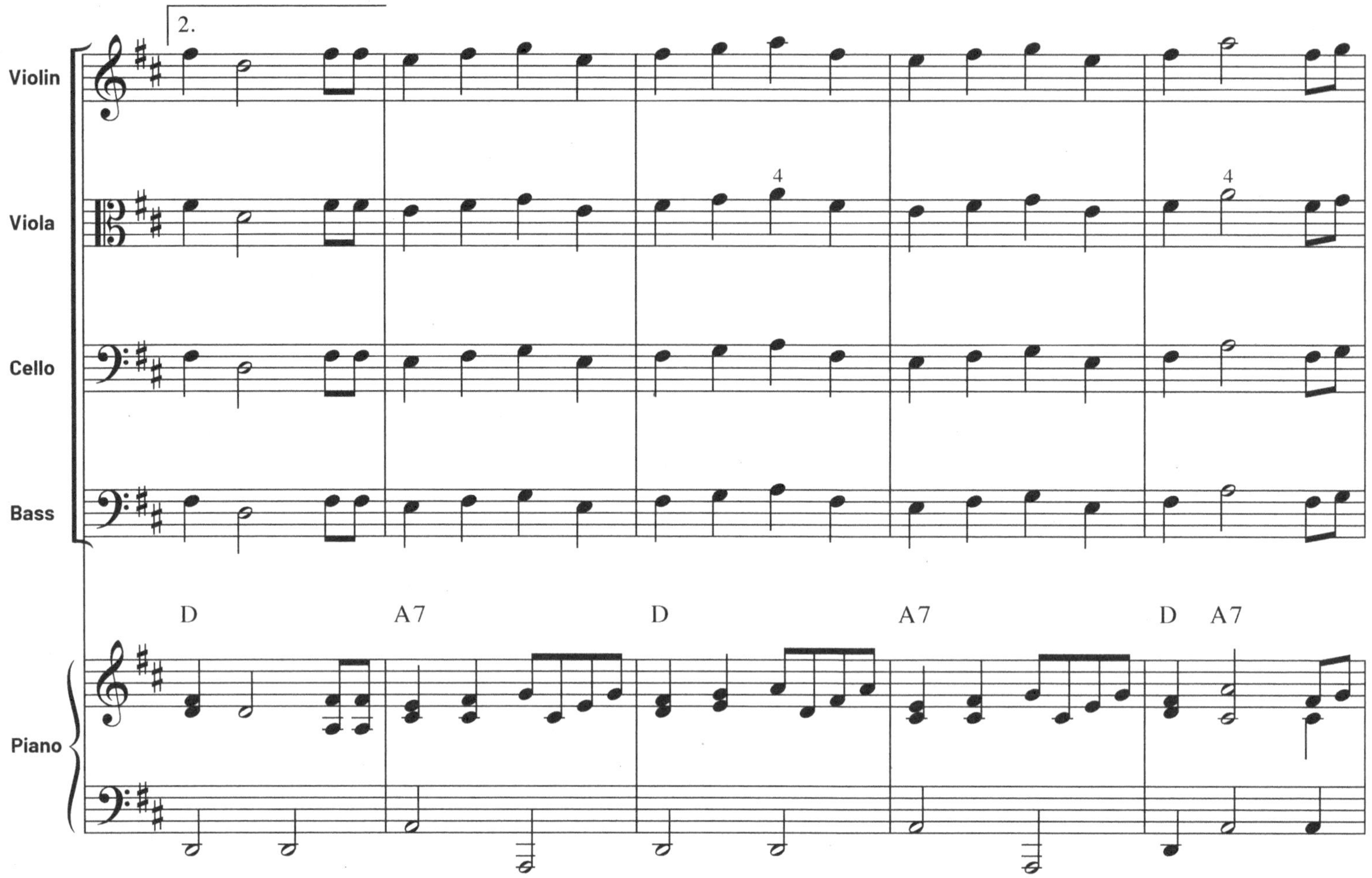

2.

Violin

Viola

Cello

Bass

D A7 D A7 D A7

Piano

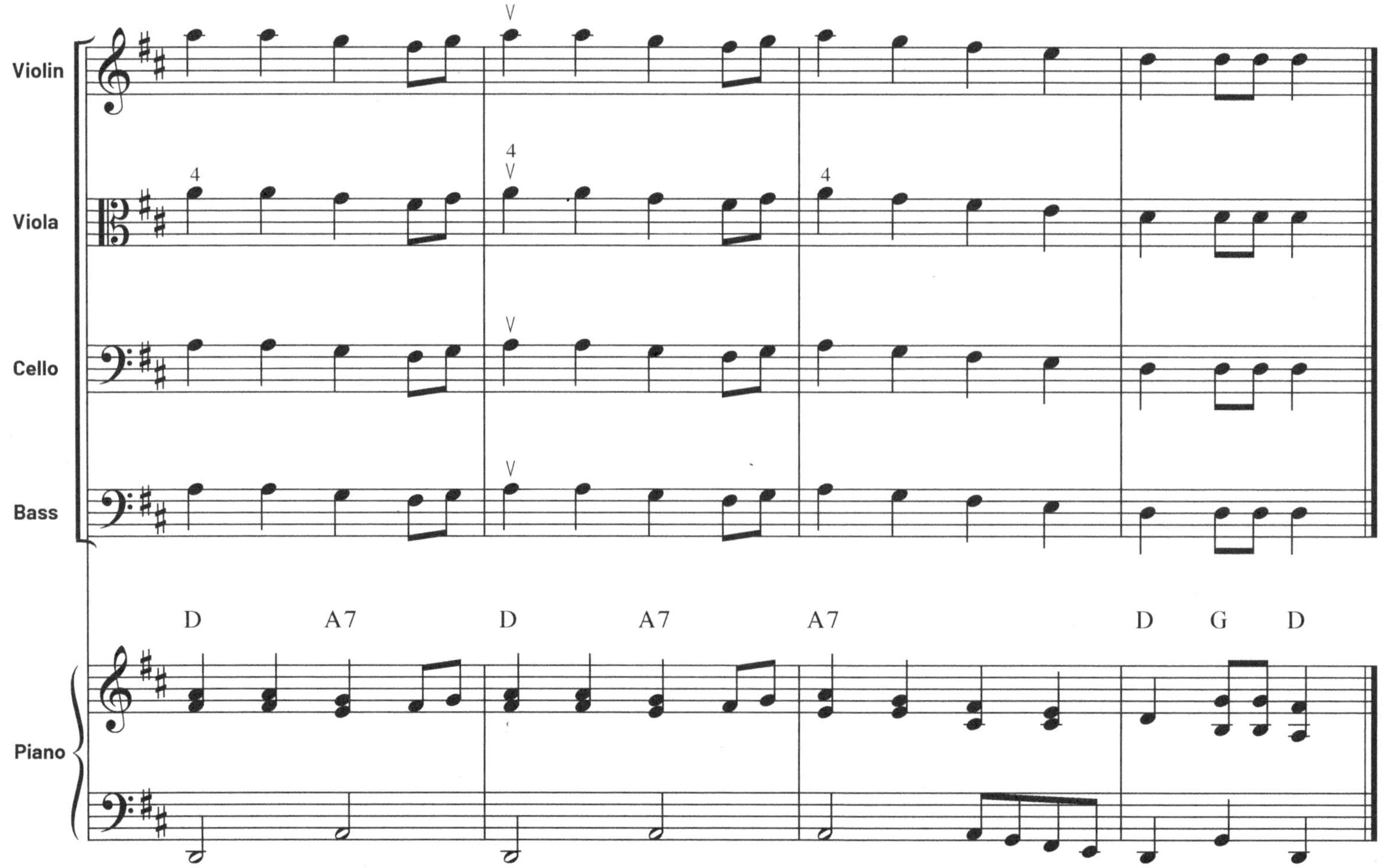

Violin

Viola

Cello

Bass

D A7 D A7 A7 D G D

Piano

Violin

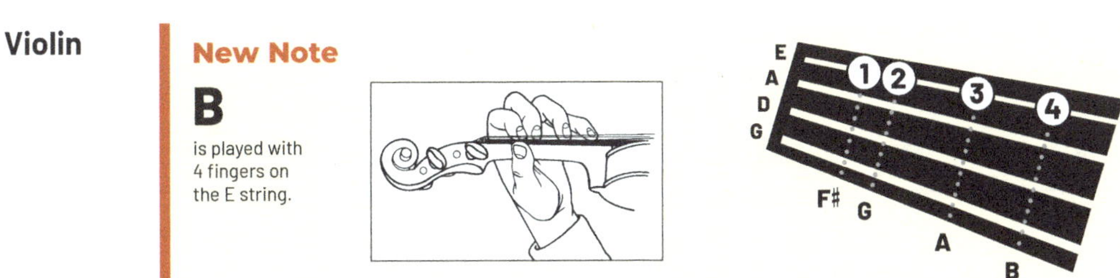

Teacher The note B is introduced for the violin on student book page 39. Use the following *Listening Skills* echo patterns to help students learn this new pitch.

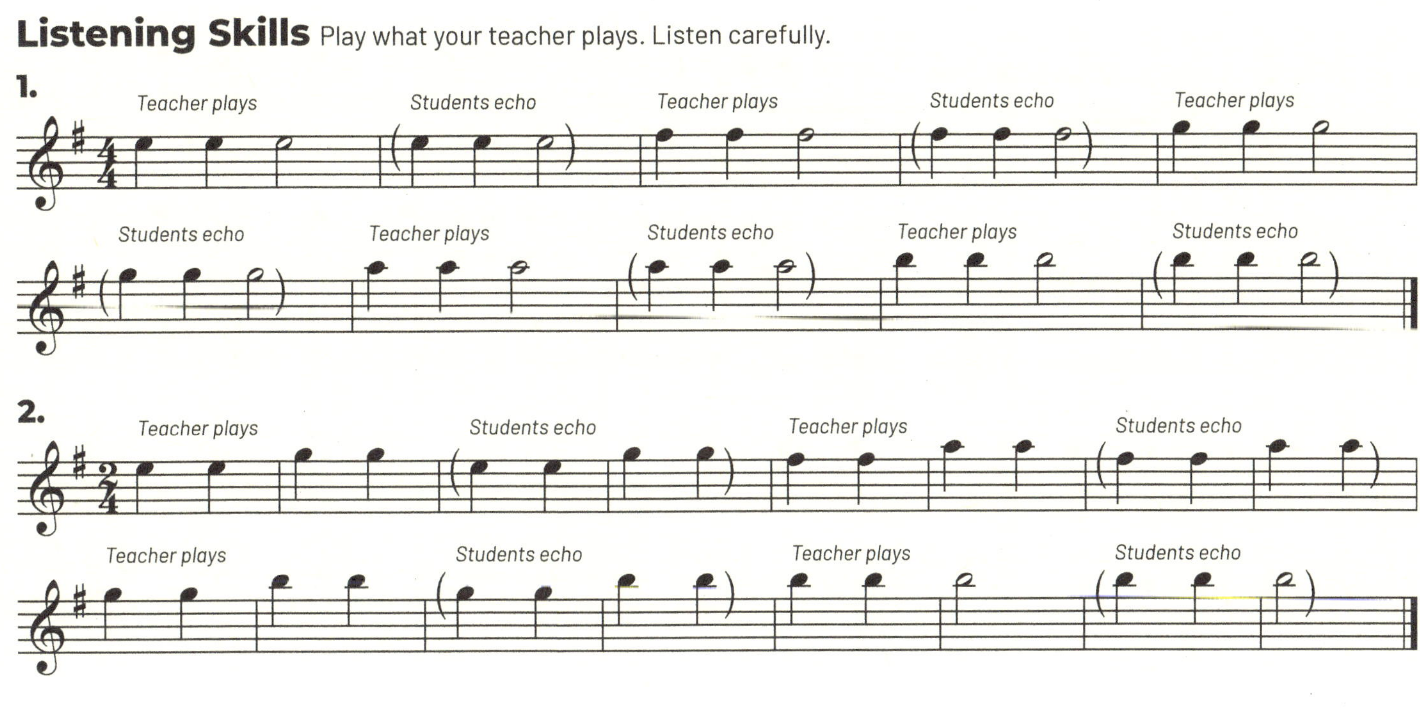

164. LET'S READ "B"

165. ICE SKATING

Moderato

Violin
Viola
Cello
Bass

D(add9) A/G Dma7 A/G D(add9)/F♯ Gma7 D(add9)/F♯ G(add9) G/A

Piano

Violin
Viola
Cello
Bass

Bmi Dma7/A A7sus Dma7/A Gma7 Emi7 G/A D(add9)

Piano

Teacher Familiarize students with different examples of music by Johannes Brahms. Play an excerpt of the melody in exercise 166 from a recording of the *Academic Festival Overture*.

QUIZ OBJECTIVES – ACADEMIC FESTIVAL OVERTURE THEME

- E string notes
- Upbeat

Review Exercises:

162. *Shepherd's Hey*
163. *Big Rock Candy Mountain*
165. *Ice Skating*

166. ESSENTIAL ELEMENTS QUIZ – ACADEMIC FESTIVAL OVERTURE THEME

Johannes Brahms

Additional bonus songs are available online. See the inside front cover for details.

Staccato notes are marked with a dot above or below the note. A staccato note is played with a stopped bow stroke. Listen for a space between staccato notes.

Teacher Staccato bowing is introduced at the top of student book page 40. Demonstrate the stroke for students. Point out how the staccato stroke begins with a slight pinch of the index finger on the bow stick. You may have students just practice the pinching motion at the balance point of their bow as a separate task before they pull the bow to start the staccato stroke. Have students practice their staccato bowing on open strings first, then on familiar scales.

167. PLAY STACCATO

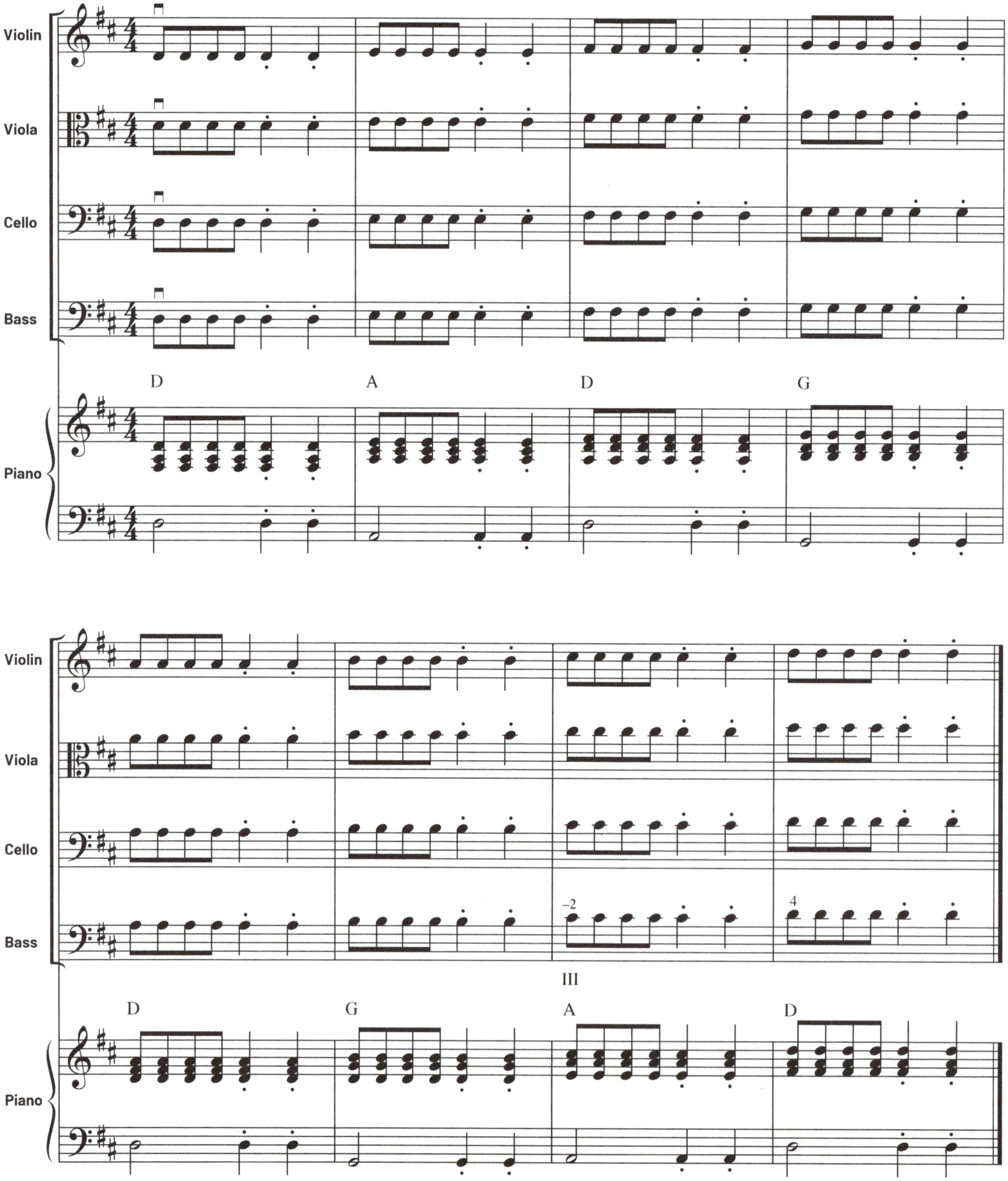

Violin

Viola

Cello

Bass

D A D G

Piano

168. ARKANSAS TRAVELER

Southern American Folk Song

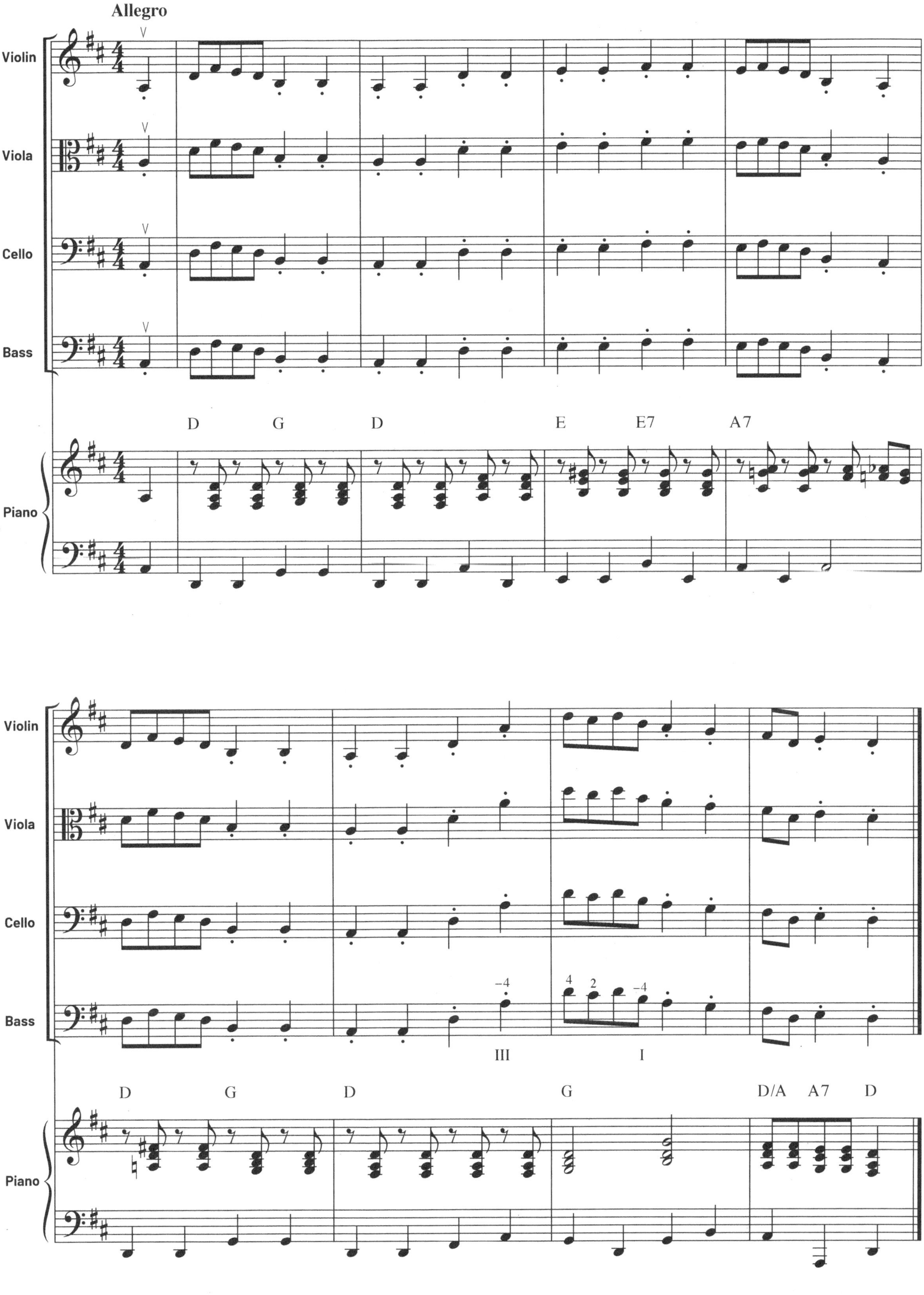
Allegro
Violin
Viola
Cello
Bass
Piano
D G D E E7 A7
Violin
Viola
Cello
Bass
−4
4 2 −4
III I
D G D G D/A A7 D
Piano

Teacher *EE SKILL BUILDERS - G MAJOR* appears on student book page 40. Its purpose is to reinforce students' understanding of G major, especially the upper octave incorporating the E string on the violin.

SKILL BUILDERS – G Major

171.

SKILL BUILDERS – G Major

Hooked Bowing

Hooked bowing is two or more notes played in the same direction with a stop between each note.

Teacher Demonstrate hooked bowing for students. Explain that hooked staccato notes simply involve bowing two staccato pitches in the same direction. As students practice their hooked bowing, their bows should completely stop between pitches. Practice hooked bowing on open strings first and then on familiar scales, as in exercises 174 and 175.

174. HOOKED ON D MAJOR

Violin

Viola

Cello

Bass

−2 4

III

Dsus D Asus A D Gsus G Dsus D Esus E A A/C♯ Dsus D

Piano

Violin

Viola

Cello

Bass

–4

I

G A/G G A/G G/A Bmi Asus A Dsus D

Piano

175. WALTZING BOWS

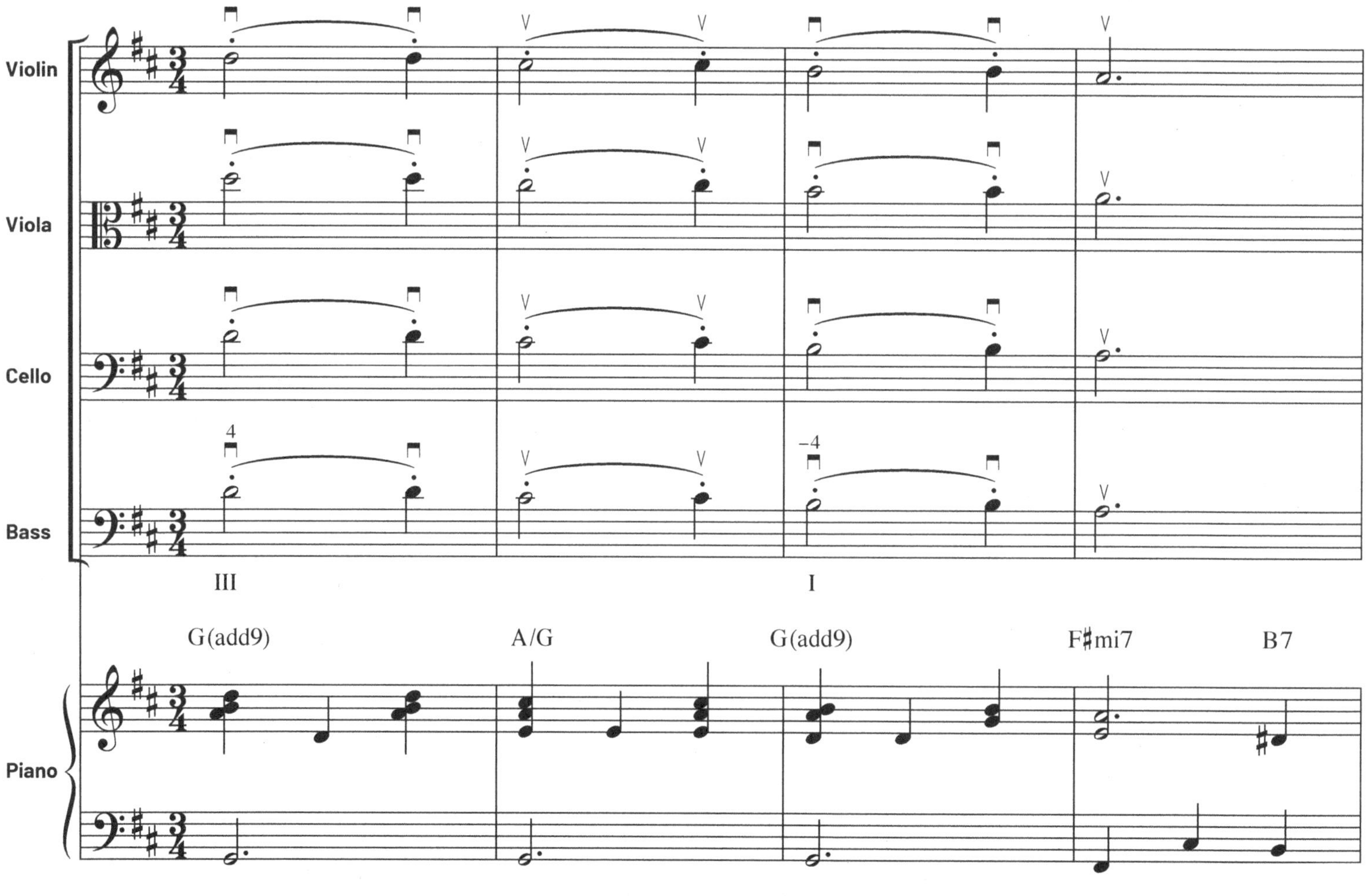

Violin

Viola

Cello

Bass

4

–4

III I

G(add9) A/G G(add9) F♯mi7 B7

Piano

Violin
Viola
Cello
Bass
Emi7
G/A
Bmi7
C
A7
D
Piano
176. POP GOES THE WEASEL
American Folk Song
Allegro
Violin
Viola
Cello
Bass
D
A7
D
Piano

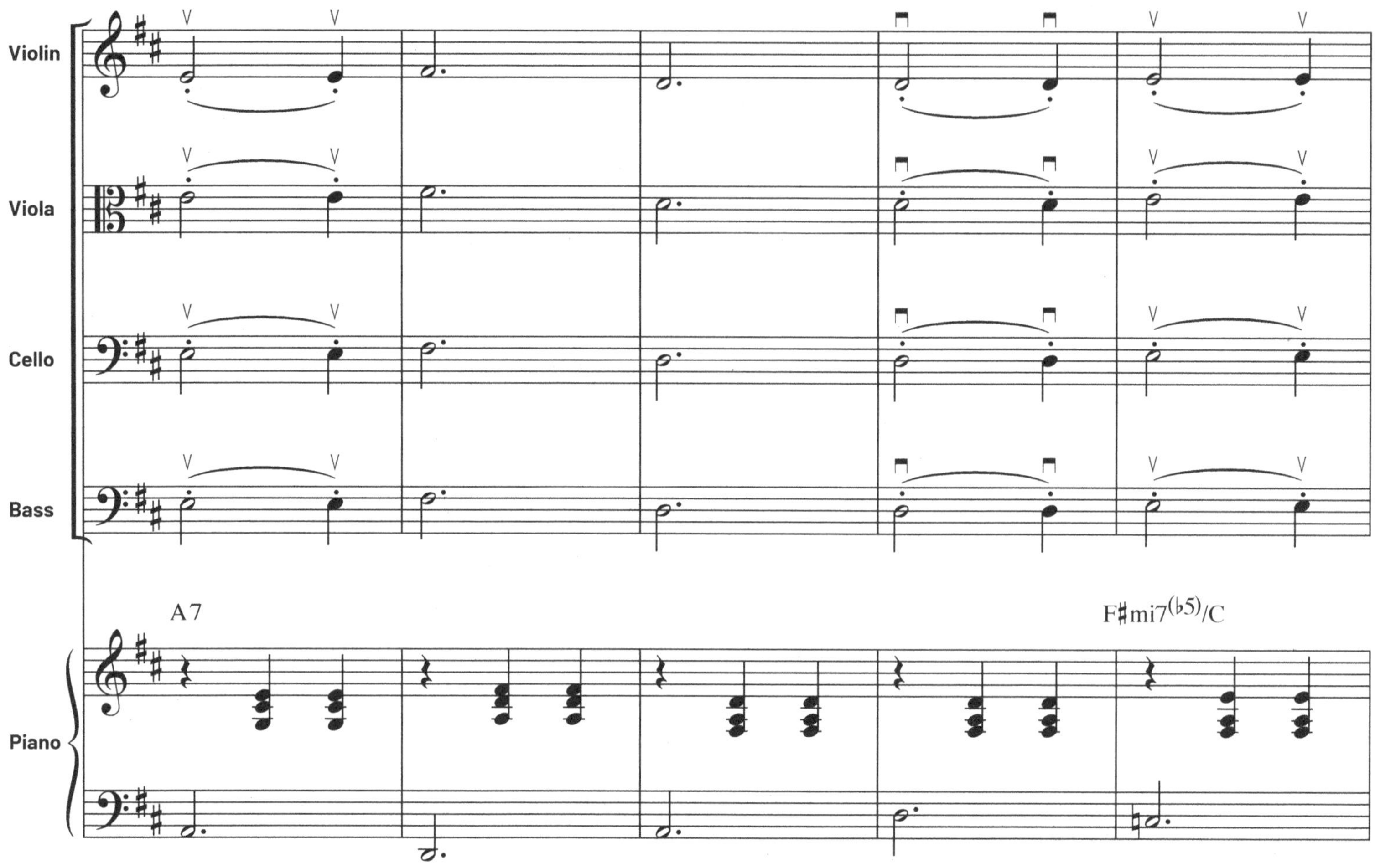

Violin
Viola
Cello
Bass

A7 F♯mi7(♭5)/C

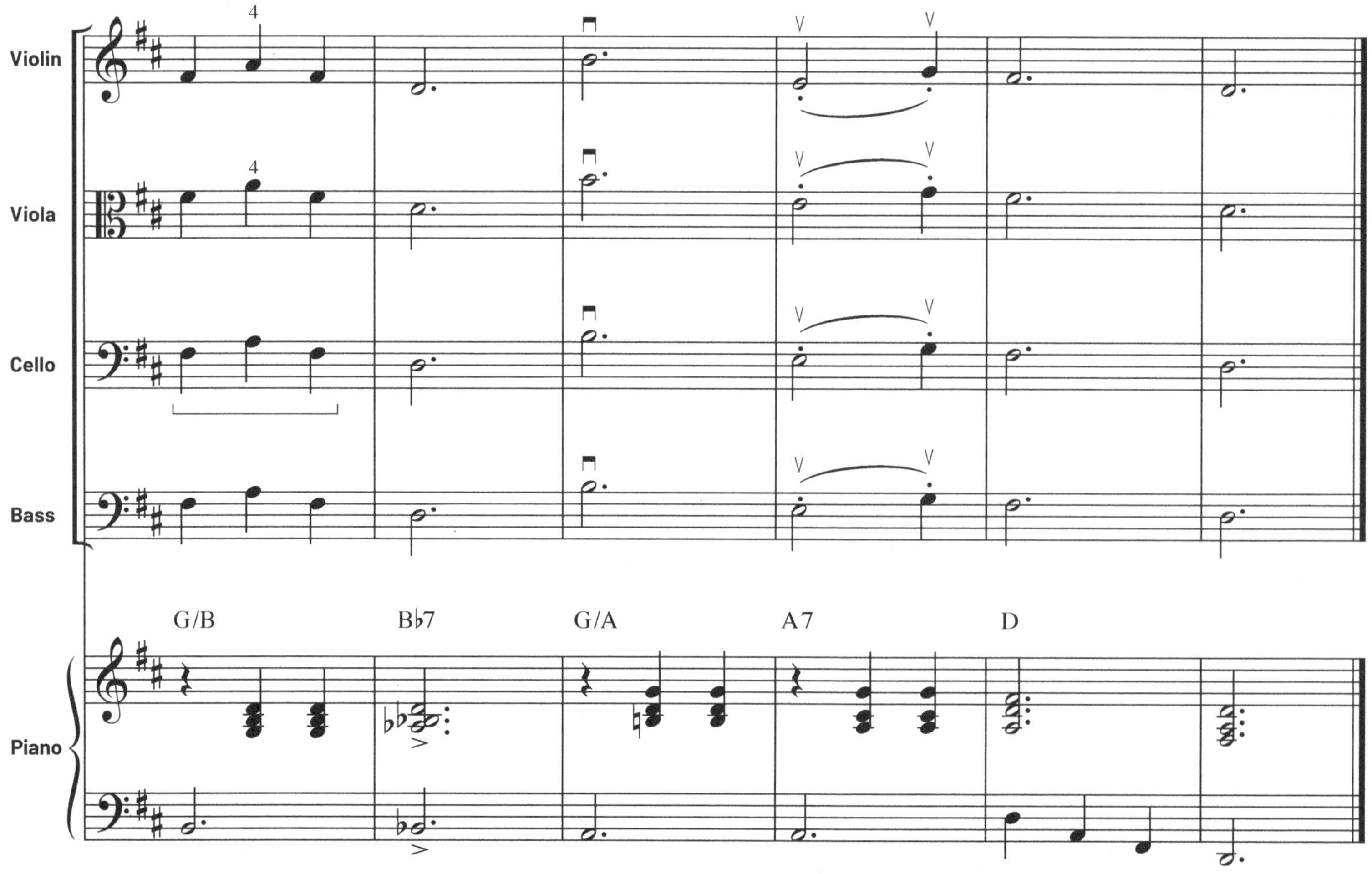

Piano

Violin
Viola
Cello
Bass

G/B B♭7 G/A A7 D

Piano

Teacher *EE SKILL BUILDERS - C MAJOR* will reinforce students' understanding of C major, especially the lower octave incorporating the C string on the viola and cello.

SKILL BUILDERS – C Major

SKILL BUILDERS – C Major

Dynamics

Dynamics tell us what volume to play or sing.

f (*forte*)	Play loudly. Add more weight to the bow.
p (*piano*)	Play softly. Remove weight from the bow.

Teacher The definition of forte and piano dynamics is given at the top of student book page 42. Play listening skill exercises incorporating different dynamic levels in preparation for exercises 181 and 182.

181. FORTE AND PIANO

Student books have repeats, not 1st and 2nd endings.

Teacher Familiarize students with the music of Franz Josef Haydn by playing recorded examples of his music, including the second movement of his Symphony No. 94 that contains The Surprise Symphony theme in exercise 182.

182. SURPRISE SYMPHONY THEME

Franz Josef Haydn

Violin
Viola
Cello
Bass
Piano

13
C F6 G7 C

Teacher *EE SKILL BUILDERS - SCALES and ARPEGGIOS* reviews and reinforces all the scales, and their related arpeggios, presented in this book.

SKILL BUILDERS – Scales and Arpeggios

Add your own dynamics to any of the lines below.

183. D MAJOR

Student books have repeats, not 1st and 2nd endings.

Violin
Viola
Cello
Bass
Piano

III I III I
D G D A D Bmi G D D

SKILL BUILDERS – Scales and Arpeggios

SKILL BUILDERS – Scales and Arpeggios

PERFORMANCE SPOTLIGHT

Teacher The following orchestra arrangements in the *PERFORMANCE SPOTLIGHT* are found on student book pages 43–44. The A and B parts for each instrument section may be combined in any way. All instruments have been provided with melody parts. However, for performance purposes the arrangements are designed for the violins to be divided between parts A and B and for all other instruments to perform part B.

188. CRIPPLE CREEK – Orchestra Arrangement (**A** = Melody and **B** = Harmony)

American Folk Song
Arr. Michael Allen

Violin
A
B
Viola
A
B
Cello
A
B
Bass
A
B
Piano
D
A7sus/D
D
D
A7sus/D
A7
D

HISTORY

Africa is a large continent made up of many nations, and African folk music is as diverse as its many cultures. This folk song is from Kenya. The words describe warriors as they prepare for battle. Listen to examples of African folk music and describe the sound.

Teacher Play recordings of African folk music and have students describe the sounds they hear.

189. TEKELE LOMERIA – Orchestra Arrangement

Kenyan Warrior Song
Arr. John Higgins

A
Violin
B
A
Viola
B
A
Cello
B
A
Bass
B
Piano
Dmi7
C5
Dmi7
C5 A5 Dmi
p
f

PERFORMANCE SPOTLIGHT

HISTORY

Italian composer **Gioachino Rossini** (1792–1868) wrote some of the world's favorite operas. "William Tell" was Rossini's last opera, and its popular theme is still heard on television.

Teacher Familiarize students with the music of Gioachino Rossini by playing recorded examples of his works in class. He wrote many lively overtures, such as the *Overture to William Tell*, which are interesting for young students to hear.

190. WILLIAM TELL OVERTURE – Orchestra Arrangement

Gioachino Rossini
Arr. John Higgins

Fine
A
Violin
B
f
A
Viola
B
f
A
Cello
B
f
A
Bass
B
f
G
D/G
G
D
Fine
Piano
III
I

9
Violin
A
B
Viola
A
B
Cello
A
B
Bass
A
B
9
Emi
B7
Emi
B7
Emi
Piano

D.C. al Fine
Violin
A
B
Viola
A
B
Cello
A
B
Bass
A
B
Piano
D A7 D
D.C. al Fine

191. ROCKIN' STRINGS – Orchestra Arrangement

John Higgins

Violin
A
B
Viola
A
B
Cello
A
B
Bass
A
B
Piano
1.
2.
II
I
G7 C/G Dmi/G C/G G7 C/G Dmi/G G D7 G/D Ami/D G/D D7 A7 D7

PERFORMANCE SPOTLIGHT

192. SIMPLE GIFTS – Orchestra Arrangement

Shaker Folk Song
Arr. John Higgins

Violin
A
B
Viola
A
B
Cello
A
B
Bass
A
B
Piano
III
I
D
Bmi7
G(add9)
D
G6/9
A

10
Violin
A
B
4
p
Viola
A
B
Cello
A
B
Bass
A
B
Piano
G
Emi7
D
N.C.
C
D5
A5

Violin
A
B
Viola
A
B
Cello
A
B
Bass
A
B
Piano
D
D/G5
A5
A
G
Emi7
D
N.C.
opt.

19
Violin
A
B
Viola
A
B
Cello
A
B
Bass
A
B
III
I
19
D
D/C♯
Bmi7
D/A
G6/9
D/F♯
A/G
Piano

Essential Elements for Strings Correlated Literature

Students will enjoy playing their own special part in string orchestra arrangements. The Explorer level of *Essential Elements for Strings* series is a collection of string orchestra arrangements that only use the rhythms, bowings, and notes that are introduced on pages student book page 1–42 (Teacher Manual pages 39–233). See your Hal Leonard dealer for the latest releases.

PERFORMANCE SPOTLIGHT – Violin

Solo with Piano Accompaniment

A solo is a composition written for one player, often with piano accompaniment. This solo was written by **Johann Sebastian Bach** (1685-1750). You and a piano accompanist can perform for the orchestra, your school, your family and other occasions. When you have learned the piece well, try memorizing it. Performing for an audience is an exciting part of being involved in music.

Teacher Each instrument has its own solo as a part of *PERFORMANCE SPOTLIGHT* on student book page 46. The solos may be used as a new musical experience for the string student and as a reward for effort and achievement. The corresponding piano accompaniments are included in each student book. Consider featuring these solos on concerts, performed by individual students or by instrument sections.

193. MINUET NO. 1 – Solo

Johann Sebastian Bach
Arr. by John Higgins

PERFORMANCE SPOTLIGHT – Viola

Solo with Piano Accompaniment

A solo is a composition written for one player, often with piano accompaniment. This solo was written by **Johann Sebastian Bach** (1685-1750). You and a piano accompanist can perform for the orchestra, your school, your family and other occasions. When you have learned the piece well, try memorizing it. Performing for an audience is an exciting part of being involved in music.

193. MINUET IN C – Solo

Johann Sebastian Bach
Arr. by John Higgins

PERFORMANCE SPOTLIGHT – Cello

Solo with Piano Accompaniment

A solo is a composition written for one player, often with piano accompaniment. This solo was written by **Johann Sebastian Bach** (1685-1750). You and a piano accompanist can perform for the orchestra, your school, your family and other occasions. When you have learned the piece well, try memorizing it. Performing for an audience is an exciting part of being involved in music.

193. MINUET NO. 2 – Solo

Johann Sebastian Bach
Arr. by John Higgins

PERFORMANCE SPOTLIGHT – Bass

Solo with Piano Accompaniment

A solo is a composition written for one player, often with piano accompaniment. This solo was written by **Johann Sebastian Bach** (1685-1750). You and a piano accompanist can perform for the orchestra, your school, your family and other occasions. When you have learned the piece well, try memorizing it. Performing for an audience is an exciting part of being involved in music.

193. MARCH IN D – Solo

Johann Sebastian Bach
Arr. by John Higgins

Improvisation

Improvisation is the art of freely creating your own music as you play.

Teacher Students are given the opportunity to apply rhythms of their choice to the pitches provided In exercise 194, *Rhythm Jam*. Remind students that there must be a total of four beats in each measure. Inform them that they can use a variety of bowings including slurs, staccato and/or hooked bowings. Give students the opportunity to perform their examples in class. Some may even be selected to perform on a concert to reinforce and reward student creativity.

194. RHYTHM JAM *Using the following notes, improvise your own rhythms.*

Violin

Viola

Cello

Bass

Teacher Give students parameters when they begin to create their improvised melody in exercise 195. For example, instruct students to select pitches only from the D major scale. Also, remind them that there must be four beats in each measure. Consider limiting rhythmic values that students may use to help them in their creativity, e.g. using only quarter and half notes, or quarter and eighth notes. Suggest that their melody will sound more natural if it begins and ends on the pitch D. Have students write out their improvised melodies to reinforce their note and rhythmic reading. Allow students to perform their melodies while accompanied by other students playing the B line. Select students to play their newly created, improvised melodies on a concert.

195. INSTANT MELODY *Using the following notes, improvise your own melody (Line A), to go with the accompaniment (Line B).*

Teacher The following fingering charts appear on page 47 of each student book.

Violin

VIOLIN FINGERING CHART

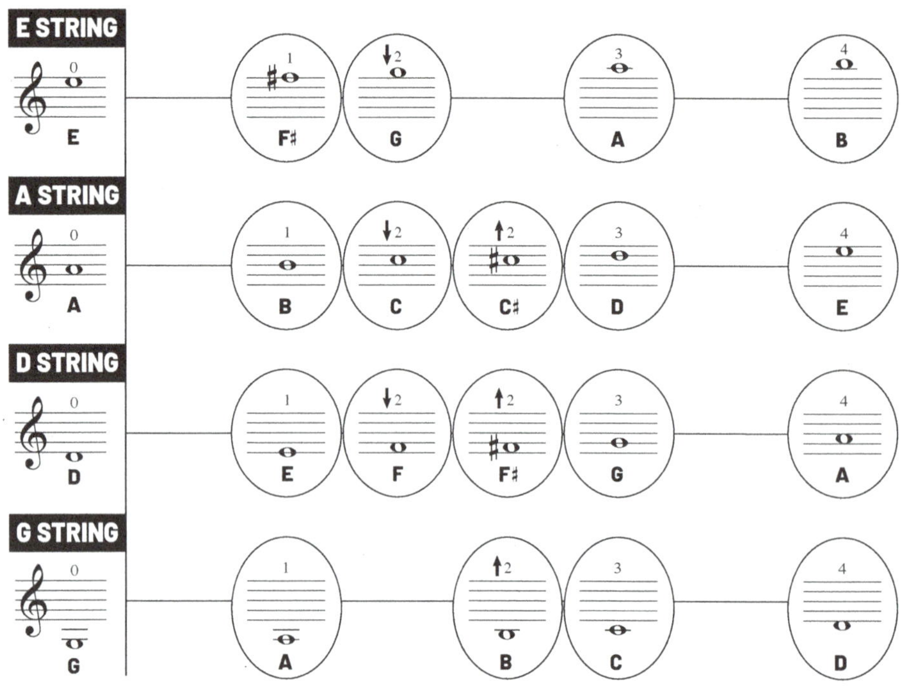

Viola

VIOLA FINGERING CHART

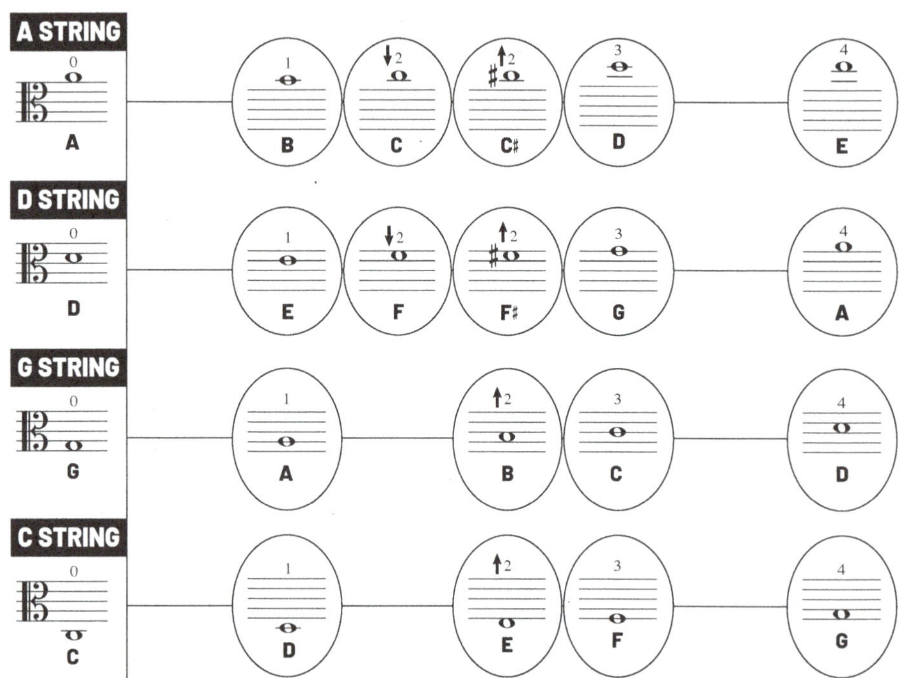

Cello

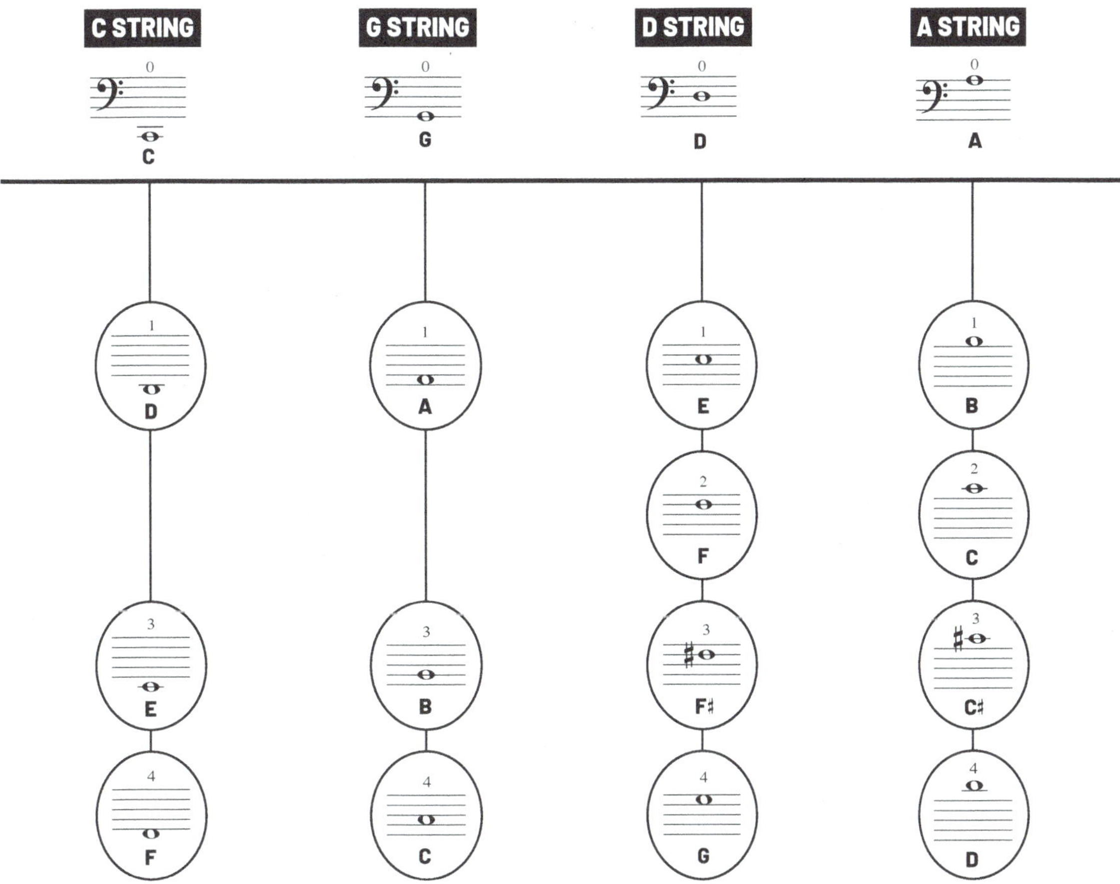

Bass

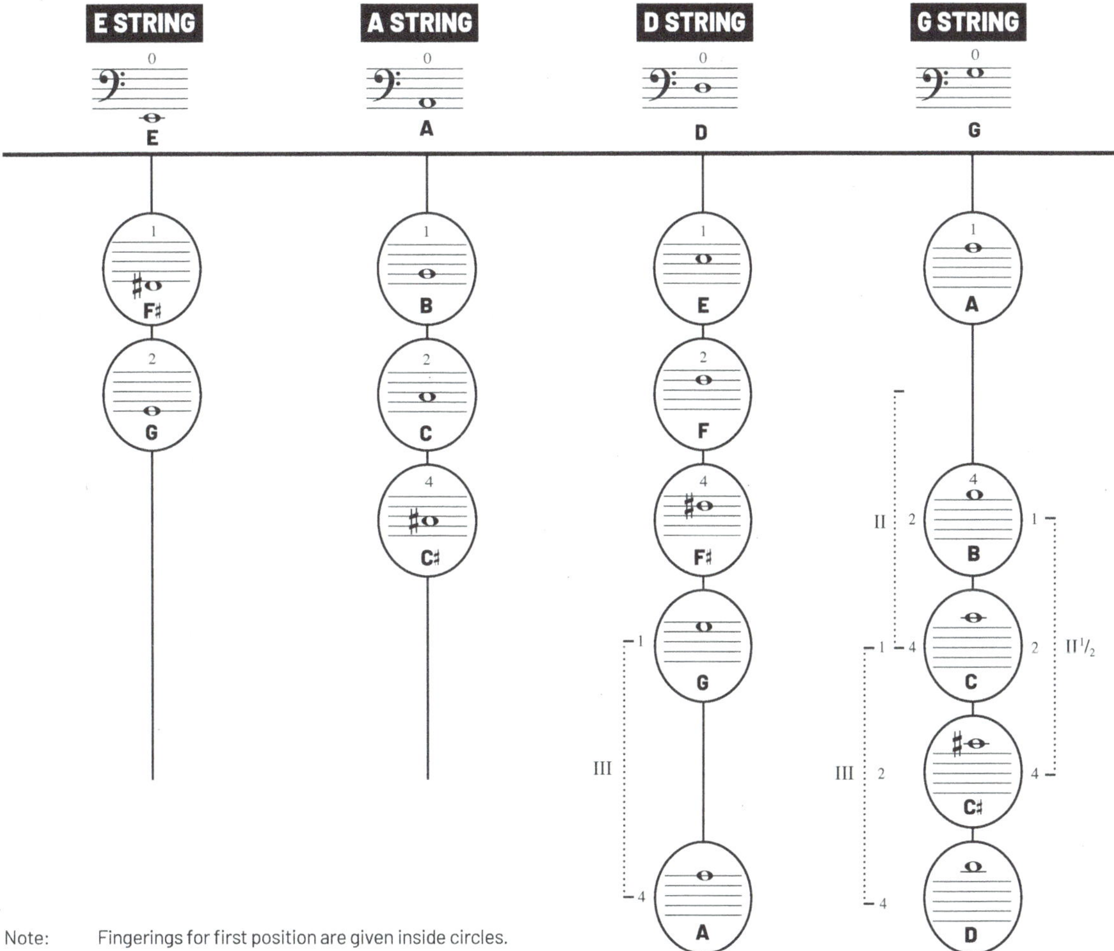

Note: Fingerings for first position are given inside circles.

Reference Index

Definitions (pg.)

Composers

World Music

Teacher The following may be photocopied and used as a student handout for instrument care.

TIPS FOR CARING FOR YOUR INSTRUMENT: WHAT TO DO AND WHAT NOT TO DO!

String instruments can last forever, but are easily damaged. To protect your instrument, be sure to follow these guidelines:

1. Never touch the bow hair, or the wooden part of the instrument with your hands.
2. Protect your instrument from extreme heat, cold, and quick temperature changes.
3. Wipe any rosin off your instrument with a soft cloth.
4. Place a cloth over your violin or viola before closing your case. Be sure to latch the case.
5. Loosen the bow hair after every use. Tighten it the same amount every time before playing.
6. Keep your instrument away from those who do not know how to properly care for it.
7. Do not attempt to repair your instrument. Tell your teacher or qualified music dealer if something needs to be fixed.

GUIDELINES FOR SELECTING THE CORRECT SIZED STRING INSTRUMENT FOR YOUR STUDENTS

Instrument	Size	Left Hand Span (Between pinky and index fingers)	Left Arm Length (From shoulder sleeve to end of middle finger)	Height
Violin	Full	5-6 inches	over 24 inches	
	3/4	4 1/2-5 inches	21-24 inches	
	1/2	4-4 1/2 inches	18-21 inches	
	1/4	3 1/2-4 inches	under 18 inches	
*Viola	16 inch	6 inches or more	28 inches or more	
	15 1/2 inch	6 inches	26-27 inches	
	15 inch	5-6 inches	25 inches	
	14 inch	5-6 inches	24 inches	
	13 1/4 inch	4 1/2-5 inches	21-24 inches	
Cello	Full	6 inches	24 inches	60 inches
	3/4	5 inches	22 inches	56 inches
	1/2	4 inches	20 inches	52 inches
	1/4	3 inches	18 inches	48 inches
Bass	3/4	6 1/2 inches	24 inches	over 60 inches
	1/2	5 3/4 inches	22 inches	56 inches
	1/4	5 inches	20 inches	52 inches

* A 3/4 violin and a junior viola are the same length. A full size violin is the same length as an intermediate viola.

Teacher This keyboard diagram can be used as a visual aid to help you explain to your students half steps and whole steps. You may make photocopies of this keyboard for use by your students.

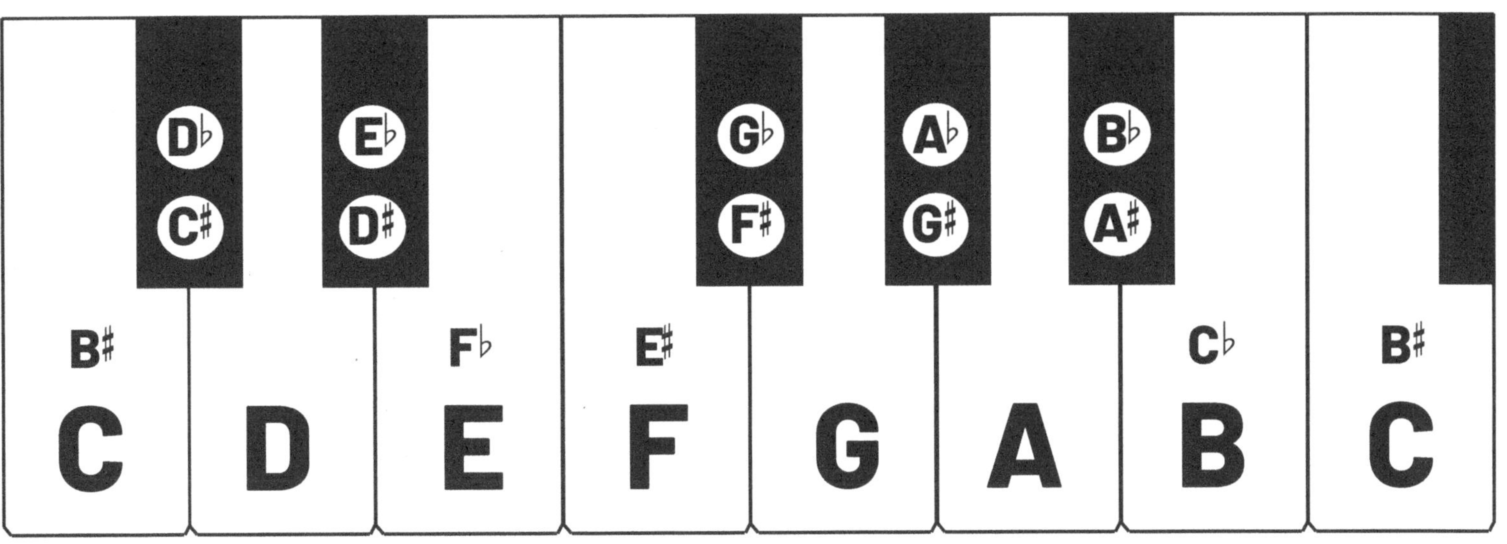

WORDS TO FAMILIAR MELODIES

The following are words to some of the familiar melodies that appear throughout this method. They are provided as a resource when teaching students to play the melodies on their string instruments.

Hot Cross Buns
Hot cross buns! Hot cross buns!
One, a pen-ny, Two, a pen-ny, Hot cross buns!

Michael Row the Boat Ashore
Mi-chael, row the boat a shore, Al-le-lu-ya
Mi-chael, row the boat a shore, Al-le-lu-ya.

Sis-ter, help to trim the sail, Al-le-lu-ya
Sis-ter, help to trim the sail, Al-le-lu-ya.

Mi-chael's boat is a gos-pel boat, Al-le-lu-ya
Mi-chael's boat is a gos-pel boat, Al-le-lu-ya.

Jor-dan's riv-er is chill-y and cold, Al-le-lu-ya
Jor-dan's riv-er is chill-y and cold, Al-le-lu-ya.

Jor-dan's riv-er is deep and wide, Al-le-lu-ya
Meet my moth-er on the oth-er side, Al-le-lu-ya.

Good King Wenceslas
Good King Wen-ces-las looked out,
On the feast of Ste-phen,
When the snow lay 'round a-bout,
deep and crisp and e-ven.

Old MacDonald
Old MacDonald had a farm, E-I-E-I-O
And on his farm he had a cow, E-I-E-I-O
With a moo-moo here, and a moo-moo there
Here a moo, there a moo
Everywhere a moo-moo
Old MacDonald had a farm, E-I-E-I-O.

Old MacDonald had a farm, E-I-E-I-O
And on his farm he had a pig, E-I-E-I-O
With a snort, snort here, and snort, snort there
Here a snort, there a snort
Everywhere a snort, snort
With a moo-moo here, and a moo-moo there
Here a moo, there a moo
Everywhere a moo-moo
Old MacDonald had a farm, E-I-E-I-O.

Pop Goes the Weasel
Round and round the cobbler's bench
The monkey chased the weasel,
The monkey thought 'twas all in fun
Pop! Goes the weasel.

Dreidel
I have a little dreidel
I made it out of clay
And when it's dry and ready
Then dreidel I shall play.

Chorus:
Dreidel, dreidel, dreidel
I made it out of clay
Dreidel, dreidel, dreidel
Then dreidel I shall play.

This Old Man
This old man, he played one
He played knick-knack on my thumb
Knick-knack paddywhack, give your dog a bone
This old man came rolling home.

This old man, he played two
He played knick-knack on my shoe
Knick-Knack paddywhack, give your dog a bone
This old man came rolling home.

Long, Long Ago
Tell me the tales
That to me were so dear,
Long, long ago,
Long, long ago:
Sing me the songs
I delighted to hear,
Long, long ago,
Long ago.

Jingle Bells
Jingle bells, jingle bells
Jingle all the way
Oh what fun it is to ride
In a one-horse open sleigh.
O Jingle bells, jingle bells
Jingle all the way
Oh what fun it is to ride
In a one-horse open sleigh.

Teacher The following are standards established by the American String Teachers Association with the National School Orchestra Association for successful string/orchestra teaching in the schools. Use the standards as goals and guidelines in evaluating and developing your teaching skills.

AMERICAN STRING TEACHERS ASSOCIATION with NATIONAL SCHOOL ORCHESTRA ASSOCIATION

STANDARDS FOR SUCCESSFUL SCHOOL STRING/ORCHESTRA TEACHING

I. As a Musician

1. demonstrates a high level of musicianship in performance
2. performs at an intermediate to advanced level on at least one string instrument
3. demonstrates at least basic to intermediate performance concepts on one string instrument and understands advanced and artistic concepts on other string instruments
4. demonstrates ability to play by ear and improvise
5. demonstrates a basic knowledge of performing and teaching the woodwind, brass, and percussion instruments at least at a basic level, with an understanding of intermediate to advanced concepts
6. demonstrates orchestral conducting skills
7. demonstrates keyboard skills of at least a basic to intermediate level and accompanies melodies using at least I-IV-V chords
8. demonstrates aural discrimination skills
9. demonstrates the understanding of prevention of performance injuries
10. demonstrates the knowledge of a wide range of music repertoire for teaching diverse styles, genres, cultures and historical periods

II. As an Educator

1. understands and applies pedagogy for violin, viola, cello and bass
2. demonstrates effective rehearsal techniques for string and full orchestra
3. demonstrates the knowledge of a variety of string and orchestral instruction materials at all levels
4. demonstrates the knowledge of repertoire for student performance, including solo literature, orchestra music, and chamber music
5. demonstrates skill in arranging music for school orchestras
6. demonstrates strategies for integrating music with other disciplines
7. understands different student learning styles, levels of maturation, special needs, and adapts instruction accordingly
8. demonstrates knowledge of comprehensive, sequential K-12 music curricula, including string and orchestra, with appropriate goals and expectations for all levels of proficiencies
9. demonstrates understanding of the principles of a variety of homogeneous and heterogeneous pedagogical approaches for teaching string classes (Suzuki, Rolland, Bornoff, e.g.)
10. exhibits effective classroom management skills and strategies
11. demonstrates understanding of how to teach students of diverse ages, socio-economic, ethnic, and geographic backgrounds
12. demonstrates effective methods of assessing and evaluating student achievement
13. knows about instrument rental and purchasing
14. knows current technology for instruction, research, and musical applications
15. knows of current music and general education policies, including current scheduling practices for successful string and orchestra programs
16. demonstrates ability to gather pertinent orchestra program data
17. understands the importance of maintaining a balance between personal and career interests
18. demonstrates ability to develop budgets for equipment and supplies
19. demonstrates understanding of effective advocacy strategies for comprehensive music programs which include string/orchestra programs
20. demonstrates clear communication in written and oral form
21. demonstrates understanding of the K-12 National Music Education Standards and other state and local standards for music

III. As a Professional

A. Musician

1. continues to perform
2. demonstrates concepts and understandings necessary for student achievement of Grade 12 National Music Education Standards
3. exhibits effective, on-going professional self-assessment
4. continues to pursue opportunities for learning as a musician

B. Professional Affiliations and Related Activities

1. maintains active involvement in professional associations, such as NAfME, ASTA/NSOA, SSA, CMA
2. continues to interact with other music educators, observes other programs
3. demonstrates professional ethics, appearance, behavior, and relationships within the profession, the school, and greater community
4. participates in ongoing professional development to improve teaching effectiveness
5. serves in leadership roles with state and local MEA's, ASTA/NSOA chapters

C. School and Community Relations

1. develops a healthy rapport with school administrators for nurturing a successful string and orchestra program
2. understands the value of positive interaction with other members of the music and arts community
3. establishes and maintains positive relations with school administrators, staff, and fellow teachers through communication and dialogue
4. articulates the positive aspects of the string/orchestra component of a school music program through writing and speaking
5. communicates effectively with parent support/booster groups, including clear and grammatically correct communication
6. advocates effectively for a strong school orchestra program

Teacher The following bibliography lists the resources considered essential by the Professional String Teaching and Playing Association (ASTA with NSOA).

AMERICAN STRING TEACHERS ASSOCIATION with NATIONAL SCHOOL ORCHESTRA ASSOCIATION

ESSENTIAL RESOURCE LIST FOR STRING TEACHERS

Stringed Instruments: Instruction and Study

The Complete String Guide: Standards, Programs, Purchase, and Maintenance. (1988). Reston, VA: Music Educators National Conference.

Dillon, J. & Kriechbaum, C. (1978). How to Design and Teach a Successful School String and Orchestra Program. San Diego, CA: Kjos West.

Dillon-Krass, J. & Straub, D. A. (Compilers). (1991). TIPS: Establishing a String and Orchestra Program. Reston, VA: Music Educators National Conference.

Green, E. A. (1966). Teaching Stringed Instruments in Classes. Englewood Cliff, NJ: Prentice-Hall, Inc. (available through ASTA).

Guidelines for Performances of School Music Groups: Expectations and Limitations. (1986) Reston, VA: Music Educators National Conference.

A Guide to Teaching Strings. Dubuque, IA: Wm. C. Brown and Co.

Mullins, S. (1998). Teaching Music: The Human Experience. Dallas, TX: Tarrant Dallas Printing.

Teaching String Instruments: A Course of Study. (1991). MENC Task Force on String Education. Reston, VA: Music Educators National Conference.

Highlights from the ASTA School Teacher's Forum. (1984-1994). Bloomington, IN: Tichenor Publishing.

String Syllabus. (revised 1997). ASTA. Bloomington, IN: Tichenor Publishing.

Straub, D. A., Bergonzi, L., & Witt, A. C. (Eds.). (1996). Strategies for Teaching Strings and Orchestra. Reston, VA: Music Educators National Conference.

Young, P. (1978). Playing the String Game - Strategies for Teaching Cello and Strings. Ann Arbor, MI: Shar Music.

Young, P. (1985). The String Play - The Drama of Playing and Teaching Strings. Austin, TX: University of Texas Press.

Strings, Winds, Brass, and Percussion
Managing the Instrumental Music Program

Colwell, R. J. and Goolsby, T. (1992). The Teaching of Instrumental Music. Englewood Cliffs, NJ: Prentice Hall.

Kohut, D. L. (1973). Instrumental Music Pedagogy: Teaching Techniques for School Band and Orchestra Directors. Englewood Cliffs, NJ: Prentice-Hall.

Strategies for Success in the Band and Orchestra. (1994). Reston, VA: Music Educators National Conference.

Walker, D. E. (1988). Teaching Music: Managing the Successful Music Program. New York, NY: Schirmer Books.

String Class Materials

Method Books

Allen, M., Gillespie, R., & Hayes, P.T. Essential Elements for Strings, (1995) Books I, II, and the Teacher Resource Kit, and Essential Techniques for Strings. Milwaukee, WI: Hal Leonard Corporation.

Anderson, G. & Frost, R. (1986). All for Strings. Kjos. Supplementary materials available.

Applebaum, S. Applebaum String Method. Books I, II, III. New York, NY: Belwin-Mills. Books I - III. Supplementary Applebaum materials include the following: Etudes for Technique and Musicianship, Chamber Music for Two String Instruments, Chamber Music for String Orchestra, and Solos with Piano Accompaniment.

Dabczynski, A., Meyer, R., & Philiips, B. (2002). String Explorer. Books I and II. Highland/Etling Pub. (a division of Alfred Music Publishing).

Dillon, J., Kjelland, J. & O'Reilly, J. Strictly Strings. Books I, II and III. Highland/Etling Pub. (a division of Alfred Music Publishing). Supplementary materials available.

Etling, F. String Method, Books I and II; Intermediate String Techniques; Solo Time for Strings, Books I, II, III, IV, and V; Workbook for Strings, Books I and II.

Froseth & Johnson (1981). Introducing the Strings, G.I.A. Publications.

Frost, R., & Fischbach, G. (2002). Artistry in Strings. Books I and II. San Diego, CA: Neil A. Kjos Music Company.

Gazda, D. & Stoutamire, A. (1997). Spotlight on Strings. San Diego, CA: Neil A. Kjos Music Company.

Isaac, M. (1962) String Class Method. Chicago, IL: M. M. Cole. Books I and II.

Matesky, R. & Womack, A. (1971). Learn to Play a Stringed Instrument. New York, NY: Alfred Music Co. Books I, II, and III.

Matesky, R. Learn to Play in the Orchestra. (1971). New York, NY: Alfred Music Co. Volumes I and II

Muller, F. & Rusch, H. Muller-Rusch String Method. (1961). Books I - V plus supplementary materials: ensembles, solos, etc. San Diego, CA: Neil A. Kjos Music Co.

Music Lists for Orchestra/String Orchestra

Non-Graded:

Farrish, M. K. (1965). String Music in Print. New York, NY: R. R. Bowker.

Farrish, M. K. (1968). Supplement to String Music in Print. New York, NY: R. R. Bowker.

Farrish, M. K. (1979). Orchestral Music in Print: Educational Section. Philadelphia, PA: Musicdata.

Littrell, D. & Racin, L. (2001) Teaching Music Through Performance in Orchestra. Chicago, IL: GIA Publications, Inc.

Graded Lists:

Matesky, R. & Smith, J. (1979). ASTA - NSOA Compendium of Orchestra & String Orchestra Literature: 1959-1977. Reston, VA: American String Teachers Association.

Mayer, F. R. (Ed.). (1993). The String Orchestra Super List. Reston, VA: Music Educators National Conference.

National School Orchestra Association - Sure-Fire Materials for the First-Year Orchestra Director.

NOTE: Many state organizations have graded music lists available.

National Standards for Arts Education

Allen, M. L. (1995). "The national standards for arts education: Implications for school string programs." American String Teacher, 45 (2), 30.

Bergonzi, L. (1996). "School teachers: The national standards in music: Access to string study for all children." American String Teacher, 46 (2), 69.

Dabczynski, A. H. (1995). "National standards for arts education: A golden opportunity for string teachers." American String Teacher, 45 (1), 73.

Daugherty, E. (1995). "Editorial: Implementing national standards in music: Context challenges and opportunities." The Quarterly of the Center for Research in Music Education, 6 (2), 3.

Kjelland, J. (1995). "String teacher preparation and the national music standards." American String Teacher, 45 (4), 34.

Mark, M. L. (1995). "Music education and the national standards: A historical review." The Quarterly of the Center for Research in Music Education, 6 (2), 34.

National Standards for Arts Education: What Every Young American Should Know and Be Able to Do in the Arts. Reston, VA: Music Educators National Conference.

Opportunity-to-Learn Standards for Music Instruction: Grades Pre K-12. (1994) Reston, VA: Music Educators National Conference.

Performance Standards for Music: Strategies and Benchmarks for Assessing Progress Toward the National Standards, Grades Pre K-12. (1996) Reston, VA: Music Educators National Conference.

The School Music Program: A New Vision. (1994). Reston, VA: Music Educators National Conference.

Shuler, S. C. (1995). "The impact of national standards on the preparation, in-service professional development, and assessment of music teachers." Arts Education Policy Review, 96 (3), 2.

Straub, D. A. (1995). "The national standards for art education: context and issues." American String Teacher, 45 (3), 24. Straub, D. A., Bergonzi, L., & Witt, A. C. (Eds.) (1996) Strategies for Teaching Strings and Orchestra. Reston, VA: Music Educators National Conference.

Advocacy

Action Kit for Music Education. (1991). Reston, VA: Music Educators National Conference. (brochures, books, videos)

Does Your School District Have an Orchestra Program? (1993). Reston, VA: Music Educators National Conference. (brochure)

Day, S. H. (1996). "Teaching orchestra on a year-round schedule." Teaching Music, 4, 33-35.

Kendall, S. (1997). "Securing our string programs." American String Teacher, 47 (2), 47.

Tellejohn, P. (1989). "Ensure your string program's success." American String Teacher, 76 (2), 30-32.

Scheduling Time for Music. (1995). Reston, VA: Music Educators National Conference.

Pedagogical Videos

From University of Wisconsin, Division of University Outreach, Department of Continuing Education.

Rabin, M. , et al. (1986). Rabin on Strings.

Rabin, M. & Smith, P. (1984). Guide to Orchestral Bowings Through Music Styles.

Paul Rolland

Rolland, P. Basic Principles of Violin Playing. (MENC Publication, 1959: ASTA, 1983).

Rolland, P. and Mutschler, M. (1974). The Teaching of Action in String Playing: Developmental and Remedial Techniques. Urbana, IL: Illinois String Research Associates.

Film

University of Illinois Film Series on Teaching of Action in String Playing. Urbana, IL: Illinois String Research Associates. Fourteen 16mm color films or videotapes; artists, teachers, and students demonstrate principles of Teaching of Action in String Playing.

String Repair

Bearden, L. & Bearden, D. (1972). Emergency String Repair Manual, 2nd Edition. AL: The University of Alabama Press.

Weisshaar, O. H. (1966). Preventative Maintenance of Stringed Instruments. Rockville Center, MD: Belwin, Inc.

Zurfluh, J. D. (Ed.). (1978). String Instrument Repair and Maintenance Manual. American String Teachers Association.

Bowing

Green, E. A. (1957). Orchestra Bowings and Routines - 2nd edition. (18th Printing). Reston, VA: American String Teachers Association.

Berman, J., Jackson and Sarah K. ASTA Dictionary of Bowing/Pizzicato Terms and Techniques (4th Edition). 1998. Bloomington, IN: Tichenor Publishing.

Video-Tape

Rabin, M. & Smith, P. (1991). Guide to Orchestral Bowings through Music Styles. Madison, WI: University of Wisconsin-Extension.

Pedagogical Concerns

From *American String Teacher*

Allen, M. L. (1994). "Introducing and integrating basic skills in the beginning string class." American String Teacher, 44 (3), 69-72.

Fischbach, G. "Getting from here to there with a smile: A sequential outline of the skills of shifting for business and pleasure." American String Teacher.
Three part article:
I. Basic Principles, Summer 1980, 30 (3), 11-12.
II. Sequential Course of Study. Autumn, 1980, 30 (4), 28-30.
III. Shifting for Pleasure, Winter 1981, 31(1), 12-13.

Gillespie, R. (1997). "String teacher training: Using history to guide the future." American String Teacher, 47 (1), 62-66.

Moskovitz, M. D. (1997). "Making the connection: Shifting through hand positions." American String Teacher, 47 (3), 55-58.

From *The Instrumentalist*

Burgess, N. (1977). "Fiddling for technical development." The Instrumentalist. 32 (5), 81-83.

Gillespie, R. (1989). "Teaching spiccato to string classes: Effective strategies for teaching your group the spiccato bounce." The Instrumentalist, 44 (4), 52, 56, 59-60.

Gillespie, R. (1992). "Building a Bass Section." The Instrumentalist, 47 (5), 66-69.

Grieve, T. (1989). "Fresh approaches to scale practice." The Instrumentalist, 43 (7), 44-46.

Rejto, G. (1978). "Strings: Producing a beautiful string tone." The Instrumentalist, 33 (2), 76.

Journals

American String Teacher
American String Teachers Association (ASTA)
with the National School Orchestra Association (NSOA)
www.astastrings.org

The Instrumentalist
www.theinstrumentalist.com

Music Educators Journal
National Association for Music Education
www.nafme.org

Teaching Music
National Association for Music Education
www.nafme.org

Professional Organizations

American String Teachers Association (ASTA) with the National School Orchestra Association (NSOA)
PO Box 551
Annapolis Junction, MD 20701
www.astastrings.org

National Association for Music Education
585 Grove Street, Suite 145 #711
Herndon, VA 20170
www.nafme.org

Suzuki Association of the Americas
P.O. Box 17310
Boulder, CO 80308
www.suzukiassociation.org

Teacher The following are video training programs for developing skills to diagnose and solve string students playing skills.

Video String Teacher Teaching Programs

Contact Robert Gillespie for these materials:
Ohio State University School of Music
110 Weigel Hall
1866 College Road
Columbus, OH 43210-1170
gillespie.5@osu.edu

Gillespie, Robert. The Violin Bowing Diagnostic Skills Program. Two videotapes and manual designed to train and evaluate teachers' abilities to recognize and solve common bowing problems of beginning violin students. Available for rent or purchase through the ASTA Media Resource Center.

Gillespie, Robert. The Violin Instrument Position and Left Hand Skills Training Program. A videotape and manual designed to train teachers to recognize common instrument position and left hand skills problems of beginning and intermediate violin students. Available for rent or purchase through the ASTA Media Resource Center.

Gillespie, Robert, William Conable, and Brent Wilson. The Cello Diagnostic Skills Training Program. A videotape and manual designed to train teachers to recognize common instrument position and left hand fingering problems of beginning and intermediate cello students. Available for rent or purchase through the ASTA Media Resource Center.

Authors

MICHAEL ALLEN
Professor of Music Education, Florida State University, Tallahassee, FL

ROBERT GILLESPIE
Professor of Music, The Ohio State University, Columbus, OH

PAMELA TELLEJOHN HAYES
Orchestra Coordinator (retired), Richland School District Two, Columbia, SC

JOHN HIGGINS
Managing Producer and Editor, Composer and Arranger, Hal Leonard Corp., Milwaukee, WI

Credits

Managing Editor and Producer	Paul Lavender
Production Editor	Stuart Malavsky Matt Wolf
Orchestra Arrangements	John Higgins
Design and Art Direction	Richard Slater Tim Bigonia Nicole Julius
Music Engraving and Typesetting	Thomas Schaller
Play Along Trax Arrangements and Production	Paul Lavender John Higgins
Additional Arrangements	John Moss
Essential Elements Rhythm Section	Steve Millikan - Keyboards Steve Potts - Keyboards Steve Dokken - Bass Sandy Williams - Guitars Steve Hanna - Percussion Larry Sauer - Drums
Recording and Mixing Engineers Aire Born Studios, Indianapolis, IN	Mark Aspinall John Bolt David Price Ben Vawter Mike Wilson
Additional Recording Production	Jared Rodin Mark Aspinall
Project Supervision Aire Born Studios, Indianapolis, IN	Nanci Milam Mike Wilson Nina Hunt
Announcer	Scott Hoke

The authors wish to give special thanks to Herman Knoll Senior, Vice President of Hal Leonard, for his dedication, leadership, and expertise in the creation of the Essential Elements educational program.